Tikal Report No. 16
EXCAVATIONS IN THE EAST PLAZA OF TIKAL

Volume I

University Museum Monograph 92

Tikal Report No. 16
EXCAVATIONS IN THE EAST PLAZA OF TIKAL

Christopher Jones

Volume I

Series Editors
William R. Coe
William A. Haviland

Published by
THE UNIVERSITY MUSEUM
University of Pennsylvania
1996

Design, editing, production
Publications Department
The University Museum

Printing
Sun Printing
Philadelphia, Pennsylvania

Library of Congress Cataloging-in-Publication Data

Jones, Christopher, 1937-
　　Excavations in the East Plaza of Tikal / Christopher Jones.
　　　　p. cm. – (Tikal report ; no. 16) (University museum monograph ; 92)
　　Includes bibliographical references.
　　ISBN (invalid) 0-924171-42-1
　　1. Tikal Site (Guatemala)　2. Mayas–Antiquities.　3. Excavations (Archaeology)–
Guatemala–Tikal Site.　4. Guatemala–Antiquities.　I. Title.　II. Series.　III. Series:
Tikal report ; no. 16.
F1435.1.T5J66 1996
972.81'2–dc20
　　　　　　　　　　　　　　　　　　　　　　　　　　　　　　　　　　　　　96-4465
　　　　　　　　　　　　　　　　　　　　　　　　　　　　　　　　　　　　　CIP

Copyright © 1996
THE UNIVERSITY OF PENNSYLVANIA MUSEUM
of Archaeology and Anthropology
Philadelphia
All rights reserved
Printed in the United States of America

Printed on acid free paper

Table of Contents

VOLUME I TEXT

LIST OF TABLES AND CHART xv
LIST OF ILLUSTRATIONS xvii

I INTRODUCTION 1

II PLATFORM 5D-2 5
  Platform 5D-2-3rd
    INTRODUCTION 5
    EXCAVATION DATA 5
      Sequence and Composition 5
      Relationship to Adjacent Stratigraphy 6
    ARCHITECTURE 6
    LOTS, GROUPING AND EVALUATION 6
      Construction 6
    TIME SPANS 7

  Platform 5D-2-2nd
    INTRODUCTION 7
    EXCAVATION DATA 7
      Sequence and Composition 7
      Evidence of Use 8
      Relationship to Adjacent Stratigraphy 8
    ARCHITECTURE 8
    LOTS, GROUPING AND EVALUATION 9
      Primary Construction 9
      Secondary Construction 9
    TIME SPANS 9

  Platform 5D-2-1st
    INTRODUCTION 9
    EXCAVATION DATA 9
      Sequence and Composition 9
      Evidence of Use 11
      Relationship to Adjacent Stratigraphy 11
    ARCHITECTURE 12
    LOTS, GROUPING AND EVALUATION 12
      Primary Construction 12
      Secondary Construction 12
      Occupation 12
    TIME SPANS 12

III STRUCTURES ON PLATFORM 5D-2 15
  Structure 5D-Sub.26
    INTRODUCTION 15

EXCAVATION DATA 15
   Relationship to Adjacent Stratigraphy 15
LOTS, GROUPING AND EVALUATION 15
   Construction 15
TIME SPANS 15

Structure 5D-Sub.27
INTRODUCTION 16
EXCAVATION DATA 16
   Construction Stages 16
   Relationship to Adjacent Stratigraphy 16
TIME SPANS 16

Structure 5D-Sub.28
INTRODUCTION 16
EXCAVATION DATA 16
TIME SPANS 16

Structure 5D-Sub.29
INTRODUCTION 16
EXCAVATION DATA 17
TIME SPANS 17

Structure 5D-Sub.16
INTRODUCTION 17
EXCAVATION DATA 17
   Construction Stages 17
   Additions and Renovations 18
   Relationship to Adjacent Stratigraphy 18
ARCHITECTURE 18
SPECIAL DEPOSITS 18
   Cache 188 18
   Cache 189 19
   Cache 192 19
   Cache 202 20
LOTS, GROUPING AND EVALUATION 20
   Construction 20
TIME SPANS 20

Structure 5E-Sub.1
INTRODUCTION 21
EXCAVATION DATA 21
   Construction Stages 21
   Additions and Renovations 21
   Relationship to Adjacent Stratigraphy 21
ARCHITECTURE 21
SPECIAL DEPOSITS 22
   Cache 195 22
   Cache 171 22
LOTS, GROUPING AND EVALUATION 22
TIME SPANS 22

Structure 5D-42
INTRODUCTION 23
EXCAVATION DATA 23
   Construction Stages 23
   Additions And Renovations 24

Relationship To Adjacent Stratigraphy 24
ARCHITECTURE 25
ASSOCIATED MONUMENTS 25
   Column Altar 2 25
LOTS, GROUPING AND EVALUATION 25
   Initial Construction 25
   Secondary Construction 25
   Occupation 26
TIME SPANS 26

Structure 5E-31
INTRODUCTION 27
EXCAVATION DATA 27
   Construction Stages 27
   Additions and Renovations 28
   Relationship to Adjacent Stratigraphy 28
ARCHITECTURE 28
ASSOCIATED MONUMENTS 28
LOTS, GROUPING AND EVALUATION 28
   Initial Construction 28
   Secondary Construction 28
   Occupation 28
TIME SPANS 28

Structure 5D-41-2ND
INTRODUCTION 29
EXCAVATION DATA 30
   Relationship to Adjacent Stratigraphy 30
ARCHITECTURE 30
LOTS, GROUPING AND EVALUATION 30
   Construction 30
TIME SPANS 30

Structure 5D-41-1ST
INTRODUCTION 31
EXCAVATION DATA 31
   Construction Stages 31
   Additions and Renovations 31
   Relationship to Adjacent Stratigraphy 31
ARCHITECTURE 31
LOTS, GROUPING AND EVALUATION 31
   Occupation 31
TIME SPANS 31

Structure 5D-43
INTRODUCTION 32
EXCAVATION DATA 32
   Construction Stages 32
   Additions and Renovations 33
   Relationship to Adjacent Stratigraphy 34
ARCHITECTURE 34
LOTS, GROUPING AND EVALUATION 35
   Initial Construction 35
   Secondary Construction 35
   Occupation 35
TIME SPANS 35

Structure 5D-135
    INTRODUCTION 36
    EXCAVATION DATA 36
        Construction Stages 36
        Relationship to Adjacent Stratigraphy 36
    ARCHITECTURE 37
    LOTS, GROUPING AND EVALUATION 37
        Construction 37
        Occupation 37
    TIME SPANS 37

Structure 5D-39
    INTRODUCTION 37
    EXCAVATION DATA 37
        Construction Stages 37
        Relationship to Adjacent Stratigraphy 38
    ARCHITECTURE 38
    LOTS, GROUPING AND EVALUATION 38
        Construction 38
        Occupation 38
    TIME SPANS 38

Structure 5D-134
    INTRODUCTION 39
    EXCAVATION DATA 39
        Construction Stages 39
        Relationship to Adjacent Stratigraphy 39
    ARCHITECTURE 39
    LOTS, GROUPING AND EVALUATION 39
        Occupation 39
    TIME SPANS 39

Structure 5D-136
    INTRODUCTION 40
    EXCAVATION DATA 40
        Construction Stages 40
        Relationship to Adjacent Stratigraphy 40
    ARCHITECTURE 40
    LOTS, GROUPING AND EVALUATION 40
        Construction 40
    TIME SPANS 40

Structure 5D-36
    INTRODUCTION 40
    EXCAVATION DATA 41
        Construction Stages 41
        Relationship to Adjacent Stratigraphy 41
    ARCHITECTURE 41
    LOTS, GROUPING AND EVALUATION 41
        Construction 41
        Occupation 41
    TIME SPANS 41

Causeway Maler A-2nd
    INTRODUCTION 42
    EXCAVATION DATA 42
        Construction Stages 42

    Relationship to Adjacent Stratigraphy 42
  ARCHITECTURE 42
  LOTS, GROUPING AND EVALUATION 42
    Construction 42
  TIME SPANS 42

Causeway Maler A-1st
  INTRODUCTION 43
  EXCAVATION DATA 43
    Construction Stages 43
    Additions and Renovations 43
    Relationship to Adjacent Stratigraphy 43
  ARCHITECTURE 43
  LOTS, GROUPING AND EVALUATION 43
    Initial Construction 43
    Secondary Construction 43
    Occupation 43
  TIME SPANS 43

Structure 5D-40
  INTRODUCTION 44
  EXCAVATION DATA 44
    Construction Stages 44
    Other Features 45
    Additions and Renovations 45
    Relationship to Adjacent Stratigraphy 45
  ARCHITECTURE 45
  SPECIAL DEPOSITS 45
    Problematical Deposit 169 45
  LOTS, GROUPING AND EVALUATION 45
    Construction 45
    Occupation 45
  TIME SPANS 45

Structure 5E-30
  INTRODUCTION 46
  EXCAVATION DATA 47
    Construction Stages 47
    Relationship to Adjacent Stratigraphy 47
  ARCHITECTURE 47
  LOTS, GROUPING AND EVALUATION 47
    Occupation 47
  TIME SPANS 47

Structure 5E-98
  INTRODUCTION 48
  EXCAVATION DATA 48
  ARCHITECTURE 48
  TIME SPANS 48

Structure 5E-92
  INTRODUCTION 48
  EXCAVATION DATA 48
  ARCHITECTURE 48
  TIME SPANS 48

Structure 5E-29

INTRODUCTION 49
EXCAVATION DATA 49
  Construction Stages 49
  Additions and Renovations 49
  Relationship to Adjacent Stratigraphy 49
ARCHITECTURE 49
LOTS, GROUPING AND EVALUATION 49
  Occupation 49
TIME SPANS 50

Structure 5E-94
INTRODUCTION 50
EXCAVATION DATA 50
ARCHITECTURE 50
LOTS, GROUPING AND EVALUATION 50
  Occupation 50
TIME SPANS 51

Structure 5E-32-2ND
INTRODUCTION 51
EXCAVATION DATA 51
  Relationship to Adjacent Stratigraphy 52
ARCHITECTURE 52
LOTS, GROUPING AND EVALUATION 52
  Construction 52
TIME SPANS 52

Structure 5E-32-1ST
INTRODUCTION 52
EXCAVATION DATA 52
  Construction Stages 52
  Additions and Renovations 53
  Relationship to Adjacent Stratigraphy 54
ARCHITECTURE 54
LOTS, GROUPING AND EVALUATION 54
  Initial Construction 54
  Secondary Construction 54
  Occupation 54
TIME SPANS 54

Structure 5E-99-2ND
INTRODUCTION 56
EXCAVATION DATA 56
  Relationship to Adjacent Stratigraphy 56
ARCHITECTURE 56
TIME SPANS 56

Structure 5E-99-1ST
INTRODUCTION 56
EXCAVATION DATA 56
  Construction Stages 56
  Relationship to Adjacent Stratigraphy 56
ARCHITECTURE 57
TIME SPANS 57

Structure 5E-34
INTRODUCTION 57

EXCAVATION DATA 57
    Construction Stages 57
    Relationship to Adjacent Stratigraphy 57
ARCHITECTURE 57
LOTS, GROUPING AND EVALUATION 58
    Construction 58
TIME SPANS 58

Structure 5E-36
INTRODUCTION 58
EXCAVATION DATA 58
ARCHITECTURE 58
TIME SPANS 58

Structure 5E-95-2ND
INTRODUCTION 59
EXCAVATION DATA 59
    Construction Stages 59
    Additions and Renovations 59
    Relationship to Adjacent Stratigraphy 59
ARCHITECTURE 59
LOTS, GROUPING AND EVALUATION 59
    Construction 59
TIME SPANS 59

Structure 5E-95-1ST
INTRODUCTION 60
EXCAVATION DATA 60
    Construction Stages 60
    Additions and Renovations 60
    Relationship to Adjacent Stratigraphy 61
ARCHITECTURE 61
LOTS, GROUPING AND EVALUATION 61
    Construction 61
    Occupation 61
TIME SPANS 61

Structure 5E-38
INTRODUCTION 62
EXCAVATION DATA 62
    Construction Stages 62
    Additions and Renovations 62
    Relationship to Adjacent Stratigraphy 63
ARCHITECTURE 63
SPECIAL DEPOSITS 63
    Problematical Deposits 260 AND 261 63
LOTS, GROUPING AND EVALUATION 63
Construction 63
Occupation 63
    TIME SPANS 63

Structure 5E-37
INTRODUCTION 64
EXCAVATION DATA 64
    Construction Stages 64
    Additions and Renovations 65
    Relationship to Adjacent Stratigraphy 65

ARCHITECTURE 65
LOTS, GROUPING AND EVALUATION 65
   Construction 65
   Initial Occupation 65
   Secondary Occupation 65
TIME SPANS 65

Structure 5D-97
   INTRODUCTION 66
   EXCAVATION DATA 66
   ARCHITECTURE 66
   LOTS, GROUPING AND EVALUATION 67
      Occupation 67
   TIME SPANS 67

Structure 5E-96
   INTRODUCTION 67
   EXCAVATION DATA 67
      Construction Stages 67
      Additions and Renovations 67
      Relationship to Adjacent Stratigraphy 67
   ARCHITECTURE 67
   TIME SPANS 68

Structure 5E-93
   INTRODUCTION 68
   EXCAVATION DATA 68
      Construction Stages 68
      Additions and Renovations 68
      Relationship to Adjacent Stratigraphy 68
   ARCHITECTURE 68
   TIME SPANS 69

Structure 5E-40

IV PLATFORM 5E-1 71
   Platform 5E-1
   INTRODUCTION 71
   EXCAVATION DATA 71
      Sequence and Composition 71
      Additions and Renovations 72
      Relationship to Adjacent Stratigraphy 72
   ARCHITECTURE 72
   LOTS, GROUPING AND EVALUATION 73
      Construction 73
      Occupation 74
   TIME SPANS 74

V STRUCTURE 5E-22 75

Structure 5E-22
   INTRODUCTION 75
   EXCAVATION DATA 75
      Construction Stages 75
      Other Features 75
      Relationship to Adjacent Stratigraphy 75
   ARCHITECTURE 76

    LOTS, GROUPING AND EVALUATION 76
        Occupation 76
    TIME SPANS 76

VI GROUP 5D-3 TIME SPANS 79
    INTRODUCTION 79
    TIME SPAN 9 79
    TIME SPAN 8 80
    TIME SPAN 7 80
    TIME SPAN 6 81
    TIME SPAN 5 83
    TIME SPAN 4 84
    TIME SPAN 3 85
    TIME SPAN 2 87
    TIME SPAN 1 89

VII CONCLUDING REMARKS 91

APPENDIX: PLATFORM UNITS 93

REFERENCES 95

VOLUME II ILLUSTRATIONS

FIGURES 1–81

Tables and Chart

Table 1.	Platform 5D-2-3rd: Time Spans	6
Table 2.	Platform 5D-2-2nd: Time Spans	8
Table 3.	Platform 5D-2-1st: Time Spans	13
Table 4.	Platform 5E-Sub26: Time Spans	15
Table 5.	Structure 5E-Sub27: Time Spans	16
Table 6.	Structure 5E-Sub28: Time Spans	17
Table 7.	Structure 5E-Sub29: Time Spans	17
Table 8.	Structure 5D-Sub16: Time Spans	20
Table 9.	Structure 5E-Sub1: Time Spans	23
Table 10.	Structure 5D-42: Time Spans	26
Table 11.	Structure 5E-31: Time Spans	29
Table 12.	Structure 5D-41-2nd: Time Spans	30
Table 13.	Structure 5D-41-1st: Time Spans	32
Table 14.	Structure 5D-43: Time Spans	36
Table 15.	Structure 5D-135: Time Spans	37
Table 16.	Structure 5D-39: Time Spans	38
Table 17.	Structure 5D-134: Time Spans	39
Table 18.	Structure 5D-136: Time Spans	40
Table 19.	Structure 5D-36: Time Spans	41
Table 20.	Causeway Maler A-2nd: Time Spans	42
Table 21.	Causeway Maler A-1st: Time Spans	44
Table 22.	Structure 5D-40: Time Spans	46
Table 23.	Structure 5E-30: Time Spans	47
Table 24.	Structure 5E-98: Time Spans	48
Table 25.	Structure 5E-92: Time Spans	49
Table 26.	Structure 5E-29: Time Spans	50
Table 27.	Structure 5E-94: Time Spans	51
Table 28.	Structure 5E-32-2nd: Time Spans	52
Table 29.	Structure 5E-32-1st: Time Spans	55
Table 30.	Structure 5E-99-2nd: Time Spans	56
Table 31.	Structure 5E-99-1st: Time Spans	57
Table 32.	Structure 5E-34: Time Spans	58
Table 33.	Structure 5E-36: Time Spans	58
Table 34.	Structure 5E-95-2nd: Time Spans	60
Table 35.	Structure 5E-95-1st: Time Spans	61
Table 36.	Structure 5E-38: Time Spans	64
Table 37.	Structure 5D-37: Time Spans	66
Table 38.	Structure 5D-97: Time Spans	67
Table 39.	Structure 5D-96: Time Spans	68
Table 40.	Structure 5E-93: Time Spans	69
Table 41.	Platform 5E-1: Time Spans	73
Table 42.	Comparative Measurements of 5E-22 with Piedras Negras Sweatbaths	76
Table 43.	Structure 5E-22: Time Spans	77
Table 44.	Volumes and Dressed Surface Areas, Time Span 9	80
Table 45.	Volumes and Dressed Surface Areas, Time Span 8	80
Table 46.	Volumes and Dressed Surface Areas, Time Span 7	81
Table 47.	Volumes and Dressed Surface Areas, Time Span 6	82

Table 48.	Volumes and Dressed Surface Areas, Time Span 5	84
Table 49.	Volumes and Dressed Surface Areas, Time Span 4	85
Table 50.	Volumes and Dressed Surface Areas, Time Span 3	87
Table 51.	Volumes and Dressed Surface Areas, Time Span 2	88
Chart 1.	Group 5D-3 Time Spans	facing page 86

Illustrations

Figure 1. Group 5D-3, Final Plan
Figure 2. Platform 5D-2, Detail Sections
Figure 3. Platform 5D-2, Detail Sections, Continued
Figure 4. Structure 5D-Sub.16-B, Plan
Figure 5. Structure 5D-Sub.1-B, Plan
Figure 6. Structure 5D-Sub.16-A, Elevation and Plan of W Side
Figure 7. Structure 5D-Sub.16-A, Plans of Special Deposits
Figure 8. Structure 5D-42 and 5E-31, Plans and Detail Section
Figure 9. Structure 5D-42 and 5E-31, E-W Axial Section
Figure 10. Structure 5E-31-A, Plan Detail, S Side
Figure 11. Structure 5D-42, Section between N Side and Structure 5D-41
Figure 12. Structure 5D-42, Details
Figure 13. Structure 5E-31, Detail Sections
Figure 14. Structure 5D-42, 5E-31, and 5D-Sub.16, Details
Figure 15. Facade Inscriptions, Str. 5D-42 and 5E-31
Figure 16. Structure 5D-41 and 5D-43, Plans, Sections, and Elevations
Figure 17. Structure 5D-41-1st, Front Elevation
Figure 18. Structure 5D-41-1st, Side Elevation
Figure 19. Structure 5D-43, Plans, Sections, and Elevations
Figure 20. Structure 5D-43-C, E Elevation Detail of Substructure
Figure 21. Structure 5D-43-C, S Elevation Detail of Upper Zone
Figure 22. Structure 5D-43, Elevation and Details
Figure 23. Structure 5D-39, Plans and Sections
Figure 24. Structure 5D-136, Plan and Section
Figure 25. Structure 5D-135, Plan and Section; Structure 5D-134, Detail Elevations
Figure 26. Structure 5D-134 Plan
Figure 27. Structure 5D-39 and 134, Sections and Elevations
Figure 28. Structure 5D-36, Plans and Sections
Figure 29. Structure 5D-36 and Maler Causeway, Details
Figure 30. Maler Causeway, Sections
Figure 31. Maler Causeway, Sequent Plans of E Parapet Gap
Figure 32. Structures 5D-40, 5E-30, Plan, Section and Elevation
Figure 33. Structure 5D-40, Side Elevation
Figure 34. Structure 5E-40, Section of E Side
Figure 35. Structure 5E-30, N-S Section, E of Axis
Figure 36. Structures 5E-29, 92, and 98, Plans
Figure 37. Structure 5E-29, 98, 92 Sections
Figure 38. Structure 5E-32, 34, Plans and Sections
Figure 39. Structures 5E-32, 34, 36, 94, Plans and Sections
Figure 40. Structure 5E-32-1st-A, Plan of SW Corner
Figure 41. Structure 5E-32-1st-B, Plan of SW Corner
Figure 42. Structure 5E-32, Detail Sections
Figure 43. Structure 5E-32, Details Continued
Figure 44. Structure 5E-32, N-S Section at SW Corner
Figure 45. Structure 5E-32, E-W Section at SW Corner
Figure 46. Structure 5E-32, N-S Section near SW Corner
Figure 47. Structure 5E-32, Elevation Details

Figure 48.	Structure 5E-32, 34, 36, 99 Detail Sections
Figure 49.	Structure 5E-38 Plan, Elevation, and Profile
Figure 50.	Structure 5E-38, Detail Sections
Figure 51.	Structure 5E-38, Details Continued
Figure 52.	Platform 5E-1 and Structure 5E-95, Plans
Figure 53.	Platform 5E-1 and Structure 5E-95, Sections
Figure 54.	Structure 5E-95, Details
Figure 55.	Structure 5E-37, N-S Section near W Side
Figure 56.	Structure 5E-37, Detail Sections
Figure 57.	Structure 5E-93, E-W Axial Section
Figure 58.	Platform 5E-1, Detail of Sculpture on W Facade
Figure 59.	Platform 5E-1, Detail Sections of W Side
Figure 60.	Platform 5E-1 and Structure 5E-23 Details
Figure 61.	Structure 5E-25, E-W Axial Section
Figure 62.	Structure 5E-22, Plan
Figure 63.	Platform 5E-1, Structures 5E-22, 27, Sections
Figure 64.	Structure 5E-22, Details
Figure 65.	Schematic Section of Platform 5D-2
Figure 66.	Platform 5D-2, Photos
Figure 67.	Structure 5D-42, Photos
Figure 68.	Structure 5D-42, Photos continued
Figure 69.	Structure 5D-42, Photos continued
Figure 70.	Structure 5E-31, Photos
Figure 71.	Structure 5E-31, Photos continued
Figure 72.	Structure 5E-Sub.1 and 5D-43, Photos
Figure 73.	Structure 5D-43, Photos
Figure 74.	Structures 5D-43 and 5E-97, Photos
Figure 75.	Structures 5D-39, 40, 134, and 136, Photos
Figure 76.	Structure 5E-32, Photos
Figure 77.	Structures 5E-29, 94, and 99, Photos
Figure 78.	Platform 5E-1, Structures 5E-95 and 37, Photos
Figure 79.	Structure 5E-38, Photos
Figure 80.	Structure 5E-22, Photos
Figure 81.	East Plaza in Maquette by Christopher Ray

I

Introduction

This volume describes excavations undertaken by the Tikal Project in the East Plaza and the large acropolis-like mound to the E (TR. 11). The East Plaza structures are supported by a single broad flat surface, *Platform 5D-2*, which extends along the N side of, and perhaps beneath, the eastern mound, *Platform 5E-1*. Hence the two aggregates are conveniently treated as a single *Group 5D-3* (Fig. 1).

Although groups have been named in Tikal Project files, they were not labeled on the TR. 11 map (1961). Only four have been defined in published excavation reports: Gp. 4F-1 and 4F-2 (TR. 19), Gp. 5D-2 (TR. 14), and Gp. 5E-11 (Larios and Orrego 1983), although others have been specified in project dissertations, articles, and TR. 12 (1982:57–61).

Group 5D-3 can be distinguished on the Project map (TR. 11) as an extensive level area. Much of its limit is formed by a sharp decline that extends E from the side of the Maler Causeway to the N and E sides of Plat. 5E-1, then presumably back along the S side of the platform to the Mendez Causeway, and finally to the corner of the Central Acropolis. The remaining S and W edges are marked by steep slopes leading up to the Central Acropolis and the Great Plaza. Thus the T-shaped Plat. 5D-2 expanse, surmounted by numerous mounds including Plat. 5E-1, delimits the group by clearly descending or ascending edges. Structures that are supported by Plat. 5D-2 or by other platform summits, such as 5D-37 (TR. 14) and 5D-44, 45, and 47 (TR. 15), are considered components of Gp. 5D-2 or 5D-11 (the Great Plaza/North Acropolis and the Central Acropolis respectively). On the other hand, those structures occupying only the platform while merely abutting the sides of other platforms (Str. 5D-36 and 43, as well as 5E-40, 93, 96, and 97) properly belong to Gp. 5D-3 and are included here. Structure 5E-22 is also included even though more logically it pertains to Gp. 4E-14 (Morley's Group F).

The map of Tikal drawn by Maudslay in 1882 (1889–1902:44–50, pl. LXVII) delineated Str. 5D-43 alone within the group. The results of Maler's 1904 mapping (1911:10, 25–26) were not published until decades later and plotted the following (Maler 1971:116–118): Str. 5E-38, the "enormous rectangular terrace with no trace of stone structures" (i.e., Plat. 5E-1), low mounds to the W (Str. 5E-32 through 37), two higher central mounds (ballcourt Str. 5E-31 and 5D-42), a broad empty area W of these, and three structures along the N edge of the East Plaza (5E-29, 30 and 5D-40). Maler's exploration also resulted in discovery of St. 17 just N of the East Plaza (1911:90–91). Alfred Tozzer and R. E. Merwin (Tozzer 1911:116–118, pl. 29) mapped the size, shape, and location of East Plaza mounds even more accurately.

Brief exploratory studies within Gp. 5D-3 were undertaken by Project staff prior to the intensive excavations of 1964 and 1965. In 1958 (Op. 14A) Linton Satterthwaite investigated the terrain around St. 17 and probed the adjacent N face of Plat. 5D-2 (TR. 8:153–160, figs. 44, 45). In 1959 (Op. 17B) Stuart Scott exposed five floors and adjacent walls in the extreme SW corner of the East Plaza (Fig. 2c). In 1960 (Op. 4G) Aubrey Trik tunneled through Str. 5D-1 from front to rear and extended his work as a trench down to the East Plaza level, where he also came upon five sequent plaster surfaces (TR. 14:fig. 254a). In the same year, Vivian Broman and Luis Luján sunk ceramic sampling pits (Op. 22B, C, E, G, K, O, Y; 23A/C) into the East Plaza and Maler Causeway (Figs. 2b, 3a,b).

As Tikal Project excavations proceeded within the Great Plaza, North Terrace, and North Acropolis, it was necessary to explore adjacent and outlying large groups for stratigraphy, dating, plan, and function (Coe 1962:502; 1965a:380–382; TR. 12:35–38). In 1962 the West Plaza was investigated, and two of the largest Central Acropolis structures were cleared (Coe 1963a:417–419; 1963b). In 1963 Jones excavated six of the Twin-Pyramid Groups in order to examine these large plazas and to complete an ongoing study of monuments and caches (Coe 1962:484–486, 492–498; 1964:412; Jones 1969). In 1964 this interest in large groups led to excavation projects in the Central Acropolis and in the plazas W of the South Acropolis, as well as a survey of large standing structures throughout central Tikal (Lowe 1966:461–463; TR. 14:35–36).

In 1964 the mounds on the E side of the East Plaza and on Plat. 5E-1 were trenched by Jones, employing a crew of 10 for two months (Op. 78A-H). In the same year Hans Hug and Andrew Nagy recorded architecture of Str. 5E-38 (Op. 92A). In 1965 Jones and Miguel Orrego excavated structures on the W side of the Plaza (Op. 78I-Q, T-U), while Nicholas Hellmuth trenched several in the NW corner (Op. 78R-S). In 1967 Stanley Loten logged further architectural details of 5E-38. Finally in 1966, 1967, and 1969 Orrego recorded information on Str. 5E-40, 93 and 5E-96 as part of the Central Acropolis excavations (Op. 107B, 107C, and 133B). From the first penetrations of the East Plaza surface it was clear that temporal depth was expressed by four or five floors analogous in thickness and composition to those of the Great Plaza. The strategies of the 1964 and 1965 seasons derived in part from the 1963 study of Twin-Pyramid Groups which relied on deep centerline trenches and corner probes to clarify structural design and stratigraphic relationships via plaza floors. Most structures in the group were excavated, but only 5D-43 and 5E-22 were consolidated and are viewable today.

The investigation of Gp. 5D-3 fulfilled many initial expectations. Platform floors proved to be fairly consistent in number and appearance E-W across the Plaza. Doubts as to the existence of a ballcourt were put to rest. In addition the court was found to possess several unusual features, such as cylindrical doorway columns, intricate paneling on vertical substructural walls, and a lengthy hieroglyphic facade text. Twin four-stairway pyramids, like those of Tikal Twin-Pyramid Groups, were discovered buried beneath the ballcourt. Structure 5D-43 at the S end of the playing alley revealed a radial four-doorway building plan, a miraculously preserved sculptured upper zone, a triple-staired substructure, a three-part substructural profile, and "Tlaloc eyes" and "Venus star" decorations. The long, low-lying buildings with close-set doorways in the eastern part of the Plaza are unknown elsewhere at Tikal and may constitute the central marketplace for the community. Finally, small late structures in the western area of the East Plaza appear to be domiciles of perishable materials built near the end of the history of the site.

Although an important goal of the excavations was the dating of structures, few trenches were excavated between them. Connections across the Plaza sometimes depended on typology and the reasonable assumption that paving projects were plaza-wide in extent. Stratigraphic links to adjacent Gp. 5D-2 constructions and floors, changes in masonry techniques, and the latest sherds in fills provided chronological estimates for changes in Gp. 5D-3 from initial paving, ca. A.D. 50, to final occupation, ca. A.D. 900. A hieroglyphic date on Str. 5E-31 possibly but not necessarily reads 9.10.0.0.0 (27 January, A.D. 633), and Column Altar 2 on Str. 5D-42, though not in its original placement, is paired stylistically with Column Altar 1, which dates to 9.15.17.10.4 (14 December, A.D. 748). Although a few carbon samples were gathered from within the group, none were considered of sufficient contextual importance to be run for radiocarbon dates.

The report follows conventions established early in the Tikal Project (TR. 5:6–13; TR. 12:42–49). Line width, scale, directional arrows, abbreviations, and use of dashed or solid line in illustrations specifically emulate those of TR. 14. Figure captions are minimal, leaving the explanation to text. Antecedent or secondary features of structures and platforms are usually the only ones to be unitized, primary constituents being referred to in text by phrases such as "the rear wall," and "the medial vault mass," "the stair." Each series of unit numbers applies to the entire platform or structure without making a distinction between 1st, 2nd, 3rd, etc. This avoids duplication of a number in a sectional drawing, except when a structure was built over a subseries structure, as was Str. 5D-42 (Fig. 9). Platform units are distinguished in illustrations from those of structures by boldface type (see listing in the Appendix).

The group plan (Fig. 1) is tied to the previously published plotting of the final phase of Gp. 5D-2 (TR. 14:fig. 61). The two drawings could be attached to each other, and Str. 5D-1, 37, and 38 are represented only by their eastern baselines. The magnetically oriented grid is an extension of the one started by Eduardo Martinez in Gp. 5D-2 (TR. 14:3). Its accuracy decreases as one moves E. The position of Str. 5E-32 has an approximate range of error of 0.30 m relative to that of Str. 5D-37; that of Plat. 5E-1 might err by as much as 0.50 m.

Several new structures were discovered in excavation, including 5D-134 through 136 and 5E-92 through 99. On the summit of Plat. 5E-1, Str. 5E-23 through 28 of TR. 11 were voided for TR. 13 (pp. 44–45, fig. 2a) and are treated here as parts of the platform itself.

The order of reporting is arbitrary at times. The first constructional entities to be described are sequential manifestations of Plat. 5D-2 from earliest to latest (Part II). Reporting of individual structures (Part III) begins at the Plaza center, moves to the W side and meanders eastward. Division of a structure into separate 1st, 2nd, and 3rd entities is made when there was almost total replacement, as in TR. 14 (whereas TR. 19 makes finer divisions). Architectural phases represented by A, B, C, etc., on the other hand, are used when a structure retained most of its original form in spite of internal changes or additions. The large eastern mound, Plat. 5E-1, and its upper protuberances are described next (Part IV), followed by Str. 5E-22 behind the platform (Part V). Finally, these various platform and structure analyses are combined to form Group Time Spans (Chart 1), in which group composition, motive for construction, and function are discussed (Part VI). Of special interest are stratigraphic links with and typological similarities to adjoining Gp. 5D-2, the only epicentral group presently published (TR. 14). The report concludes with general observations (Part VII).

In the platform and structure descriptions of Parts II–V, the segments labeled Excavation Data describe stages of assembly and modifications from the start of construction to disintegration or replacement, ending with a summary of stratigraphic connections. The topic called Architecture is devoted to aspects of design and also quantifies construction material and trimmed masonry surface. Summarized under the subject of Lots, Grouping and Evaluation are assessments of sherd and artifact collections, emphasizing the latest sealed ceramics. The final topic, Time Spans, presents a synthesis of information, including chronological placement and function. Numbered time spans include periods of use following each construction or modification, as well as a period of collapse (TS. 1) after the abandonment of an unsuperseded structure. Demolition of earlier entities is described in the initial time span of the superimposed structure.

I am most grateful for the help I received in the preparation of this report. Independently conducted excavations within Gp. 5D-3 by Linton Satterthwaite, Aubrey Trik, Stuart Scott, William Coe, Vivian Broman, Luis Luján, Edward Sisson, Hans Hug, Andrew Nagy, and Stanley Loten have been extensively utilized. Miguel Orrego helped supervise and record the excavations of Str. 5D-43, 5D-40, 5E-30, and many others in 1965. Nicholas Hellmuth excavated Str. 5D-36, 39, and 134 and submitted a full report for Project files. Sally Bates drew sections of the Plat. 5E-1 mounds. Amilcar Ordóñez and Rudy Larios recorded the axial section of Str. 5D-41. I would also like to thank Nina Mandel, who researched Mesoamerican marketplaces and submitted a paper to me in 1983.

William Coe provided guidance throughout, suggesting that I excavate the East Plaza in 1964 and continue in 1965, supervising the excavations during both seasons, teaching me to ink the illustrations, and providing drafting assistance. Finally, he read and commented on early drafts of the report, pointing out errors and inconsistencies on every level, from organization to interpretation.

More than half the illustrations were expertly inked in Philadelphia by Jane Homiller. Carl Bates inked the drawings of Str. 5E-38. Coe drafted the facade text of 5E-31 and 5D-42 and the coquille rendering of the upper zone of Str. 5D-43. Barbara Hayden inked Chart 1, Figures 1 and 65, improved and completed many other inked figures, reviewed the manuscript several times, and oversaw preparation for publication. Tobia L. Worth was responsible for final manuscript editing. In the last stages, William Haviland and William Coe kindly read or reread the manuscript and offered additional valuable suggestions.

II

Platform 5D-2

PLATFORM 5D-2-3RD

INTRODUCTION

Platform 5D-2 is the broad horizontal surface extending eastward from the Great Plaza to the rear of Plat. 5E-1 (Fig. 1; TR. 11). The integrity of the flat surface shown on the TR. 11 map was confirmed in excavation. For the most part, borders are demarcated by steep ascents and declines, although it was not certain exactly where the 5D-2 pavement merged with the Maler and Mendez Causeways. The final dimensions of the platform are larger than the earlier ones, especially along the N edge. Three staged developments were defined as 3rd, 2nd, and 1st, dating roughly to the conventionally defined Preclassic, Early Classic, and Late Classic periods.

The first two stages of the platform, 3rd-B and A, are represented by bottom floors in E-W trenches across the Plaza (Table 1). No side walls were seen for these surfaces. See Figs. 2b,c, 9, 19d, 48c, 53a, 66a,b, TR. 14:fig. 254a.

EXCAVATION DATA

SEQUENCE AND COMPOSITION

PLATFORM 5D-2-3RD-B

Five pavements were encountered by Trik in the 1960 trench below Str. 5D-1 (TR. 14:fig. 254a). *Floor 5*, at the bottom, was composed of a 0.10 m thick mortar layer containing small light and dark stones above 0.60 m of marl fill with variably sized stones. This fill covered yellow bedrock with no soil in between and extended W under Plat. 5D-1:U. 17, of which only a single course of large sloping faced header blocks survived (TR. 14:170–171, 821). The fill, floor, and facing were apparently constructed as a single project. In the Op. 17B trench at the SW corner of the East Plaza (Figs. 2c, 66a), the lowest of five pavements over bedrock was almost certainly this Fl. 5. Here it covered 0.20 m of fill and abutted a course of east-facing stones of the same size and shape as U. 17 (Fig. 66b).

Unit 78, the 0.10 m thick basal floor in the trench and tunnel through Str. 5D-42 and 5E-31, contained softer stone inclusions than later floors (Fig. 9). It covered 0.05–0.25 m of white marl interleaved with dark earth lenses on bedrock. In the 7 m length of the trench, the floor sloped 0.40 m to compensate for the bedrock slope of 0.80 m. *Unit 8*, the lowest floor under Str. 5D-43 (Fig. 19d), faded against a bedrock slope that rose steeply S to a 2 m high plateau, in front of which were the remains of the frontal stair of Str. 5D-Sub.27. The plaster surface of U. 8 did not abut the structure.

At the E end of the plaza (Figs. 48c, 53a) the lowest floor, *Unit 71*, was 0.10 m thick and contained less aggregate than later ones. The condition of the area prior to construction of U. 71 was recorded in a 1960 ceramic test pit (Op. 23B) on the same centerline location as the later trench (Fig. 2b). Uneven yellow-and-white bedrock was blanketed by 0.20 m of soft, white, disintegrated rock (*Unit 88*) and then by 0.40 m of stoneless dark brown soil. These natural strata supported 1 m of lensed gray-and-brown fill. Although the U. 71 floor went undetected in this earlier probe, it was recorded in the 1964 excavation (Fig. 53a). The floor continued E beyond the trench, either to turn down over a wall or abut an unseen earlier version of Plat. 5E-1. Bedrock was not reached at the foot of Str. 5E-38 (Fig. 49c); therefore a floor belonging to Plat. 5D-2-3rd was not securely identified.

Floor 5 dipped from three sides of the plaza to an elevation of 240.9 m in the central area, probably draining off the N side. The SW corner floor stood at 244.4 m, the W side at 243.5 m, the S side at 242.6 m, and the E side at 241.1 m.

PLATFORM 5D-2-3RD-A

Floor 4 was first identified as a thin 0.10 m repaving of Fl. 5, either badly weathered or purposely roughened before being covered by Fl. 3 (TR. 14:fig. 254a). Like its predecessor it abutted the stub of Plat. 5D-1:U. 17. In the nearby Op. 17B trench (Fig. 2c) the fourth surface down also turned up to an east-facing U. 17 and was probably Fl. 4. Farther E under Str. 5D-42 and 5E-31, *Unit 79* capped 1.00 m of white marl interspersed by dark lenses (Fig. 9). The fill was thickened in the center of the platform to produce a more level plaza. The soft white plaster containing red, yellow, and white chips was spread over 0.12 m of gray mortar. *Unit 10* in the Str. 5D-43 trench on the S edge of the Plaza consisted of thin mortar and small stones covering 0.10 m of larger aggregate (Fig. 19d). *Unit 72* at the E end of the platform was identified as Fl. 4 by its thinness and its position on U. 71 (Figs. 48c, 53a).

In the central area under Str. 5D-42, U. 79 was resurfaced by 0.10 m thick *Unit 4*, which feathered out onto the plaster surface and apparently did not extend over the entire plaza (Fig. 9).

RELATIONSHIP TO ADJACENT STRATIGRAPHY

Floor 5 and U. 8, 71, and 78 were the only components of Plat. 5D-2-3rd-B seen in excavation. Their composition, relationship to bedrock, and number of overlying floors linked the separate exposures. The W edge of the floor turned up to the U. 17 wall of Plat. 5D-1-4th-A, and the S border abutted Str. 5D-Sub.27. Structures 5D-Sub.28 and 29 were built on its surface.

Floor 4 and U. 10, 72, and 79 constituted Plat. 5D-2-3rd-A. Thin at the platform edges, the 1 m thickness of the fill in the plaza center buried the remains of Str. 5D-Sub.28 and 29. Like the earlier pavement, the edges turned up to both Str. 5D-Sub.27 and U. 17 of Plat. 5D-1. The final U. 4 floor was confined to the central area and had no contact with other platforms and structures.

ARCHITECTURE

Fills of Plat. 5D-2-3rd-B and A were stoneless white marls containing dark lenses and no retaining walls. The floors contained fewer and softer inclusions than later pavements. Presumably, platform sides had stairs and facade walls, but none were encountered. (Subsequent floors lay on wet-laid marl fills studded with horizontally laid blocks and strengthened by fill walls.)

In calculating the quantity of material used in construction, a smaller paved area is assumed than for that of the final platform, extending N no farther than the N side of Str. 5E-32. Even so, Plat. 5D-2-3rd-B covered at least 2.18 ha to an average 0.30 m thickness, requiring 6,540 m^3 of material as well as 420 m^2 of trimmed facing surface for the hypothetical side walls. Platform 5D-2-3rd-A, 1 m thick at the center and thin on the peripheries, used ca. 2,180 m^3 of material, whereas U. 4 subsumed only 100 m^3.

LOTS, GROUPING AND EVALUATION

CONSTRUCTION

4G/10, a small lot from within Fl. 5, 78K/46 from U. 78, and 23B/5–9 and 78G/7 from U. 71 contained sherds no later than the Cimi Ceramic Complex (except for one stray Imix sherd in 78G/7). Absence of sealed Manik pottery in these sizable samples favors a Preclassic date for Plat. 5D-2-3rd-B.

TABLE 1
Platform 5D-2-3rd: Time Spans

Time Span	Architectural Addition	Floor, Unit	Special Deposit	Lot	Other Data
1	—	—	—	—	Use
2	—	U. 4	—	—	Partial resurfacing
3	—	—	—	—	Use
4	A	Fl. 4; U. 10, 72, 79	—	—	Repaving with Str. 5D-Sub.26
5	—	—	—	—	Use
6	B	Fl. 5; U.8, 71, 78, 88	—	4G/10; 23B/5–9; 78G/7; 78K/46	Assembly (6,540 m^3) with Str. 5D-Sub.27 and Plat. 5D-1:U. 17; Cauac ceramics

TIME SPANS

Time spans of Plat. 5D-2-3rd are outlined in Table 1. The TS. 6 cutting of bedrock, filling of low areas, and construction of peripheral walls and pavement in TS. 6 provided a broad concourse E of the Great Plaza. The side walls or stairs were at least 1 m high on the S, N, and E edges. Terrace facings and a possible stair (U. 17) descended for the first time all the way from the Great Plaza. The first platform floor was built at the same time as U. 17, part of Plat. 5D-1-4th-A of Gp. 5D-2:TS. 11 for which a date of ca. A.D. 50 was estimated on the basis of radiocarbon determinations (TR. 14:168, 821; Chart 1). Soft inclusions in the floor and lensed fills below it are characteristics of both plazas during these time spans (cf. Fig. 9; TR. 14:fig. 10). Absence of Manik sherds in several sealed lots further supports an early date. Public use of Plat. 5D-2 during TS. 5 is implied by its great expanse and location adjacent to the Great Plaza. Structures 5D-Sub.28 and 29, built in the center of the earliest platform, anticipated the later location and duality of the twin pyramids and the ballcourt. The Fl. 4 resurfacing of the summit (TS. 4) obliterated Str. 5D-Sub.28 and 29, and left Sub.26 as the only known structure on the floor. This pavement correlates roughly with Plat. 5D-1-3rd-B, which is estimated as only a few years later within Gp. 5D-2:TS. 11 at ca. A.D. 75 (TR. 14:176, 822, chart 1). Unit 4 of TS. 2 was a relatively insignificant patching of the plaza center.

PLATFORM 5D-2-2ND

INTRODUCTION

Two platform developments, 2nd-B and 2nd-A, are represented by plaza-wide floors first identified as Fl. 3 and 2 on the W side of the platform; elsewhere they are labeled with separate unit numbers to express an absence of physical connection. See Figs. 2c, 9, 19d, 23b, 38c, 48c, 51c, 53a, 59a,c, 60b, 66a,b, Table 2, and TR. 14:fig. 254a.

EXCAVATION DATA

SEQUENCE AND COMPOSITION

PLATFORM 5D-2-2ND-B

Floor 3 in the base of the trench behind Str. 5D-1 (TR. 14:fig. 254) was composed of hard-surfaced 0.06 m thick plaster over 0.25 m of compact marl and stone ballast. Flint chips in the surface gave off an ozone smell when scraped by a trowel, and this is characteristic of the middle pavements of Plat. 5D-1 and 5D-4 (TR. 14:103, 176, 179). The floor turned up to the U. 17 wall of Plat. 5D-1, which had previously been abutted by Fl. 5 and 4 (TR. 14:178–179). In the trench to the S (Fig. 2c), the third pavement from the bottom also turned up to the east-facing wall and was surely the same Fl. 3 (Fig. 66a,b). *Unit 91* under Str. 5D-39 corresponds to Fl. 3 in position (Fig. 23b).

Unit 80 was the third plaster surface above bedrock (not counting U. 4) beneath Str. 5D-42 in the central plaza trench (Fig. 9). Like Fl. 3, its surface plaster had a flinty sharp-edged surface aggregate and overlay 0.25 m of marl fill. *Unit 94* in the Str. 5D-43 trench to the S (Fig. 19d) was 0.20 m thick but missing its plaster surface through erosion. Covering it was the flinty aggregate and plaster of U. 18.

Unit 49 was the third floor from the bottom on the E side of the East Plaza. As the first to contain flint aggregate (Figs. 48c, 53a), it was identified as Fl. 3. Surface plaster became thin or absent as the floor ran eastward because of weathering or because of deliberate terminal roughening. *Unit 60* at the front of Str. 5D-38 (Fig. 49c) and *Unit 67* beneath 5E-32 (Fig. 38c) were also judged to be Fl. 3 by their sequential relationship below the top floors, even though bedrock was not reached. Marginal walls and stairs of Plat. 5D-2-2nd-B were not encountered.

PLATFORM 5D-2-2ND-A

In the trench at the E edge of the plaza (TR. 14:179, 839, fig. 254), *Floor 2* was 0.15 m thick and contained the same flint aggregate as Fl. 3 below it. The pavement was laid over remains of Plat. 5D-1:U. 17, which had been dismantled to its basal course. The new U. 18 wall erected on the rip-out would have looked unfinished without Fl. 2 against it and probably immediately preceded it. Although U. 18 was surmised to be a terrace wall in TR. 14 (179), its vertically fronted header stones are identical to stair stones on Str. 5D-22-1st (TR. 14:fig. 9a). In the Op. 17A trench to the S, Fl. 2 abutted an east-facing course probably related to U. 18 (Fig. 2c). In the trench beneath Str. 5D-39 to the N, *Unit 92* should be Fl. 2 by stratigraphic position (Fig. 23b). In the center of the platform *Unit 83* and *Unit 21* was a 0.10 m thick pavement that resembled Fl. 2 in thickness, flinty composition, and position in the sequence (Figs. 9, 38c). The floor turned up to pyramidal Str. 5D-Sub.16 and 5E-Sub.1 just after their construction. *Unit 18* beneath Str. 5D-43 (Fig. 19d) was the last to abut Str. 5D-Sub.27, and also extended (as *Unit 15*) over the rip-out of Str. 5D-Sub.26. *Unit 47* at the E end of the platform was in the proper sequential position and had the thinness of Fl. 2 (Fig. 53a). The erosion of the plaster surface kept the floor from being detected in the nearby Str. 5E-99 trench (Fig. 48c). *Unit 59* in front of Str. 5E-38 (Fig. 51c) is a likely Fl. 2 equivalent, as is *Unit 32*, apparently laid with Plat. 5E-1 (Figs. 59a,c, 60b).

Unit 2, a resurfacing of U. 83 that turned up to secondary stairs of Str. 5D-Sub.16 (Fig. 9), had the compact flinty aggregate of its two predecessors. Although the floor did not survive between Sub.16 and 5E-Sub.1, it probably once covered Ca. 202 and 195 and the area around the pyramids before eroding.

EVIDENCE OF USE

Unit 3 was an ancient pit 0.20 m in diameter and 0.25 m deep cut through the U. 80 floor in front of the W stair of Str. 5D-Sub.16 (Fig. 9). Roughly the dimension of the later Ca. 192 repository, it contained charcoal-flecked dirt and was sealed by the U. 83 floor without patching.

Unit 13 was a larger pit cutting through U. 80 and Unit 95 in front of the W stair of Str. 5D-Sub.16 (Fig. 9). The E edge was vertical and the inclined W edge reduced the E-W breadth from 1.00 to 0.60 m. Of unknown function, the pit was sealed much later by the U. 1 floor of Plat. 5D-2-1st. The socket for a missing stela comes to mind.

RELATIONSHIP TO ADJACENT STRATIGRAPHY

The Plat. 5D-2-2nd-B floor turned up to Plat. 5D-1:U. 17 and Str. 5D-Sub.27 and was coeval with Str. 5D-Sub.26. As the third and last floor to abut U. 17, it may be a contemporary of Fl. 2B in the Great Plaza (Plat. 5D-1-2nd-B), estimated at A.D. 325 (TR. 14:chart 1).

The Plat. 5D-2-2nd-A floor was accompanied by several important constructions: Plat. 5D-1:U. 18, Plat. 5E-1 on the W and E sides, and twin-pyramid Str. 5D-Sub.16 and 5E-Sub.1 in the center. Structure 5D-Sub.27 continued in view and Sub.26 was demolished. The platform correlates stratigraphically through U. 18 with Plat. 5D-1-2nd-A (Great Plaza Fl. 2A), estimated at A.D. 475 (TR. 14:839). The later U. 2 floor was confined to the area of Str. 5D-Sub.16 and 5E-Sub.1 on the occasion of their extensive revision and does not tie in with other floors.

ARCHITECTURE

Like Plat. 5D-2-3rd, 2nd was known through a pair of pavements stretching from the E to W edge of the East Plaza. Construction techniques, consisting of a wet-laid tamped marl ballast reinforced with oblong blocks and small, angular flint chips in the surface plaster, differed from those of prior floors. Side walls and stairs, if any were built for these platforms, were not seen.

The average 0.25 m thickness of Plat. 5D-2-2nd-B over 2.18 ha required 5,450 m^3 of material. For 2nd-A, the average 0.15 m thickness on the same expanse contained 3,270 m^3. If the unseen N and SE sides were rebuilt at either stage, their 1 m average height

TABLE 2
Platform 5D-2-2nd: Time Spans

Time Span	Architectural Addition	Floor, Unit	Special Deposit	Lot	Other Data
1	—	—	—	—	Use
2	—	U. 2	—	—	Local flooring with Str. 5D-Sub.16-A, 5E-Sub.1-A
3	—	U. 13	—	—	Use
4	A	Fl. 2; U. 15, 18, 21, 32, 47, 59, 83, 92	—	78G/3,6; 78P/32	Assembly (3,270 m^3) with Plat. 5D-1-2nd-A, Plat. 5E-1, Str. 5D-Sub.16-B, 5E-Sub.1-B; Manik ceramics
5	—	U. 3	—	—	Use
6	B	Fl. 3; U. 49, 60, 67, 80, 91, 94, 95	—	4G/9; 78M/50; 78K/16,38	Assembly (5,450 m^3); Manik ceramics

and 330 m length necessitated 330 m² of dressed facing. Unit 2 used an additional 100 m³ of material.

LOTS, GROUPING AND EVALUATION

PRIMARY CONSTRUCTION

4G/9, sealed within Fl. 3 on the W side of the plaza, was a small lot containing Manik and earlier sherds. 78M/50 from U. 80 had Manik sherds, an hourglass censer fragment, human teeth and bone, and a green obsidian flake-blade often found with Manik material. 78K/16 and 38, also sealed by U. 80, were large lots containing nothing later than Manik sherds. Platform 5D-2-2nd-B was certainly built during the period of Manik ceramic production.

SECONDARY CONSTRUCTION

78P/32 sealed in U. 18 of Plat. 5D-2-2nd-A and 78G/3 and 6 from U. 47 contained no certain sherds later than Manik (though contamination by Imix sherds occurred during excavation).

TIME SPANS

Platform 5D-2-2nd time spans are presented in Table 2. The hypothesis that there was a plaza-wide floor in TS. 6 is based on aggregate, thickness, and sequential position. New structures were not built with the pavement, at least within the probed areas of the edges and center. Certainly, the W facade of the Plaza, U. 17 of Plat. 5D-1, was not rebuilt with the floor, and perhaps the N and E edges of Plat. 5D-2 also remained as they were. Floors under Str. 5E-38 demonstrate that the platform extended into the SE sector at least by this time. Great Plaza Fl. 2B (Plat. 5D-1-2nd-B) was roughly synchronous and almost identical to Fl. 3 in thickness, flinty aggregate, and underlying foundation material (TR. 14:832–835).

Floor 2 and separately unitized equivalents comprising Plat. 5D-2-2nd-A abutted several newly built entities in TS. 4: pyramidal Str. 5D-Sub.16 and 5E-Sub.1 in the center of the platform, acropolis-like Plat. 5E-1 on the E, and the new U. 18 facing of Plat. 5D-1-2nd-A on the W. Although the pavement itself was relatively thin, these three constructions greatly altered the appearance and use of the Plaza. Like its predecessor, the platform was probably constructed during Manik Ceramic Complex production, at least no later ceramics were found sealed in its floors or associated structures. In TS. 2, a thin floor abutted new stairs on Str. 5D-Sub.16 and Str. 5E-Sub.1. Muul and Leum Complex caches within the pyramid revisions, which include a Manik cache vessel, confirm this date.

PLATFORM 5D-2-1ST

INTRODUCTION

Culminating elements of Plat. 5D-2 can be broken down into three sequent developments: 1st-C, a new surfacing of the plaza and northward enlargement toward the Maler Causeway; 1st-B, repaving of the eastern Plaza and expansion to the present N limit; and 1st-A, a final surfacing. See Figs. 2a–c, 3a,b, 8f, 9, 11, 12a–c, 13a,b, 16d, 19d, 22c, 23b, 24b, 25b, 27c,d, 28b, 29b, 30a–c, 32c, 34, 35, 37a–c, 38b,c, 39b, 42a,c, 43b, 44–46, 48a–c, 50a, 51c, 53a,b, 54a, 55, 57, 59a,c, 60b, 62, 63b, 66a–e, and TR. 14:figs. 246a,b, 248, 250a,b, 252a,b, 254a.

EXCAVATION DATA

SEQUENCE AND COMPOSITION

PLATFORM 5D-2-1ST-C

Floor 1 is the upper plaster surface in the trench behind Str. 5D-1 (TR. 14:184–185, fig. 254a). In preparation Plat. 5D-1:U. 18 was reduced to its basal course and a 0.10 m thick ballast, *Unit 65*, and 0.06 m thick Fl. 1 body were laid over the remains. Round, soft-edged, and occasionally calcined inclusions within Fl. 1 differed from the flinty aggregates of Fl. 2 and 3. The floor surface, which was plasterless through erosion, supported the smooth U. 20 plastered slope, a Plat. 5D-1 construction in its own right or merely a nuclear element of a torn-out facade (TR. 14:184–185, fig. 254a). The sloping face lacked the finish masonry suitable for a ballcourt bench like that of Str. 5D-74 (see TR. 14:fig. 288). Floor 1 was also seen as the upper of the five floor surfaces at the SW plaza corner (Figs. 2c, 66a). Here it overlay remains of an east-facing Plat. 5D-1 wall and turned up to the base of a north-facing Central Acropolis wall that in profile and masonry resembles the Central Acropolis wall farther E (Fig. 19d). The floor and the wall were probably built together, as no plaster surface directly underlay the facing.

In the center of the plaza a thick final floor overrode the remains of Str. 5D-Sub.16 and 5E-Sub.1 and abutted the sides of 5D-42 and 5E-31 (Fig. 9). Destruction of the pyramids immediately preceded the floor and the ballcourt structures. The floor is composed of two layers labeled *Unit 1* and U. 35. These could be distinguished from each other where the S addition on 5E-31 separated them (here called U. 1 and U. 11; Fig. 13b) and farther E where Str. 5E-32 preserved the equivalent of U. 1, *Unit 5* (Figs. 9, 38c). Unit 5 sustained 32-2nd-B in these excavations and at the S end of the structure (Fig. 44). The pavement reappeared as *Unit 20* (Fig. 46) beneath 32-2nd-A immediately to the SE. Unit 5 continued E from Str. 5E-32 to 5E-34 and to the central court of the quadrangle, where it was called *Unit 26* (Fig. 48a) as well as *Unit 68* and *Unit 33* (Fig. 38c). Another appearance of the floor was *Unit 19* in the Str. 5D-43 trench (Fig. 19d, 22c). The 0.10 m thick pavement covered remains of Str. 5D-Sub.27 and faded out against a rising rip-out line as did Fl. 1 to the W (cf. TR. 14:fig. 254a). A thin Unit 17 plaster turned up against the front and E sides of 5D-43 as well and to the Central Acropolis wall, again like Fl. 1 (Fig. 2c). Finally, *Unit 7* beneath Str. 5D-41-2nd was comparable to U. 5 in thickness and composition (Fig. 16d), emerging from the SE corner of 41-1st and running up against Str. 5D-42 like U. 2.

In contrast to the deep five-floor sequences described above, excavations in the NW corner of the platform revealed only two floors above the level bedrock surface (TR. 14:figs. 246a, 248, 250a,b, 252a,b). The lower *Unit 41* supported fill and walls of Str. 5D-37 and probably ran against the base of U. 71 behind the structure, a two-tiered Plat. 5D-1 buried facing (TR. 14:fig. 248) that resembled in profile and masonry the Central Acropolis wall abutted by Fl. 1 (Figs. 2c, 19d). Interlocking masonry on 5D-37 and the adjacent Plat. 5D-1:U. 72 stair to the S ensured their contemporaneity. Because U. 41 supported the N end of the stair, it must be the pavement underneath the U. 72 centerline (Fig. 23b). Nevertheless, the floor had weathered away in front of this protective stair and did not survive under the axis of 5D-39 (Fig. 27c) as it did under the N end (Fig. 27d), where U. 41 was identified by tracing it to 5D-37. *Unit 27*, covering deep *Unit 28* fill between Str. 5D-40 and 41, is probably this flooring (Fig. 2a), as is *Unit 81* (Fig. 25b).

Unit 41 was followed N from Str. 5D-37 to where it turned up to the base of stair U. 75/80 that descended to the East Plaza beside 5D-37. From there the floor continued N to become U. 4 of the Maler Causeway, the lower of its two floors. Across the causeway, the rear wall of Str. 5D-40 stood on this U. 4, and therefore the flooring that supports the front stair of the structure should also be U. 41 (Fig. 32c). This floor was cut before the stair had been built, and a stratum of jumbled blocks and earth may fill an uninvestigated burial pit beneath the structural fill.

Unit 44 appears to be a side wall of the U. 41 platform (Fig. 34), distinguished by its vertical facing from the incline of the substructure above it. The top of U. 44 at the E side of the structure was 1 m lower than U. 41 at the centerline, probably for drainage. *Unit 53* was a broad stair found in widely separated trenches beneath the N side of Str. 5E-32 (Fig. 42a,c). The top of the stair formed a raised landing comparable to that on the U. 7 stair of the Maler Causeway (Fig. 30a). The 0.28 m high stair stones of U. 53 rested directly on earth fill without supporting blocks (Fig. 42c). In the W trench, a coeval Unit 56 pavement was laid against the S base of the landing (Fig. 42a).

Unit 73, the third floor from the top and the first with marl aggregate, turned up to the long Str. 5E-95-2nd building that blocked the stair of Plat. 5E-1 (Fig. 2b, 53a). The same floor preceded Str. 5E-99-2nd to the W (Fig. 48c). The second floor down in front of and behind Str. 5E-38 (Figs. 50a, 51c), *Unit 58* and *Unit 63* were first to abut the structure and cover the centerline caches, probably with the construction of 38. *Unit 76* is the equivalent flooring at the S end of Str. 5E-95-2nd (Fig. 54a)

PLATFORM 5D-2-1ST-B

In two excavations beneath the N side of Str. 5E-32, *Unit 36* covered the U. 53 stair of Plat. 5D-2-1st-C or its destruction line, *Unit 52*, with deep fill and a plaster floor containing calcined gravel (Fig. 42a,c). *Unit 25* was laid at the same level against the S side of U. 53, eliminating its raised landing altogether. Because of the identical profile of the two floors across the space to the N (Fig. 37c), U. 36 can also be identified as the lower pavement abutting Str. 5E-29 there. The *Unit 54* pavement a half meter below the structure either was a component of Plat. 5D-2 or belonged to an earlier construction. In front of Str. 5E-30, the pair of floors are 0.15 m apart and cover a fill at least 0.40 m thick (Fig. 35). In this case, however, the lower floor ran beneath Str. 5E-30 and thus preceded it. The two floors that abut the W end of 5E-30 are later pavements, however, and U. 36 seems to have weathered away where it emerged from the structure at the elevation of the U. 44 plaza edge (Fig. 34) and probably had extended the older plaza level. The skin coat on U. 41 under the front stair of Str. 5D-40 (drawn but not labeled in Fig. 32c) might have been a thinly spread extension of U. 36 over the earlier U. 41 summit plaster.

Within the Str. 5E-32 quadrangle (Figs. 38c, 42c, 46, 48a), *Unit 25* was the penultimate surface and, like the other floors pertaining to Plat. 5D-2-1st-B, was 0.15 m thick and contained marl inclusions. The floor was the base for construction of 5E-32-1st-A (Figs. 38c, 46), 5E-34 and 36 (Fig. 48a). Abutting 32-2nd-B, it also should equate with *Unit 34* farther S (Fig. 44). Less certain was correlation with *Unit 50*, the second-to-top floor between 5E-32 and 37 (Figs. 46, 55), which ran up against the U. 12 stair of 32-2nd-A and must have succeeded U. 5 of Plat. 5D-2-1st-C. *Unit 74*, the next-to-last surface on the E side of the Plaza, turned up to both 5E-99-2nd (Fig. 48c) and 5E-95-2nd (Fig. 53a).

PLATFORM 5D-2-1ST-A

The final plaza-wide platform floor was first seen on the W side of the Plaza as *Unit 93*, a thin stratum of gravel overriding Fl. 1 and lying against the Plat. 5D-1:U. 16 stair (TR. 14:fig. 254a). This stair, built with Str. 5D-1-1st, may already have existed for some time before the floor was laid. A comparable surface was not seen on top of Fl. 1 in the plaza corner trench to the S (Fig. 2c). In the many excavations in the NW corner of the Plaza, however (TR. 14:figs. 246a,b, 248, 250a,b, 252a,b), Unit 40 was the uppermost of the two floors on bedrock (U. 41 was the lower). It is described by Hellmuth as 3 cm of hard lime plaster over 5 cm of mortar and 4 cm of small stones and dirt. *Unit 40* abutted Str. 5D-37 and the concurrent U. 72 stair of Plat. 5D-1 after these had stood on U. 41 for some time with plaster turndowns onto the floor (TR. 14:656–657). Structure 5D-134 and the N end of 5D-39 were constructed on U. 40 (Fig. 27d), and although U. 41 can be seen beneath the U. 72 stair at its axis, both it and U. 40 had weathered away in front of the stair before 5D-39 was built (Fig. 23b).

Appearing in trenches N of Str. 5D-37 (Figs. 28b, 29b, 30c), the U. 40 floor became *Unit 3* of Maler Causeway. The upper of the two causeway pavements, U. 3 turned up to final parapet walls on both sides of the road (Fig. 30a,b) and then (as U. 40) to the rear walls, front stair, and E end of 5D-40 (Fig. 32c) and the W side of 5E-30 (Fig. 34). Farther E, *Unit 35* is equivalent to 40 as the first pavement to strike the front of Str. 5E-30 (Fig. 35) and the N side of 32-1st-A across the way (Fig. 42a,c). The pavement can also be identified in nearby trenches by its relationship to 32-1st-A (Figs. 9, 38c, 39b, 43b, 45) and to the U. 10 step that had been built with 1st-A (Fig. 38c). In the axial ballcourt trench nearby (Fig. 9) the earlier floor (U. 5 and U. 1) was hard to distinguish from U. 35 except where protected under fills. The Unit 11 skin-coat abutted the S addition of Str. 5E-31 (Fig. 13b), and the *Unit 16* plaster turned up to stair additions of Str. 5D-43 (unillustrated). The pavement against the front and rear of Str. 5D-41-1st was labeled U. 35 because of proximity to the ballcourt (Figs. 8f, 11, 12a–c, 13a, 16d). Pavements under Str. 5D-136 (Fig. 24b), 5E-92 (Fig. 37a), and 5E-98 (Fig. 37b) were termed U. 40 or 35 as terminal plaza surfaces in their respective trenches. *Unit 82* under Str. 5D-135 (Fig. 25b) might also be this final platform plaster, despite the presence of later U. 39. *Unit 37* on the S side of Str. 5E-32 (Fig. 46) should also be equivalent to U. 35, if U. 50 beneath it equates to Plat. 5D-2-1st-B. The upper flooring of comparable thickness and composition just to the S was also designated U. 37 (Fig. 55). *Unit 24*, the final pavement inside the quadrangle, abutted the inside walls of 32-1st-A and 99-1st in several trenches (Figs. 38c, 39b, 43b, 46, 48a,b). Although connecting trenches traced the floor from 5E-32 to 34 and 36, the pavement was eroded away at the center of the quadrangle (Figs. 38c, 48a).

Unit 75 was the upper floor on the E side of the plaza. Similar to U. 35 in thickness and inclusions, the pavement turned up to both Str. 5E-99-1st and 95-1st on either side of the narrow space between these structures (Figs. 48c, 53a). *Unit 29* at the S end of 5E-95-1st raised Plat. 5D-2 at least 0.65 m (Figs. 53b, 54a, 59a,c, 60b) and continued onto the Mendez Causeway in the same way that U. 40 became U. 3 of the Maler Causeway. *Unit 45* at Str. 5E-93 (Fig. 57), *Unit 57* in front of Str. 5E-38 (Fig. 51c) and *Unit 62* at the rear (Fig. 50a) are considered equivalent to U. 29 because of position. The floor and side wall were also seen as *Unit 97* behind Str. 5E-22 (Figs. 62, 63b).

The facade wall of Plat. 5D-2-1st-A was probably seen as *Unit 51* in the Op. 220 trench (Figs. 3b, 66c,d). The lower portions of the wall were quarried from bedrock. A basal molding stood 0.80 m above the wall base. The total 10 m height of the facade may have been divided into equal 5 m terraces, though little was seen of an upper terrace except for a core wall in the trench behind Str. 5E-29 (Fig. 37c).

The platform received patch surfaces in the areas around structures and units that were erected on its surface. *Unit 43* raised the N side of the plaza 0.40 m at the SE corner of Str. 5D-40 (Figs. 32c, 34), but was not seen in the axial excavations of either 5D-40 or 5E-30 (Figs. 32c, 35). *Unit 42* between 5D-134 and 39 (Fig. 27d) and *Unit 39* against 5D-135 (Fig. 25b) were apparently restricted to those structures and were not parts of any plaza-wide restoration.

EVIDENCE OF USE

Unit 55 was a cylindrical hole 0.20 m in diameter and a surprising 0.80 m deep penetrating the U. 53 stair landing (Fig. 42c). Its nearly central position on the landing precluded reconstruction of two parallel rows of posts, though a fence or even a roof supported by a single row of posts are possibilities. Another hole, labeled U. 11 of Str. 5E-32 and discussed under that structural designation, was 0.20 m in diameter, 0.44 m deep, and cut through U. 34 near the S end of 32-2nd-B (Figs. 38b, 44). This is almost certainly a posthole and probably supported a perishable roof beside the building.

RELATIONSHIP TO ADJACENT STRATIGRAPHY

Platform 5D-2-1st-C immediately followed demolition of Plat. 5D-1:U. 18, Str. 5D-Sub.16, 5E-Sub.1, 5D-Sub.27, and Plat. 5E-1 and construction of their replacements: Plat. 5D-1:U. 71 (estimated at A.D. 600; TR 14:841 and chart 1), Str. 5D-42, 5E-31, 5D-43, and 5E-95-2nd. Maler Causeway A-2nd, a possible early Mendez Causeway, and a huge new Central Acropolis facade were also built at this time. Structures erected on the platform, not necessarily contemporaneously, were 5D-37, 5D-41-2nd, 5E-32-2nd-B and A, and the Plat. 5D-1:U. 72 stair. Platform 5D-2-1st-B was a repaving and an expansion N of the plaza edge. Structures 5E-29, 99-2nd, 37-B, and 32-1st:U. 1 were built on it. Platform 5D-2-1st-A finished a multitude of newly built constructions: Str. 5D-40, 5E-30, 32-1st-A, 33, 34, 35, 36, 99-1st, and 95-1st, Plat. 5E-1:U. 5, and new Maler and Mendez Causeways. The structures, especially the elongate ones, provided important stratigraphic links between separate appearances of the floor across the plaza. In the final stages of the plaza, several structures were built on the floor: 5D-39, 134, 135, 136, 5E-92, 98, and 94, and three presumably restricted surfaces surrounded some of these.

ARCHITECTURE

More is known of 1st-C peripheries than of preceding ones. A broad stair, U. 53, rose from the unpaved area to the N, and a wide landing at its summit was similar to one on the side of the Maler Causeway. The platform covered a larger area than the earlier one, reaching for the first time the NW corner of the plaza. Elsewhere the floor was relatively thin. Platform 5D-2-1st-B broadened the N edge once more, using a large amount of fill and supporting Str. 5E-29 at its edge. Platform 5D-2-1st-A consisted of thin summit resurfacing around new galleries and other structures. The side terrace walls of the platform might have been rebuilt again.

Averaging 0.10 m in thickness across most of the plaza and perhaps 3 m in the new fill near the Maler Causeway, Plat. 5D-2-1st-C required ca. 8,500 m^3 of material and 762 m^2 of surface dressing. Platform 5D-2-1st-B, averaging 7 m in thickness in the N area and 0.07 m on the rest of the platform, utilized an even larger 16,500 m^3 and 1,040 m^2, whereas Plat. 5D-2-1st-A expended only ca. 1,300 m^3 and 1,640 m^2.

LOTS, GROUPING AND EVALUATION

PRIMARY CONSTRUCTION

4G/7 and 17B/7, sealed within Fl. 1 of Plat. 5D-2-1st-C, contained Manik sherds and one Ik. 78P/4 and 6 from U. 53 had mostly Ik and Imix ceramics. 78O/10, 11, and 12, sealed in platform fill in the pit between Str. 5D-40 and 41 (Fig. 2a), contained late Manik and Ik. These collections indicate that at least Ik and perhaps early Imix ceramics were in use at the time of construction, confirming the ceramic collections sealed in Str. 5D-42, 43, and 5E-31.

SECONDARY CONSTRUCTION

78D/3 sealed in U. 36, and 78A/13, 14, 78C/2, and 78M/8 from U. 25 contained Manik, Ik, and Imix sherds, ensuring that Imix was being produced by the time of 1st-B assembly. Platform 5D-2-1st-A had no sealed lots.

OCCUPATION

22O/1-49 were collected in deep trenching through inclined strata that had accumulated beside a projecting stair of 1st-A (Figs. 3a,b, 66c,d). A 1960 ceramic test report by Vivian Broman stated:

> Operation 22O was enlarged after the initial test showed a quantity of sherds of [Imix] types. A most satisfactory quantity of sherds was recovered from this test: much polychrome, most in fairly delicate condition and requiring special care in cleaning, as well as large sherds representing whole sections in many cases. The extended trench revealed that the bedrock surface had been quarried, later filled with construction fill to bring it up to a certain level, and subsequently loaded with dump debris. Some Early Classic elements occurred in the construction fill, but the main bulk of ceramic material from surface to bedrock was that of the [Imix Ceramic Complex].

Notes on individual lots mention large jar sherds, polychromes, cut and/or polished bone, including "fan handles" and flutes, cut shell tinklers, pendants made from sherds, figurine heads, and censers. The bone, shell, and lithics were suggestive of workshop activity that presumably derived from occupation of the platform summit. Perhaps the material came from Str. 5E-32 and the E half of the platform, because the absence of Eznab sherds makes it clear that the deposit was not associated with the Eznab middens on and around the western structures.

TIME SPANS

Platform 5D-2-1st began with paving most of the summit (Table 3:TS. 9). The center of the Plaza was occupied by ballcourt Str. 5D-42 and 5E-31 and Str. 5D-43 at the S end of the court. The W edge of the plaza is poorly understood, U. 20 perhaps being an interior construction for a now-missing wall (TR. 14:184–185). Farther N the Plaza side was more clearly demarcated by two-tiered U. 71 of Plat. 5D-1-1st-E (TR. 14:194; fig. 248) and the S side was defined by a Central Acropolis wall of identical profile and masonry. The platform was extended to meet the head of the new Maler Causeway approaching it from the N.

On the E edge of the Plaza Str. 5E-95-2nd cut off the only known stair of Plat. 5E-1, rendering it obsolete. The floors which abut Str. 5E-38 and cover dedicatory skull caches are likely of this time span though the structure may be earlier.

Platform 5D-2 was extended N once more in TS. 7 and thereby gave the Plaza a single border reaching from the Maler Causeway to Plat. 5E-1. The platform now supported vaulted gallery Str. 5E-29, 99-2nd, 37, and 32-1st-C. Because none of the floors in the W part of the Plaza were of this time, a stratigraphic link was not made to Gp. 5D-2. Nonetheless, assembly of Str. 5D-1-1st (Temple I, ca. A.D. 734) could have been the incentive for this development.

The principal component of Plat. 5D-2-1st-A (TS. 5) was a new Plaza floor seen in every part of the summit, sometime after erection of Str. 5D-1-1st. In addition, the U. 8 stair descending from the causeway edge behind Str. 5D-40 (Fig. 30a) and U. 62 terrace behind 5E-38 (Fig. 50a) were indications that the platform sides also underwent extensive reconstruction. Many new structures were built on the platform in the beginning of the time span with the pavement turning up to their bases and serving to complete them. Most were gallery buildings with multiple doorways covering the E half of the plaza. In TS. 3 several small substructures were built on the floor. Limited patch floors were probably not components of widespread resurfacing. The collapse of the N face in TS. 1 buried thick deposits of cultural debris.

TABLE 3
Platform 5D-2-1st: Time Spans

Time Span	Architectural Addition	Floor, Unit	Special Deposit	Lot	Other Data
1	—	—	—	—	Collapse
2	—	—	—	—	Use
3	—	U. 39,42,43	—	—	Local patch floors with Str. 5D-39,134–136; 5E-92,94,98; Eznab ceramics
4	—	—	—	22O/1–49	Use
5	A	U. 11,16,24,29,35, 37,40,51,57,62, 75,82,93	—	—	Assembly (1,300 m^3) with Str. 5D-40,43-A; 5E-30,32-1st-A, 33–36,93,95-1st,96,97,99-1st; Cswy. Maler A-1st; Imix ceramics
6	—	—	—	—	Use
7	B	U. 25,36,50,54,74	—	78A/13,14; 78C/2; 78D/3; 78M/8	NE expansion (15,500 m^3) with Str. 5D-41-1st; 5E-29,32-1st-C,B, 37,99-2nd; Imix ceramics
8	—	—	—	—	Use
9	C	Fl. 1; U. 1,5,7,17, 19,20,26,33,41,44, 53,55,56,58,63,65, 68,73,76	—	4G/7; 17B/7; 78O/10,11,12; 78/4,6	Assembly (8,500 m^3) with Str. 5D-42,43; 5E-31,32-2nd,38; Cswy. Maler A-2nd; Imix ceramics?

III

Structures on Platform 5D-2

STRUCTURE 5D-SUB.26

INTRODUCTION

A wall stub and fill were all that was seen of a possible structure beneath Str. 5D-43 and two plaza floors (Op. 78P). See Fig. 19d.

EXCAVATION DATA

A single south-facing course of stones sitting on a thin layer of fill over U. 8 (the lowest of five Plat. 5D-2 floors) was abutted by two pavements, U. 10 and U. 93 (Fig. 19d). The thin stratum of mortar that runs beneath both the U. 10 floor and the wall indicates that the pavement was laid with the structure. The wall stones lie flat (an early trait for Gp. 5D-3) rather than on their sides; one measures 0.17 m high and 0.34 m long. The face of the course has a slight slope suitable for the rear of a north-oriented substructure. Seen only within the meter width of the trench, interior fill extended N for 2.35 m.

RELATIONSHIP TO ADJACENT STRATIGRAPHY

The U. 10 floor abutting Sub.26 corresponds in its stratigraphic position to Fl. 4 of Plat. 5D-2-3rd-A. After a secondary abutment by U. 93 (Plat. 5D-2-2nd-B), Sub.26 was demolished and covered by U. 18 of 2nd-A. Structure 5D-Sub.27 to the S survived until later.

LOTS, GROUPING AND EVALUATION

CONSTRUCTION

78P/31 from within structural fill contained Cimi and Manik sherds and a "Preclassic" Holom spiked censer rim sherd (Ferree 1972:38–53).

TIME SPANS

Table 4 outlines the time spans. The structure was erected (TS. 2) in front of 5D-Sub.27 with both entities probably facing N. Structures 5D-Sub.28 and 29 to the N had been demolished by this time, and 5D-Sub.16 and 5E-Sub.1 were not yet built. Although the dimensions and form of the structure are unknown, Sub.26 in front of Sub.27 might have covered a burial pit and chamber (as did Str. 5D-Sub.10, located above Bu. 164 and in front of 5D-Sub.9, TR. 14:fig. 30c).

TABLE 4
Structure 5D-Sub.26: Time Spans

Time Span	Architectural Addition	Floor, Unit	Special Deposit	Lot	Other Data
1	—	—	—	—	Use
2	—	—	—	78P/31	Assembly with Plat. 5D-2: U. 10; Manik ceramics

STRUCTURE 5D-SUB.27

INTRODUCTION

A row of masonry beneath Str. 5D-43 was recorded by Orrego and Jones in 1965 (Op. 78P), but not recognized as a structure at the time. See Fig. 19d.

EXCAVATION DATA

CONSTRUCTION STAGES

A basal course of headers 0.60 m long facing N on the unplastered surface of Plat. 5D-2:U. 8 had a slightly inclined front surface suitable for either a substructural wall or a stair (Fig. 19d). No plaster was observed on the facing. Interior fill was supported by U. 8 and rising bedrock. A possible second step may have survived as a single large stone. Structural plan is unknown.

RELATIONSHIP TO ADJACENT STRATIGRAPHY

Analogous by position to Fl. 5 of Plat. 5D-2-3rd-B, the unplastered U. 8 floor supported the structure with its plaster surface running up against the base. Units 10, 93 and 18 (Fl. 4, 3 and 2) also turned up against the structure, and U. 19 (Fl. 1 of Plat. 5D-2-1st-C) and Str. 5D-43 later covered it.

TIME SPANS

Time spans are outlined in Table 5. Projecting from the S edge of the plaza, Str. 5D-Sub.27 might have anticipated 5D-43 in form and function. The structure stood for a time with Sub.28 and 29 and later with 5D-Sub.16 and 5E-Sub.1 at the same locations. Although the frontal plaza was always paved, the area to the E lacked a plaster floor and may have remained unpaved until construction of 5D-43 and the Central Acropolis facade behind it.

TABLE 5
Structure 5D-Sub.27: Time Spans

Time Span	Architectural Addition	Floor, Unit	Special Deposit	Lot	Other Data
1	—	—	—	—	Use with Plat. 5D-2:U. 10,93,18
2	—	—	—	—	Assembly with Plat. 5D-2:U. 8 (Fl. 5)

STRUCTURE 5D-SUB.28

INTRODUCTION

A west-facing wall on the U. 78 floor is interpreted as the remnant of a structure, Sub.28, because of its similarity to the corresponding E wall of Sub.29 (Fig. 9). Both were poorly recorded, however, and had not been recognized in the field. See Fig. 9.

EXCAVATION DATA

The W faces of the two surviving courses formed a vertical, unplastered facade with a height of 0.27 m and a flat upper surface suitable for a bottom step of a stair rather than for the base of a wall. The deep fill of floor U. 79 buried the stones.

TIME SPANS

Assembled in TS. 2 (Table 6), Str. 5D-Sub.28 and its twin Sub.29 might have been either opposing stairs of structures anticipating in placement and function the superimposed twin pyramids (5D-Sub.16 and 5E-Sub.1), or opposing bench faces of a ballcourt, anticipating Strs. 5D-42 and 5E-31.

STRUCTURE 5D-SUB.29

INTRODUCTION

A wall deep below Str. 5E-31 on Plat. 5D-2 floor U. 78 was recorded in a 1960 ceramic test pit (Op. 23A), but was unnoticed in 1965 trenching (Op. 78K). Excavation control was poor because neither it nor

TABLE 6
Structure 5E-Sub.28: Time Spans

Time Span	Architectural Addition	Floor, Unit	Special Deposit	Lot	Other Data
1	—	—	—	—	Use
2	—	—	—	—	Assembly on Plat. 5D-2:U. 78 (Fl. 5)

Sub.28 was recognized as a possible structure until after the excavations had ended. See Fig. 9.

EXCAVATION DATA

The 1960 field notes described the two-course retaining wall as oriented E, but the W faces of the stones appear to be vertical and well aligned, and the marly earth E of the wall looks like structural fill. The stones were laid on their largest surfaces. The two courses and interior fill were 0.30 m high, appropriate for a step as in the case of Sub.28. Both structures were buried by Plat. 5D-2:U. 79, which raised the plaza level 1 m.

TIME SPANS

Two courses of masonry are interpreted as a west-oriented stair or wall opposite a similar feature across an 8.5 m space. Accordingly, twin pyramids or a ball-court might have existed here at this early period (TS. 2:Table 7). Evidence is scanty, however, even for the existence of these structures, much less their forms.

TABLE 7
Structure 5E-Sub.29: Time Spans

Time Span	Architectural Addition	Floor, Unit	Special Deposit	Lot	Other Data
1	—	—	—	—	Use
2	—	—	—	—	Assembly on Plat. 5D-2:U. 78 (Fl. 5)

STRUCTURE 5D-SUB.16

INTRODUCTION

During the 1965 investigations into Str. 5D-42 (Op. 78M), Jones and Orrego found the well-preserved terraces and stairs of a buried pyramidal structure; identical features under 5E-31 proved the existence of twin pyramids. A preliminary description appeared in Jones 1969 (pp. 31–32, 85–87, 93–95, 107–109, fig. 10). See Figs. 4 (plan), 6a,b, 7a–c, 9 (section), 12c, 14h, 67b–d, 68a,b,d.

EXCAVATION DATA

CONSTRUCTION STAGES

CONSTRUCTION STAGE 3

The axial tunnel through Str. 5D-42 revealed the several stages of Sub.16 construction. *Unit 4* is the pyramidal core, assembled on the Plat. 5D-2:U. 80 floor (Fig. 9). At least two terrace-levels high, the nucleus of gray-brown earth and roughly hewn, oblong blocks was faced with sloping E and W walls of undressed, flat, evenly coursed blocks. A crude uneven plaster floor capped the lowest terrace of the E side and ran under the next higher terrace wall.

CONSTRUCTION STAGE 2

Short sets of masons' stairs were built against both sides of the U. 4 nucleus: *Unit 3* on the W, *Unit 5* on the E. These differ from the finish stairs in their irregular construction, single-course steps, and absence of plaster. Fill stones were similar to those of U. 4.

CONSTRUCTION STAGE 1

Unit 7 and *Unit 2*, the E and W stairs of the pyramid, were built 1.20 m in front of the core stairs (Fig. 9). Interior fill contained the same rough oblong stones as the core units. Each step in U. 2 (Figs. 14h, 67b, 68a,b) was made of two courses laid flat, the lower one with blocks ca. 0.50 by 0.30 by 0.15 m, the upper one of smaller slabs 0.35 by 0.20 by 0.10 m. Faces were trimmed before installation. Thick, hard yellow plaster on the risers turned down over slightly sloping tread plaster. No traces of paint were seen on plaster, either here or on twin Str. 5E-Sub.1. Average stair height of 0.295 m and depth of 0.318 m were calculated from the nine lower steps. These differ little from the 0.296 and 0.313 m averages of six steps on 5E-Sub.1 and allow 18 or 19 steps in the 5.5 m rise. Stair width (Fig. 4) was extrapolated from that of 5E-Sub.1 (Fig. 5). The U. 7 stair on the W side of the structure was torn down to its lowest course (Fig. 9). The remnant was compositionally identical to U. 2 and was built on the same U. 80 floor that had been followed under the structure. The stair wall and terraces on the W side of the pyramid resembled counterparts on 5E-Sub.1 (Figs. 4, 6a). Plaster still adhered to masonry, and a slight outward slope could be seen on the stair wall.

ADDITIONS AND RENOVATIONS

Apparently part of a full-scale renovation of the pyramid (Sub.16-A), *Unit 1* was a new flight of stairs covering the W stair of Sub.16 and sealing Ca. 188, 189, and 192 (Figs. 6a,b, 9, 67b). The two courses of the bottom step were laid on their larger surfaces, like original Sub.16-B stonework. The stair blocks, as long as 0.78 m, were roughly shaped, but had flat vertical faces. Inner fill was hard brown marl closely packed with long, roughly hewn blocks. The N end wall of U. 1 was probably *Unit 8*, discovered within the stair wall of later Str. 5D-42 (Figs. 6a,b, 12c, 68d). The slightly inclined U. 8 appears to have been a stair-side border. Together U. 1 and 8 may have reached only the height shown in Fig. 6a,b, but might also have encased the pyramid stair to full height. During excavation U. 1 and 8 had been the only additions recognized for Sub.16. *Unit 6* can now be seen as a comparable E stair addition that had been dismantled to a single facing course (Fig. 9). The 0.35 by 0.25 by 0.15 m stones were identical to those of U. 1 and were 1.90 m in front of the pyramid stair, as was U. 4 of Str. 5E-Sub.1. Although no floor turned up to U. 6 corresponding to the U. 2 floor against U. 1, a plaster turn across the alley (5E-Sub.1:U. 4) was probably a U.2 remnant surrounding the structures and covering Ca. 202 and 195. Taken together, Units 1 and 6 are evidence for a major revision of the pyramid (Str. 5D-Sub.16-A).

RELATIONSHIP TO ADJACENT STRATIGRAPHY

Structure 5D-Sub.16-B was built on Plat. 5D-2:U. 80, the floor of which was traced by tunnel from side to side and beyond to Str. 5E-Sub.1. Both pyramids were completed by floor U. 83 of Plat. 5D-2-2nd-A. The 5D-Sub.16-A additions were built with floor U. 2, which survived on the W side of the pyramid and probably once paved the area to the E as well.

ARCHITECTURE

As far as could be discerned, Str. 5D-Sub.16 was a close twin to 5E-Sub.1, just E of it. The W stair and terraces and a stub of the E flight were the only surfaces exposed, but existence of N and S stairs was implied from the S stair found on the other pyramid. The five undecorated, inclined terrace faces were like those on 5E-Sub.1 and later twin pyramids. Soft-edged stair and wall stones were laid on their largest surfaces, as on Str. 5E-Sub.1, Plat. 5D-1:U. 18 and Plat. 5E-1, in contrast to later sharply edged stretchers and headers laid on edge. Pyramid height measured 5.5 m; the base was 12 by 12.5 m and the summit 6 by 6.5 m. Volume was ca. 600 m^3 and the area of dressed surface 200 m^2. Assuming that Sub.16-A modifications reached full height, an additional 381 m^3 of fill material and 314 m^2 of dressed surface would have been needed.

SPECIAL DEPOSITS

CACHE 188

LOCATION

Str. 5D-Sub.16, W side, centerline, sealed by secondary U. 1 of Sub.16-A (cf. Ca. 189 and 192). 78M/26. See Figs. 6b, 7a, 9, 67b–d.

CONTENT

2 eccentric flints (TR. 27A:fig. 9c); 7 eccentric obsidians (ibid., figs. 26e, 28f); 435 gray obsidian flake-blades, apparently from the same or matched cores, most chipped on edges; 326 used obsidian flakes; 71 unused obsidian flakes; 3 jade beads (ibid., fig. 125i); 112 jade mosaic elements (ibid., fig. 77*a*1); 9 *Spondylus*, and 32 white and nacreous shell mosaic elements (ibid., fig. 77*a*3); 2 specular hematite mosaic elements (ibid., fig. 77*a*2); 90 jade particles (ibid., fig. 136c); 1 *Spondylus* valve, complete, each hinge perforated in two or three places; 16 shell figurines (ibid., fig. 160 concordance); 98 shell fragments, unworked; 1 bone imitation stingray spine (ibid., fig. 184*d*9); 1 pottery cache vessel and cover, Balanza Black, round-sided variety (TR. 25A:fig. 102c).

ARRANGEMENT

Cache 188 occupied a repository dug out of the stone and earth fill of U. 1 (Figs. 7a, 9, 67c). The side of a large stone was cut to form part of the pit wall. The cache vessel was set in the center of the hole after the bottom of the pit was charred by fire. The lid collapsed and the pot filled with dirt. Pieces on the bottom of the vessel included two jade beads (Fig. 7a; locus 3), a complete *Spondylus* shell closed upon another jade bead (locus 1), and four obsidian eccentrics (locus 5). Shell figurines were placed E of the rim after earth and obsidian flakes had filled the pit around the vessel. A Type EF-12 eccentric flint (locus 4) and a type EO-11 eccentric obsidian (locus 2) lay respectively above and beside the vessel.

SEQUENTIAL POSITION

The cache was sealed by Str. 5D-Sub.16-A stair fill. The vessel belongs to the Manik Ceramic Complex (TR. 25A) and the cache was assigned to the Early Classic Muul Offertory Assemblage (TR. 35).

CACHE 189

LOCATION

In the Str. 5D-Sub.16 W side, centerline, sealed by secondary U. 1 of Sub.16-A (cf. Ca. 188 and 192). 78M/33. See Figs. 6b, 7b, 9.

CONTENT

3 flint eccentrics (TR. 27A:figs. 9d, 11a5); 1 obsidian eccentric (ibid., fig. 26f); ca. 100 used obsidian flake-blade fragments; ca. 50 used obsidian flakes; 25 jade mosaic elements (ibid., fig. 77*f*1); 12 *Spondylus*, white and nacreous mosaic elements (ibid., fig. 77*f*2); 3 polished jade chunks (ibid., fig. 132h); 54 jade particles (ibid., fig. 136c); 14 standard *Spondylus* figurines (ibid., fig. 160 concordance) and 5 disks (ibid., fig. 77*f*3); 4 unworked *Spondylus* fragments; 1 eccentrically perforated sherd, perhaps not from the cache.

ARRANGEMENT

The bulk of material was centrally placed at the bottom of a circular pit, on a thin layer of earth and obsidian chips (Fig. 7b). Most of the mosaic pieces (locus 9) were grouped between two shell elements (loci 5, 12) as though once articulated as an object. The larger obsidian and flint eccentrics (loci 1, 8, 10, 11) were positioned last. In Ca. 188 and 189 they were oriented NW-SE as though placed by a right-handed person facing E.

SEQUENTIAL POSITION

The repository within the U. 1 stair hearting of Str. 5D-Sub.16-A was better sealed than Ca. 188. The cache was assigned to the Muul Offertory Assemblage (TR. 35).

CACHE 192

LOCATION

In a pit in the Plat. 5D-2:U. 83 floor, sealed by U. 1 of 5D-Sub.16-A (cf. Ca. 188 and 189). 78M/35. See Figs. 6b, 7c, 9.

CONTENT

16 jade particles; 5 slightly modified Spondylus sp. valves; 7 standard *Spondylus* figurines (TR. 27A:fig. 160 concordance); unworked shell chips; 1 weathered piece of branch coral.

ARRANGEMENT

The figurines lay face down on or near the bottom of the cylindrical pit, and the shells and coral were placed above them (Fig. 6b).

SEQUENTIAL POSITION

The pit cut through the U. 83 platform floor that turned up to Str. 5D-Sub.16-B, and was capped by thin rough plaster. This plaster seal, subsequently covered by the U. 1 fill of Sub.16-A, might indicate that the cache significantly predates U. 1 construction. The cache was assigned to the Leum Offertory Assemblage, which is contemporary to Muul Offertory Assemblages such as Ca. 188 and 189 (TR. 35).

CACHE 202

LOCATION

On Plat. 5D-2:U. 83 just E of U. 6 of Str. 5D-Sub.16-A, perhaps once sealed by a now-missing Plat. 5D-2:U. 2 floor and certainly by U. 1 and 35 floors.

CONTENT

2 whole standard *Spondylus* figurines and 1 incomplete (TR. 27A); 1 small *Spondylus* disk (ibid., fig. 84l). The cache seems to be a portion of a "split" cache, the rest of which may be Cache 195.

ARRANGEMENT

In a 0.10 by 0.10 m area of the weathered U. 83 surface of U. 83 within 0.15 m of the E stair of Str. 5D-Sub.16-A (cf. Ca. 195 at 5E-Sub.1).

SEQUENTIAL POSITION

Cache 202 was sealed by the Plat. 5D-2:U. 1 and 35 floors. Because of plaster turning up to twin Str. 5E-Sub.1-A just to the E, it is likely that the cache had been covered by a thin floor equivalent to Plat. 5D-2:U. 2 and was therefore coeval with Ca. 188, 189, and 192 as well as 171 and 195 of 5E-Sub.1. These caches (of Muul and Leum Offertory Assemblages; TR. 35) contained shell figurines and disks similar to those of Ca. 202.

LOTS, GROUPING AND EVALUATION

CONSTRUCTION

78M/37, 41, 42, and 43 sealed within nuclear constructions U. 4 and 5 contained Manik pottery with some Cauac sherds. The lack of Ik and Imix sherds within more than 10 lbs of pottery strongly implied that construction occurred during Manik production.

TIME SPANS

The Str. 5D-Sub.16-B pyramid was assembled on weathered Plat. 5D-2:U. 80 flooring (Table 8:TS. 4). Shortly after completion, floor U. 83 was spread against the stair bases. By typology and position this floor belongs to Plat. 5D-2-2nd-B. The masonry was distinct from that of later East Plaza construction. Large collections of Manik sherds from the structural fill suggest an early date for the structure. Excavation sufficed to reconstruct a five-terrace, four-stair pyramid and its twin, conforming in most details to later twin pyramids (Jones 1969) but more closely spaced. No evidence was found of a N enclosure or a S building. Wear on floor U. 83 and the stair points to some passage of time prior to the renovations of TS. 2. Although these additions are depicted as only 1.75 m high (Fig. 6b), they might have risen to the full height of the pyramids. Caches 188, 189, and 192 on the W side of the pyramid and Ca. 202 on the E of the Muul and Leum Offertory Assemblages (TR. 35) include a Manik Ceramic Complex cache vessel (TR. 25A). The four-stairway pyramid plan seems to have been retained, hence the structures were probably used for longer than the single katun implied for later Twin Pyramids Groups. The renovations themselves possibly marked a new katun of use. With the decision to build Str. 5D-42 and 5E-31, Sub.16 was partially dismantled and completely buried beneath the new ballcourt.

TABLE 8
Structure 5D-Sub.16: Time Spans

Time Span	Architectural Addition	Floor, Unit	Special Deposit	Lot	Other Data
1	—	—	—	—	Use
2	A	U. 1,6,8	Ca. 188,189, 192,202	—	Additions (380 m^3) with Plat. 5D-2:U. 2; Muul and Leum caches; Manik ceramics
3	—	—	—	—	Use
4	B	U. 2–5,7	—	78M/37,41–43	Assembly (600 m^3) with Plat. 5D-2:U.83; Manik ceramics

STRUCTURE 5E-SUB.1

INTRODUCTION

A 1960 test pit (Op. 23A) unexpectedly uncovered a stair on the W side of Str. 5E-31. When reexamined in 1964 (Op. 78K), its undeniable presence negated for a short time the conviction that the pair of mounds in the center of the East Plaza constituted a ballcourt. When East Plaza excavations were expanded in 1965 by Jones and Orrego (Op. 78K), the stair was seen to belong to an earlier pyramid buried within the ballcourt bench. The W stair and terraces, NW and SW corners, and S stair of the pyramid were subsequently uncovered in excavation. See Figs. 5(plan), 9 (section), 70a, 72a,b.

EXCAVATION DATA

CONSTRUCTION STAGES

CONSTRUCTION STAGE 3

The first stage in construction of Sub.1 was a nucleus built in rough terraces. Sloping walls of the core were seen at the top of the E side (Fig. 9).

CONSTRUCTION STAGE 2

As on Str. 5D-Sub.16, a construction stair, *Unit 2* (not to be confused with the U. 2 rip-out line of Str. 5E-31), was built over the pyramidal core.

CONSTRUCTION STAGE 1

Floor U. 83 of Plat. 5D-2 turned up to a course of flat stones, helping to identify it as the basal course of the *Unit 1* stair (Figs. 9, 70a). Although the upper course and the entire second step had been torn out for placement of the 5E-31 bench, the third through sixth steps survived. An average 0.313 m rise was calculated from these 6 steps and enabled reconstruction of 18 steps in the 5.71 m pyramid height. The stair stones were laid flat; they measured 0.35–0.50 m long, 0.20–0.30 m wide, and 0.15–0.20 high m, and were identical to those of Str. 5D-Sub.16.

Terraces were partially preserved on both sides of the W stair (Figs. 5, 72b). The second level inclined gently 0.12 m from the N corner to the S, corresponding to the plaza slope below. The first and second terraces together were 2.25 m high, and the third 1.06 m, leaving 2.20 m for the combined fourth and fifth stages. The 0.32 m summit depth and 15° slope recorded on one terrace were used in reconstruction of both pyramids (Figs. 4, 5, 6a). Wall stones laid on their flat surfaces corresponded in dimensions to those of the stairs. Their fronts were cut to the 15° angle of the walls themselves. This masonry has been termed "bread-loaf" (Jones 1969) because of the rounded edges and horizontal setting.

The axial trench strayed considerably S of centerline on the E side of the structure, missing the E stair entirely (Figs. 5, 9). Nevertheless, floor U. 83 was seen to turn up to *Unit 3*, a line of stones belonging to the pyramid wall. The SW corner terrace levels were followed E in a narrow tunnel to a S stair wall on which were seen the corners of two thickly plastered steps. A corresponding N stair and radially symmetrical pyramid are likely.

ADDITIONS AND RENOVATIONS

Unit 4 is interpreted as an addition like that of U. 1 and 6 of 5D-Sub.16. All that remains, however, is west-facing plaster rising from the U. 83 floor (Figs. 9, 72a). The masonry of the U. 4 wall itself, which once stood as the first step, had been removed in ancient times. As with the Str. 5D-Sub.16 additions, U. 4 may have extended only partway up the pyramids, (cf. Fig. 6a,b), or to full height. The fact that the U. 83 floor is better preserved under rather than in front of U. 4 demonstrates that the new stair was in use for a long time.

RELATIONSHIP TO ADJACENT STRATIGRAPHY

Original Str. 5E-Sub.1-B was built on the worn surface of Plat. 5D-2:U. 80 and was immediately abutted by U. 83, which probably belonged to Plat. 5D-2-2nd-A. The structure was buried during assembly of Str. 5E-31 and the Plat. 5D-2-1st-C floor.

ARCHITECTURE

Structure 5E-Sub.1-B was identical to 5D-Sub.16 in measurements and assembly technique. Excavators did not look for the pyramid summit beneath the ballcourt structure. Masonry was identical to that of Str. 5D-Sub.16, Plat. 5D-1:U. 18 (TR. 14:fig. 254) and Plat. 5E-1 (Figs. 53a, 59a). The pyramid did not deviate in any known way from those in later Twin Pyramid Groups at Tikal, except for its proximity to the W pyramid. Primary Sub.1-B required ca. 600 m^3 of material and 200 m^2 of dressed surface. The Sub.1-A rebuilding would have added another 380 m^3 of material and yet another 310 m^2 of trimmed outer surface.

SPECIAL DEPOSITS

CACHE 195

LOCATION

Cache 195 lay on Plat. 5D-2:U. 83, 0.10 m W of U. 4 of Str. 5E-Sub.1-A, probably sealed by a now-missing U. 2 floor and subsequently by U. 1 and U. 35. 78K/17. See Fig. 9.

CONTENT

5 standard *Spondylus* figurines (TR. 27A:fig. 160 concordance); 1 jade fragment, apparently small and unworked (lost in the field). The contents appear to be part of a "split" cache along with Ca. 202.

ARRANGEMENT

Contents were confined to a small oval area in front of the plaster turnup to U. 4 of 5E-Sub.1-A. All lay flat on eroded U. 83, four of them parallel to each other and perpendicular to the U. 4 rise. The arrangement suggests that the objects were sealed immediately by a floor equivalent to Plat. 5D-2:U. 2 on the W side of Sub.16-A.

SEQUENTIAL POSITION

Association of the cache with Sub.1-A remains hypothetical because the pieces were not sealed by the plaster that turned up to the structure. The deposit was located at the centerline base of the structure, however, and the figurines are identical to those in Ca. 202 in front of U. 6 of Str. 5D-Sub.16-A and in Ca. 188, 189, and 191 on the W side of Sub.16-A.

CACHE 171

LOCATION

Most of the cache was centered on the fourth tread of the W stair of Str. 5E-Sub.1-B, probably sealed first by missing fills of 5E-Sub.1-A and subsequently by 5E-31. A trident eccentric flint now considered part of Ca. 171 was found higher on the stair and was also probably once sealed within Sub.1-A. 78K/1, 18. See Fig. 9.

CONTENT

6 eccentric flints (TR. 27A:fig. 8j); 25 unmodified obsidian flake-blades; obsidian flakes and flake-blade and core fragments.

ARRANGEMENT

5 eccentric flints were grouped on the fourth step and one was found higher up. Arrangement and orientation were not recorded. The 78K/18 eccentric flint was lost in the field.

SEQUENTIAL POSITION

The cache lay within a thin layer of undisturbed fill probably pertaining to Str. 5E-Sub.1-A.

LOTS, GROUPING AND EVALUATION

78K/33 and 34 from Str. 5E-Sub.1-B fill contained sherds no later than Manik and corroborated assessments of the larger Sub.16-B lots.

TIME SPANS

Structure 5E-Sub.1 time spans are summarized in Table 9. The structure was unequivocally a pyramid with five undecorated terrace levels. The presence of stairs on three sides necessitates the assumption of a fourth, making the whole a radially symmetrical structure identical to later twin pyramids. The summit was not investigated for evidence of a building. Techniques of assembly were those of Str. 5D-Sub.16-B: a terraced pyramidal nucleus with construction stairs, thick plastered walls, and round-edged, oblong masonry laid flat. The E-W setting of twin pyramids of this form on the broad platform surface conforms to plans of later Tikal twin pyramids, though here the two are unaccountably crowded into the center of the plaza. A N enclosure, S building, and monuments of a complete Twin Pyramid Group were not searched for, however, and the expected pit for a centerline stela between the structures was not evident in the trench. Good preservation of U. 83 flooring underneath the additions to the pyramid in TS. 2 suggests that exposure during TS. 3 possibly lasted only the 20 years of a katun of use. Renovation perhaps occurred on all four stairs of the pyramid, but is only evidenced by a plaster turnup running parallel to the W stair. Caches associated with this plaster and the additions on Str. 5D-Sub.16 help to place them within the time of Manik ceramic production.

TABLE 9
Structure 5E-Sub.1: Time Spans

Time Span	Architectural Addition	Floor, Unit	Special Deposit	Lot	Other Data
1	—	—	—	—	Use
2	A	U. 4	Ca. 195,171	—	Additions (380 m^3) with Plat. 5D-2:U. 2?
3	—	—	—	—	Use
4	B	U. 1–3	—	78K/33,34	Assembly (600 m^3) with Plat. 5D-2:U. 83; Manik ceramics

STRUCTURE 5D-42

INTRODUCTION

The project map (TR. 11:Great Plaza Sheet) shows the mound of this structure as a twin to 5E-31, suitable for a ballcourt, but test trenching in 1960 on the W side of 5E-31 (Op. 23A) uncovered a stair in place of a ballcourt bench. In 1965, however, sloping ballcourt benches were found on both structures, confirming the presence of a ballcourt (Op. 78M for this structure, 78K for 5E-31). See Figs. 1, 8a–c (plan), e,f, 9 (section), 11, 12a–c, 14a,b,d,g, 15a–c, 67a,b, 68b,c, 69a–d.

EXCAVATION DATA

CONSTRUCTION STAGES

CONSTRUCTION STAGE 3

Assembly necessitated removal of large portions of Str. 5D-Sub.16. Demolition of the E stair (U. 6) to the *Unit 12* rip-out line spared only the lowest step and penetrated deeply into the structural core (Fig. 9). Although the upper half of the W stair was also torn out (*Unit 11*) to make way for the ballcourt side wall, the lower steps were preserved. Plans of 42 and Sub.16 (Figs. 4, 8a) demonstrate that the N and S stairs of the pyramid did not need to be demolished and might be intact within the ballcourt.

CONSTRUCTION STAGE 2

Unit 3 is a five-step stair of massive blocks leading to a narrow landing from which two more steps, *Unit 4*, mounted to a broader platform surface turning up to the W wall of the substructure (Figs. 8a,e, 9, 14d, 67a,b, 68b). Unit 3 was constructed of exceptionally large stones, with sample lengths of 1.55 and 1.40 m, heights of 0.44, 0.45, and 0.49 m, and thicknesses of 0.60 and 0.70 m. The front and upper surfaces of the chalky limestone blocks were smoothly finished with rounded noses. Deep carving was seen on one block displaced from the third or fourth step of the N end (Fig. 68c). The N end of the stair was flanked by a 2.90 m wide *Unit 13* stair set back from the main stair. The stretcher stones of U. 13 are distinguishable from the headers of the later U. 9 stairs beside it (Figs. 8a,e, 12c, 68d). Blocks averaged 0.50 by 0.30 by 0.20 m, and lengths ranged from 0.35 to 0.60 m.

Despite careful exposure of the substructural upper zone on the N, S, and W sides (Figs. 8d,e, 69a–c), no evidence was found of stair insets or outsets such as on ballcourt Str. 5D-74 and 80. No access stairs to the buildings were located on 5E-31, although it is difficult to imagine the ballcourt without access to upper buildings. The substructure had two upper levels, the rear one 0.30 m higher than the front, laterally outset, and possessing a central outset (Fig. 8d,e). Upper and lower zones on the ends of the substructure had inset panels edged with vertical grooves (Figs. 8d,e, 69c). A three-step overhang extended under the lip of the ballcourt bench. These features are identical on all four ends of the ballcourt ranges.

Two stones carved with hieroglyphics were found fallen onto the bench top in the narrow centerline trench (Fig. 15a–c). One block portrayed a profile head with a snake-rattle prefix (Fig. 15a,b). The carving is identical in size and style to that on similar blocks from 5E-31, where a central panel of 24 glyph blocks in two rows was flanked by non-glyphic side panels (Fig. 8b). The inscription, if read as a unit on both structures, probably began on 5D-42 because the Tikal Emblem Glyph that often ends inscriptions formed the final block on the opposing structure.

Substructural walls were built with standing stretcher and header blocks varying in size from 0.25–0.40 m high and 0.40–0.70 m long. Irregularities of shape were common, with coursing undulating as if trimmed after installation. Panel and molding tops were made level by short courses of stones laid flat. The outer surfaces of installed blocks were smoothed and coated with thin plaster. Blocks tapered back from tightly fitted outer edges. These techniques were also seen in Str. 5E-31 and 5D-43.

Both corners of the ballcourt bench were excavated, as were those on Str. 5E-31. Length of the bench front was 24.75 m; that on Str. 5E-31 was 24.4 m long, and a centerline alley length can be averaged at 24.6 m. Depth of the bench top was 4.1 m, almost equal to the 3.9 m on 5E-31. The 20° slope was projected forward to an estimated bench-front height of 1.35 m above the U. 1 floor. The width of the alley at centerline was 8.4 m, the S end the same, and the N end 8.25 m. The alley dimensions are thus very close to a 1:3 ratio. Scarborough (1991:fig. 7.3) estimated an 8 by 28 m alleyway, probably based on Str. 5E-31 mound length in TR. 11. Masonry of the ballcourt bench front was especially large, with corner blocks measuring 0.57-0.67 m long, 0.36 m high, and 0.20 m thick.

CONSTRUCTION STAGE 1

The building walls stood directly on the building platform with no intervening plaster (Fig. 9 illustrates the room floor within the E and W doorways). The single long narrow room was entered through a central W doorway or seven E doorways separated by cylindrical masonry columns (Fig. 8a). Positions and sizes of these doorways were confidently reconstructed from three excavated examples. Vault stones fallen within the room confirm that the building had a stone roof.

ADDITIONS AND RENOVATIONS

UNIT 9

As mentioned, permanent masonry stairs could not be identified on 5D-42 and 5E-31 as originally built. On Str. 5D-42 this was rectified by *Unit 9*, a broad stair that was erected against the standing W side of the substructure (Figs. 8c,f, 14g, 67b, 69a,c). The new flight extended the old U. 13 lateral stairs to the summit and to the sides of the substructure and almost completely engulfed the projecting U. 3 and U. 4 central flights. An overlap with U. 16 proved that U. 9 preceded. Step stones were headers measuring ca. 0.55 by 0.25 by 0.25 m, distinct from the stretchers of U. 13.

UNIT 16

Terraced additions, *Unit 16* of 5D-42 and U. 6 of 5E-31, were constructed against the S ends of the ballcourt ranges (Figs. 8c,d, 10, 13b). Both of these buttress-like constructions attained the front level of the substructure summit in five corniced walls. Stretcher and header blocks averaged 0.55 by 0.25 by 0.20 m, often laid with bedding planes horizontal. Terrace corners were rounded to a radius of 0.25 m. The E wall of the addition was the same distance back from the ballcourt bench face as U. 6 of 5E-31, resulting in an end zone 14.30 m wide. Unit 16 apparently buttressed the collapsing, extensively cracked and shifted end of the structure. Inset stairs were not detected on the unit, but might have existed on the W side.

UNITS 6–8, 15, 17

Earth accumulated in layers within the narrow alley between Str. 5D-41 and 42 before being covered by masonry debris (Figs. 11, 12a,b). A lens of reddish earth, light gray ash, and charcoal more than a meter above floor level (Fig. 11) could be evidence of a hearth. Above the layers of dirt was a jumble of broken masonry strewn with charcoal flecks, one block having the distinctive curve of the column doorways. Near the summit, the filled alley was capped by floor *Unit 6*, running S from Str. 5D-41 to *Unit 7*, a one-course step from which a higher floor, *Unit 8*, stretched to 5D-42 (Fig. 11). The U. 7 step perhaps maintained a visual separation between the structures. On the W side of the addition, the Unit 15 stair extended the U. 9 stair, differing from it by use of stretchers rather than headers (Figs. 12a, 14b). Because the stair stones rested on soft earth without underlying blocks for support, they sank deeply into the fill. The E side of the addition was *Unit 17*, three terraces high (Figs. 12b, 14a, 69d). The basal terrace wall had a pronounced batter whereas upper ones were vertical. Cornice stones from the collapsed building were reused in this construction. The unit aligns with the rear wall of 5D-41 but does not match it in height or slope. Nevertheless, the setback from the ballcourt alley was the same as that of 5D-41 and would not have impeded the ball game.

RELATIONSHIP TO ADJACENT STRATIGRAPHY

Although composed of two visually separate elements, the ballcourt and the megalithic W stair, Str. 5D-42 was built as a unit with the ballcourt wall terminating just below the stair-top floor (Fig. 9). Both entities covered Str. 5D-Sub.16 and were abutted contemporaneously by floor U. 1 of Plat. 5D-2-1st-C.

ARCHITECTURE

In almost every detail Str. 5D-42 was a mirror twin to 5E-31, in substructural length and height, vertical substructural walls, complexities of paneling, bench height and slope, building dimensions, number of front and rear entries, and rounded columns. The projecting W stair of Str. 5D-42 was probably not related to the ball game. The massive stones and carving on the stair were identical to those of the N stair of Str. 5D-65 in the Central Acropolis, hinting at contemporaneity.

Several features of the ballcourt were remarkable. The substructures imitated the form of buildings with basal moldings, vertical walls, corniced upper zones, and side and rear outsets. Although intricate lower zone paneling was not found elsewhere at Tikal, the Str. 5D-74 ballcourt in the Great Plaza had basal moldings, rear outsets, and vertical substructural walls (TR. 14:fig. 286). Cylindrical columns on the buildings were without precedent in Tikal and may be the earliest known in the Maya area. The ballcourt as a whole, with its vertical bench front and sloping bench top, falls into Type A of Acosta and Koer (1946) and Type I in the typology of Taladoire (1981:pls. 28–36), specifically Type I, Variety I (open courts without benches, one axial structure). Taladoire, however, placed the court in his Type II (open courts with benches), not aware that the profile matches those of Type I courts at Copan, Uaxactun, Balakbal, Becan, Naachtun, Sayil, Quirigua, Calakmul, and other sites (ibid.:141–153; pls. 28–30). The other ballcourts at Tikal, Str. 5D-74 and the three courts comprising Str. 5D-78-81, have the very different flat-topped benches with inclined fronts and tall inclined back-stop walls of Type II courts. The profile of the East Plaza court matches that drawn as graffiti on a room wall of Str. 5D-43, which is listed by Taladoire as a Type I profile (TR. 31:fig. 46; Taladoire 1981:146, pl. 5).

Structure 5D-42-D was built on Sub.16 and used 1,100 m^3 of material and 700 m^2 of surface dressing; U. 9 (42-C), 190 m^3 and 125 m^2; U. 16 (42-B), 100 m^3 and 70 m^2; and the merging with 5D-41 (42-A), 45 m^3 and 20 m^2.

ASSOCIATED MONUMENTS

COLUMN ALTAR 2

EXCAVATION

Column Altar 2 (TR. 33A:84, figs. 62c, 110b) was found horizontally set into the second step of U. 3, with the carved scene facing outward (Figs. 8a,c, 9, 67a). Composed of hard white crystalline limestone with no visible bedding planes, the 0.66 m long cylindrical shaft tapered from a 0.36 m front diameter to 0.25 m, all surfaces carefully rounded and smoothed. The scene on the large end depicted within a rope border a human figure seated on a ground line with arms tied behind the back and one knee raised. A large upper portion of carving, possibly carrying a hieroglyphic text, was broken off and is missing. The stone was placed into the stair so that the front was aligned with the stair riser and the carved ground line was correctly oriented. The stair blocks on both sides were hacked away to accommodate the stone.

DISCUSSION

One of three known Tikal column altars (TR. 33A:fig. 62), Col. Alt. 2 resembled Col. Alt. 1 in dimensions, rope border, and basic motif of a bound seated human figure. The latter was discovered in a horizontal, front-facing position on the centerline second step of Str. 5D-15 in the West Plaza. This setting was similar to that of Col. Alt. 2, though not securely incorporated into the step.

Tikal column altars are comparable in shape to vertically placed column altars of Uxmal and other Puuc sites (Pollock 1980:583), except that carving occurs on end surfaces rather than on upper peripheries. Uncarved column altars were also set vertically in Piedras Negras (Satterthwaite 1939:fig. A). Three ballcourt markers on the centerline of the Court II alley at Copan are tapered cylinders with carved scenes on the larger ends. In Strömsvik's (1952) sectional drawing of the court they are ca. 0.50 m in length and 0.60 m in diameter, only slightly shorter and wider than the Tikal stones. Even though their shafts are also well formed, they were set vertically in the court floor with only the carved surfaces exposed. The Tikal column altars might also have once stood vertically within a ballcourt floor. Socket holes have not been located in the five Tikal courts, however, and the East Plaza court in particular yielded no evidence of a marker socket in the center or end positions of the alley.

LOTS, GROUPING AND EVALUATION

INITIAL CONSTRUCTION

78M/6 and 12 from within the substructure contained primarily Manik with some Ik and possibly Imix sherds.

SECONDARY CONSTRUCTION

78M/39, 40, and 45–47 from the U. 9 stair addition covering the W side of the substructure contained Manik, Ik, and probable but poorly sealed Imix sherds.

OCCUPATION

78M/1, 4, 5, 13–16, 18–25, 27–30, 36, 38, 44, 48, and 49 from contexts of mixed collapse and occupation held Preclassic, Manik, Ik, and Imix sherds. 78M/13, 14, 19, 24, and 29 from the top of the W stair, 78M/19 from the SW corner, 78M/30 from the ballcourt alley, 78M/21 and 22 from the bench surface, and 78M/4 from the substructural summit included Eznab sherds. 78M/7 and 9–11 from layers of earth between Str. 5D-42 and 41 sealed under late floors contained Eznab ceramics, including Sahcaba Modeled-Carved sherds and disarticulated human vertebrae like those found between Str. 5D-40 and 5E-30.

TIME SPANS

The history of Str. 5D-42 is summarized in Table 10. The long-standing twin pyramids were partially demolished to make way for the new ballcourt. Possibly, however, the oddly projecting U. 3 stair was a reminder of the ancient four-stair structures. The court was accompanied by Plat. 5D-2-1st-C pavement and by Str. 5D-43, the radial building that looks down the alley and was probably an important adjunct to the ballcourt. The inscription above the 5D-42 and 5E-31 benches, probably original to the structures, incorporated a 1 Ahau date that might refer to Katun 1 Ahau at 9.10.0.0.0 (A.D. 633), suitable for the stratigraphic link to Plat. 5D-1-1st-E around A.D. 600 (TR. 14:chart 1). (Secondarily installed Col. Alt. 2 stylistically matches Col. Alt. 1 with its hieroglyphic date of 9.15.17.10.4 [A.D. 748].) In TS. 7, the U. 9 stair covered the W side of the substructure and provided a wide ascent to the building. In TS. 5, the S ends of both ballcourt ranges were reinforced by terraced additions (U. 16 on 5D-42), apparently after signs of cracking and collapse. These terraces possibly included inset stairs. In TS. 4 there occurred a gradual deposition of Eznab-rich refuse in the narrow alley between Str. 5D-42 and 41, followed in TS. 3 by collapse of the 5D-42 building and deliberate closure of the alley with stairs, terrace walls, and summit floors. These additions are rare examples of substantial architecture at Tikal that seals Eznab pottery. It is evident that ball play was allowed to continue during TS. 2. Carved stones lying undisturbed on the ballcourt bench indicate continued collapse without robbery in TS. 1.

TABLE 10
Structure 5D-42: Time Spans

Time Span	Architectural Addition	Floor, Unit	Special Deposit	Lot	Other Data
1	—	—	—	78M/1,4,5,13–16, 18–25,27–30,36, 38,44,48,49	Continued collapse
2	—	—	—	—	Use
3	A	U. 6–8,15,17	—	78M/7,9–11	Collapse and addition on N; Eznab ceramics
4	—	—	—	—	Use
5	B	U. 16	—	—	S buttress with Plat. 5D-2:U. 35
6	—	—	—	—	Use
7	C	U. 9	—	78M/39,40,45–47	W stair, Col. Alt. 2?; Imix ceramics
8	—	—	—	—	Use
9	D	U. 2–4,12–13	—	78M/6,12	Assembly (1,100m^3) with Plat. 5D-2:U. 1; Ik ceramics

STRUCTURE 5E-31

INTRODUCTION

In 1960, a stair was exposed on the W side of Str. 5E-31 (Op. 23A) discrediting the existence of a ballcourt. In 1964 the steps were reexamined and a profile was drawn of the standing rear wall (Op. 78K). A year later, Jones and Orrego excavated the structure more intensively and established that the stair pertained to underlying Str. 5E-Sub.1 (Op. 78K). See Figs. 1, 8a (plan), b,d, 9 (section), 10, 13a,b, 14c,e,f, 15d–ff, 70a–d, 71a–d, 74b.

EXCAVATION DATA

CONSTRUCTION STAGES

CONSTRUCTION STAGE 3

Demolition of pyramidal Str. 5E-Sub.1 was severe. On the E side the three lower terraces and projecting stair were completely removed in order to build the rear wall of 5E-31 (Figs. 5, 8a, 9). On the W side the lowest step and the upper half of the stair were demolished to make room for the ballcourt bench. The N and S stairs of the pyramid might still be intact within the fill of 5E-31.

CONSTRUCTION STAGE 2

Though badly cracked and in danger of falling, the rear of the substructure survived to cornice level (Fig. 71a). The N and S ends of the substructure (the latter buttressed by U. 6) exhibited the complex paneling of upper and lower zones seen on 5D-42 (Figs. 8d, 13a, 14e, 70d). The close-fitting wall blocks averaged 0.55 by 0.30 by 0.20 m, with one or two stretchers set between headers (Fig. 14e). The wall face was trimmed and smoothed after construction, with blocks often cut for inset panels. Coursing lines were undulating and even broken at times by changes in level. As was the case for Str. 5D-42 in its original form, no stair from plaza level to the building could be found, even though large stretches of the upper zone were exposed, including the end walls, on which inset stairs are located on Str. 5D-74 and 5D-81. Perhaps complete excavation will one day resolve this mystery.

The front face of the ballcourt bench was built of larger blocks than the rest of the substructure, two of them measuring 0.65 by 0.37 by 0.20 m and 0.72 by 0.53 by 0.21 m. The lower block on the W corner was set on end, and a fallen block of similar size lay on top. When upright, both would reach 1.32 m above the U. 1 floor to match the reconstructed face height at centerline (Fig. 9). (See Str. 5D-42 for other bench and alley dimensions.)

Header stones with carving on the ends were found in place in the upper zone panel above a plain molding, confirming the original position of the hieroglyphic panel (Figs. 8d, 9, 14c, 70c). Many stretchers fallen on the bench were carved and plastered, some in excellent shape and others disintegrated beyond recovery (Fig. 15d–ff). Stones were labeled by letter and number, the letter indicating the meter-wide area on the bench in which they were discovered (area M being at centerline), the number listing the order of discovery. Thus block P4 was the fourth block found and was in Area P, 4 m S from the axial trench (Fig. 15x). The inset panel was composed of three courses. Upper edges of glyphs can be seen on several 0.15 m high blocks (Fig. 15m,o) and bottom edges at the bases of full-height stones (Fig. 15h,aa). An intermediate course carried parts of both glyph rows (Fig. 15l,r,x). Stones from areas G and R, respectively 6 and 5 m N and S of axis, showed broad plain vertical borders (Fig. 15e,i,y,z,aa), and figurative (non-hieroglyphic) carving appeared on blocks at or beyond these areas (Fig. 15e,f,i,bb–ee). Five blocks from area M were assembled into a readable text segment in which a Distance Number of 1 katun and 15 tuns (35 tun-years) with uinals and kins missing led forward by a Posterior Date Indicator to a 1 Ahau day (Figs. 15l, 65b–d). An attempted reconstruction of the inscription appears in the elevation drawing (Fig. 8d). It ends next to a plain border with the Tikal Emblem Glyph in the bottom row (Fig. 15aa). Two unlabeled blocks (Fig. 15ff) came from the N end of the glyph panel. Glyph columns probably numbered 12, though 10 or 14 are possible. Because carved blocks were not found more than 7 m on either side of the axis, sculpture may not have extended to the ends of the facade.

CONSTRUCTION STAGE 1

Building walls were assembled on the substructure without intervening plaster (Fig. 9 shows the room floor at centerline within the doorways). The room floor turned up to the walls, and a basal molding defined the building platform in front with a step up to the front doorways of the W side (Fig. 8a,b,d). The long narrow room had a central E entry and seven W openings separated by cylindrical columns. The curved stretchers and headers were found in place on several columns, with as many as three courses surviving N of the central doorway (Figs. 14f, 70b). These blocks had the dimensions and trimming techniques of building and substructural wall masonry, measuring 0.45–0.55 m by 0.30–0.35 m by 0.20–0.25 m. The number of doorways was based on excavation of two central columns and the S doorway with its square-cornered end jamb. The N end of the building was assumed to fall the same distance from the substructural end as on the S, even though this makes a shorter N half. Doorway width varied from 1.82 m at the center to 1.26 m at the S end, and the 1.46 m diameter of the N central column matched 1.43, 1.45, and 1.50 m diameters on 5D-42. A vault stone in room debris measured 0.50 by 0.30 by 0.20 m and had a 29° soffit angle. Three cylindrical fragments of masonry 0.10 m in diameter and 0.17 m in maximum length found inside the central doorway and at plaza level might have been roof ornaments or small relief columns on the upper facade.

ADDITIONS AND RENOVATIONS

Unit 6 was a terraced addition to the S end of the substructure, identical in all but width to U. 16 of 5D-42 (Figs. 8d, 10, 13b). Interior fill consisted of large horizontally laid stones in hard earth. Pause-lines show at each terrace top. Blocks were a little longer (average 55 m) and coursing was more level than on the original structure. Cornices were still in place on the two lower terraces. No inset stair was seen either on this addition or that of 5D-42, although excavations may have missed them on the E side. The W side was placed far enough back from the ballcourt bench face to allow continued use of the end zone.

Unit 3 consisted of a poorly understood wall face extending S from the corner of U. 6 and covering an accumulation of ash and debris on the U. 11 floor (Figs. 10, 13b). Collapse on the surface defined a height of 0.90 m. Two courses survived and the wall extended 4.00 m, although no search was made for the S or E limits. The addition is aligned with U. 6 so that the ball game could have continued. Possibly U. 3 extended to Str. 5D-43 to cut off entry to the plaza from the E, but this was never explored. A carved architectural element with ray designs was found among the jumbled blocks of the fill (Fig. 74b).

RELATIONSHIP TO ADJACENT STRATIGRAPHY

The ballcourt ranges, Str. 5E-31 and 5D-42, were abutted by paving topped by U. 35. Where protected by additions (Figs. 9, 13b) a contemporaneous abutting floor, U. 1, could be seen within this thick mass of pavement. Unit 1 pertains to Plat. 5D-2-1st-C, linking the structure with 5D-42, 5D-43, and Plat. 5D-1-1st-E. Unit 35 was the later widespread surfacing seen elsewhere as Plat. 5D-2-1st-A.

ARCHITECTURE

Str. 5D-42 and 5E-31 possess the characteristics of a typical Mesoamerican ballcourt. The bench profile is different, however, from those of the other Tikal courts, Str. 5D-74 (TR. 14) and Str. 5D-78 through 81, as is the presence of masonry buildings, elaborate paneling, and carved hieroglyphic texts. Doorway columns are unique at Tikal and throughout the Maya Southern Lowland. See Str. 5D-42 for more comparisons.

Structure 5E-31 required slightly less material than 5D-42. The substructure and building together utilized 1,000 m^3 of material in addition to the material required for Sub.1 and 680 m^2 of surface trimming. The U. 6 buttress on the S end of the substructure consumed an additional 80 m^3 and 60 m^2, and U. 3 used only 7 m^3 and 9 m^2.

ASSOCIATED MONUMENTS

Miscellaneous Stone 90 (TR. 33A:92, fig. 65x), a fragment of a compact limestone stela displaying part of a belt pendant of early style, was found near the surface, probably weathering out of 5E-31 or Sub.1 fill.

LOTS, GROUPING AND EVALUATION

INITIAL CONSTRUCTION

78K/41 sealed within the bench contained Manik and one Ik or early Imix sherd.

SECONDARY CONSTRUCTION

78K/30 and 32 from the U. 6 addition contained unweathered Manik, Ik, and Imix ceramics; 78K/11, 14, and 15 from U. 3 had Manik, Imix, and Eznab.

OCCUPATION

78K/4, 5, 8–10, 31, 36, and 44, from surrounding floor surfaces, contained predominately Imix sherds but also Sahcaba Modeled-carved sherds of the Eznab Ceramic Complex. 78K/6, 7, 19, 29, and 43, from talus at the base of the structure, 78K/2, 13, and 40 from the room floor, and 78K/3 and 35 from the bench floor held sherds of all ceramic complexes except Eznab. Lots from the bench surface included a large number of flint and obsidian flakes plus two small fragments of stucco with orange-red paint on modeled surfaces, perhaps derived from carved panels or the upper zone of the building above.

TIME SPANS

Structure 5E-31 time spans are outlined in Table 11. Assembly in TS. 7 necessitated the partial destruction and covering of 5E-Sub.1. The U. 1 floor that turned up to 5E-31 linked it to 5D-42 as well as to nearby 5D-43, the Central Acropolis facade behind 5D-43, and the Plat. 5D-1:U. 72 facing. The latest sherds sealed within 5E-31 are Manik. Structure 5D-32-1st, which can possibly be dated to 9.8.0.0.0 (A.D. 593) or thereafter by the hieroglyphic text on wooden boards within Bu. 195 (TR. 14:196–197), has been cited as a means of dating the East Plaza ballcourt by stratigraphic connection (Jones 1991:116). The standing header and stretcher masonry, however, does not match that of 32-1st as well as 33-1st, although both structures fall within TS. 7 of Plat. 5D-4 and are guess-dated on non-hieroglyphic grounds to A.D. 600 and 660 respectively (TR. 14:158). In this light, the 1 Ahau date on 5E-31 would be suitable as a katun-ending Dedication Date for the ballcourt at 9.10.0.0.0 1 Ahau 8 Kayab (A.D. 633). The reading is not conclusive, however, as a Vague Year or period-ending fix is missing.

The terraced U. 6 addition built in TS. 5 on the S end of Str. 5E-31 appears designed primarily to retain the collapsing substructure and could also have housed rear inset stairs ascending to the buildings above. The position of U. 6 and corresponding U. 16 of 5D-42 allowed continued ball play during TS. 4. Eznab sherds accumulated in layers of dirt against the side of U. 6 and at the N end of 5D-42 before the U. 3 wall was built on the debris, perhaps at the same time as U. 6–8, 15, and 17 of 5D-42. Again, neither of these constructions interfered with the ballcourt end zones. Structure 5E-31 stood less protected from weathering and failure than 5D-42, but fared surprisingly well. There is no evidence that collapse was due to other than natural causes or that masonry was robbed.

TABLE 11
Structure 5E-31: Time Spans

Time Span	Architectural Addition	Floor, Unit	Special Deposit	Lot	Other Data
1	—	—	—	78K/2,4,5,8–10, 13,19,29,31,35,36, 40,43,44	Collapse
2	—	—	—	—	Use
3	A	U.3	—	78K/11,14,15	S addition, Eznab ceramics
4	—	—	—	—	Use
5	B	U.6	—	78K/30,32	S addition with Plat. 5D-2. U. 11,35; Imix ceramics
6	—	—	—	—	Use
7	C	U.2–5	—	78K/41	Assembly (1,000 m^3) with Plat. 5D-2:U. 1; Manik ceramic, possible Ik or Imix

STRUCTURE 5D-41-2ND

INTRODUCTION

It was fortunate that separate numbers were assigned to the 5D-41 and 42 mound on the Tikal Project map (TR. 11) because 1965 excavations uncovered the gap between these two entities closed in ancient times. Investigation (as Op. 78N) by Jones with the assistance of Ordóñez, Orrego, and Larios included a shallow centerline trench across the 5D-41 mound, probes at the SE and SW corners, and a tunnel into the front stair. Inquiry focused on form, chronology, presence or absence of special deposits and prior structures, and function as related to the ballcourt. Structure 5D-41-2nd was known solely through its interior fill and rear wall within the 41-1st tunnel. See Fig. 16d.

EXCAVATION DATA

The centerline tunnel into the W side of 41-1st ended after breaking through the back (E) wall of 2nd (Fig. 16d). Flooring did not abut the wall, and perhaps for that reason the front of the structure was not located. Interior fill assignable to 41-2nd consisted of large stones and broken chunks in hard light earth (Fig. 16d). The rear wall, seen only within the tunnel width, was exposed up to its narrow summit floor and the base of the second-terrace face. Wall block measurements were 0.56 m long to 0.36 m high and 0.19 to 0.24 m thick. These dimensions differed little from those of 41-1st. The shallow basal and upper moldings were cut into installed blocks, sometimes between course divisions. Basically it appears that this earlier structure had at least the orientation and form of its successor. The height and number of terraces reconstructed in Fig. 16d is purely speculative.

RELATIONSHIP TO ADJACENT STRATIGRAPHY

Structure 5D-41-2nd stood on the same Plat. 5D-2:U. 7 floor as 1st, without an abutting plaster surface. The floor, which emerged from the S rear corner of 41-1st and abutted Str. 5D-42 as U. 1, was therefore U. 7. Thus 41-2nd was built later than the 5D-42 ballcourt beside it, and the next floor, U. 35, was not laid until the assembly of 41-1st had been accomplished.

ARCHITECTURE

The front stair was missing and lateral dimensions are unknown. Height and setback of the rear terraces were almost identical to those of 41-1st, however, leading one to suppose that 2nd was similar in form. Assuming that 41-2nd was 5 m high and proportioned like 1st, volume amounted to 280 m^3 and dressed surface area to 150 m^2.

LOTS, GROUPING AND EVALUATION

CONSTRUCTION

78N/6, sealed within the tunnel, contained Preclassic, Manik, and probable Ik or Imix sherds, whereas 78N/7, also from tunnel fill of 2nd, had 2 lbs of solely Manik material.

TIME SPANS

Known only by its interior fill and rear wall within a narrow tunnel, the size and form of Str. 5D-41-2nd are poorly understood. When built (Table 12:TS 2), the structure stood on Plat. 5D-2-1st-C, which had expanded the W part of the platform N to shift the Plaza axis N from the old Str. 5D-Sub.16 and 5E-Sub.1 centerline. The proximity of 5D-41 to the ballcourt might be explained by this new axis, which lay approximately halfway between the Central Acropolis on the S and the new causeway head on the N (Fig. 1).

Across from 41-2nd, the broad U. 72 stair of Plat. 5D-1 led to a structureless summit on which was later erected nine-doorway Str. 5D-38. Unit 72 and Str. 5D-37 beside it were both built on the Plat. 5D-2-1st-C pavement without a floor immediately abutting them, and 5D-37 and 41-2nd terrace profile and post-installation molding cuts.

TABLE 12
Structure 5D-41-2nd: Time Spans

Time Span	Architectural Addition	Floor, Unit	Special Deposit	Lot	Other Data
1	—	—	—	—	Use
2	—	U. 2,3	—	78N/6,7	Assembly (280 m^3) on Plat. 5D-2:U. 1

STRUCTURE 5D-41-1ST

INTRODUCTION

Investigation of the mound was described in the introduction to 41-2nd. See Figs. 1, 8c, 11, 16a (plan), b–d (section) 17, 18.

EXCAVATION DATA

CONSTRUCTION STAGES

In preparation for assembly of 41-1st, the rear wall of 2nd was left intact while the front stair was stripped of masonry (Fig. 16d). Fill placed in front and back of the old structure consisted of hard earth and many flat-laid blocks, not unlike that of 41-2nd. Only two basal steps of the W stair of 41-1st survived, but the rear wall was better preserved. The S side terrace wall was 1.65 m high and 0.40 m wide and protected by later construction (Fig. 11). A higher terrace face, flooring, and adjacent stair wall also survived on the SW corner (Fig. 16c). These allowed a confident reconstruction of the five terrace levels (Figs. 16a, 17, 18). A stair balustrade was detected, its base in line with the stair and the terrace wall.

Stair stones were laid on edge as stretchers and occasional headers, averaging 0.45 by 0.30 by 0.20 m. Rear wall blocks were identical, ranging from 0.45 to 0.60 m in length (Fig. 16b). Their outer faces were trimmed and smoothed after installation, and the ends taper inward from close-fitting edges.

The summit was briefly excavated with a narrow centerline trench (Fig. 16a,d). The flat fill surface marked a probable summit floor level. A building platform was not detected, but the area at the top of the stair was too damaged to know whether or not the summit had separate front and rear levels. A narrow perishable superstructure (presumably pole and thatch) would fit the oblong top. Interestingly, it would have been close in size and proportions to the building platform on Str. 5D-37 across the plaza (TR. 14:fig. 247).

ADDITIONS AND RENOVATIONS

Unit 1 was a small platform or buttress of unknown height, ca. 3.30 m wide and 0.60 m thick, built against the rear wall (Fig. 16a,d).

RELATIONSHIP TO ADJACENT STRATIGRAPHY

Platform 5D-2:U. 7 beneath 41-1st (Fig. 16d) was traced from the SW corner of the structure to where it abutted 5D-42 as U. 1 of Plat. 5D-2-1st-C. The rear wall and stair were flanked by floor U. 35 immediately after assembly, arguing for the contemporaneity of 41-1st with Plat. 5D-2-1st-A.

ARCHITECTURE

Structure 5D-41-1st was a five-terrace substructure with a W stair and no evidence of masonry superstructure (Figs. 1, 8c, 16a, 17, 18). A rear outset was drawn in the plan because of nonalignment with the SW corner; side outsets did not seem to be present. The unusually broad W stair did not project forward from the terrace line, but rose at the same angle as the substructure. The raised stair margins (stair sides) were unique for the East Plaza, but were seen on earlier 5D-35 and perhaps on 5D-33-1st (TR. 14:886). The oblong summit possibly supported a perishable structure. The material used to erect 41-1st over the remains of 41-2nd was ca. 1,000 m^3, and the area of surface dressing, was 415 m^2.

LOTS, GROUPING AND EVALUATION

OCCUPATION

78N/1 from the summit surface contained Preclassic, Manik, probable Ik or Imix, and one Eznab sherd. 78N/2 from the stair base, 78N/3 from the NW corner base, and 78N/4 and 5 from the rear trench contained primarily Manik pottery with some Ik or Imix. Several Eznab Modeled-Carved sherds were in 78N/5. These are surface mixtures of fill and occupation debris.

TIME SPANS

Structure 5D-41-1st was assembled in TS. 5 (Table 13) over an earlier version which was apparently related to it in form as well as orientation. Location of both the later structure and its predecessor might have been dictated by a new E-W centerline of Plat. 5D-2-1st (Fig. 1). This axis is shared by Str. 5D-38 and stair U. 71 of Plat. 5D-1. Although it was positioned close to the East Plaza ballcourt, the structure faced away from the playing alley and did not intrude into the end zone any more than did the additions to the ballcourt ranges themselves. The game could have been viewed from the substructure if there were no summit building, or one without a rear wall. The only known addition to the structure in TS. 3 was U. 1, a small platform or buttress against the rear wall. Collapse in TS. 1 was probably gradual, with the possibility that stair stone was robbed.

TABLE 13
Structure 5D-41-1st: Time Spans

Time Span	Architectural Addition	Floor, Unit	Special Deposit	Lot	Other Data
1	—	—	—	—	Collapse
2	—	—	—	78N/1–5	Use, including Eznab ceramics
3	—	U. 1	—	—	Rear platform
4	—	—	—	—	Use
5	—	—	—	—	Assembly (1,000 m^3) with Plat. 5D-2:U. 35

STRUCTURE 5D-43

INTRODUCTION

This mound projecting from the S side of the Central Acropolis is not mentioned in text by Maler (1911) or Tozzer (1911). Maler's map (1971) does not depict it either, although it is shown in Tozzer's map (1911:pl. 29). Tikal Report 11, of course, places it in proper scale and position. Excavation by Jones and Orrego lasted from May through August 1965 (Op. 78P). Following a deep N-S axial cut, exploration at the NE corner revealed the unusual substructure and decorations. Rooms were cleared, a tunnel penetrated the back wall, and the substructural base was entirely exposed along its E, W, and N sides. The structure was consolidated and partially restored in 1965 and 1966 under the direction of Guillemin. See Figs. 1, 19a,b (plans), c,d (section), 20, 21, 22a–c, 72c,d, 73a–d, 74a,b.

EXCAVATION DATA

CONSTRUCTION STAGES

CONSTRUCTION STAGE 7

Site preparation toward assembly of Str. 5D-43-C involved almost complete removal of Sub.27 and laying of Plat. 5D-2:U. 19 over the remains and against a steep bedrock outcrop (Figs. 19d, 22c).

CONSTRUCTION STAGE 6

The *Unit 2* nucleus was built on unplastered U. 19 and sheathed the bedrock outcrop with fill containing many chips of red and white marl derived from the rock (Figs. 19d, 22c). Stones in this fill were smaller than those within the building platform. The summit was level but not plastered. A crude S stair was made of untrimmed stones laid either on their larger surfaces or their sides.

CONSTRUCTION STAGE 5

After completion of the nucleus, work began on substructural facings (Figs. 20, 22a,c, 72c,d, 73c). Although the complex three-part profile of *talud*, *tablero*, and negatively battered cornice was unusual, masonry dimensions and installation were identical to those of Str. 5D-42 and 5E-31. The wall was constructed ca. 0.60 m beyond the core wall with hard concrete rubble placed between to secure the facing stones (Fig. 22c). A typical block measured 0.50 by 0.30 by 0.25 m, and two stretcher stones were placed between headers to achieve a 2:1 bond. Shaving down the tops of installed rows resulted in undulating coursing. Courses of horizontally laid stone of variable height were therefore employed to level the summits of walls and cornices (Fig. 20). These techniques were utilized in assembly of Str. 5D-42 and 5E-31 but not in later structures such as 5D-40 and 5E-32-1st-A. The unusual Venus ray designs of both the talud and the overhanging cornice extended across several blocks and must therefore have been carved after installation. On the other hand, the paired Tlaloc eye motifs on the *tablero* were carved on single stretchers and possibly sculpted beforehand (Figs. 20, 73c; Coe 1965b:40, photo).

CONSTRUCTION STAGE 4

Stairs were built on the E, N, and W sides of the substructure against finished facades, the N side wall of the S stair actually overlapping a carved element (Figs. 19a,d, 20, 72d). *Unit 11*, the N stair, was made with a solid fill and few large fill blocks. The risers were only 0.20 m. high, probably worn down by use from the 0.30 m height seen on the E flight. The coeval *Unit 12* building platform fill incorporated large blocks and was walled by dressed blocks laid on edge (Fig. 19d).

CONSTRUCTION STAGE 3

The building walls rose on the rough unplastered surface of U. 12 with the room floor abutting them and passing through doorways (Figs. 19d, 22b, 73d). Stretcher and header blocks in the walls were 0.50 by 0.30 by 0.20 m, with variation in length. Coursing levels were visible running from the outside to the inside of the wall (Fig. 22b). A change in coursing level near the SE corner may have been a juncture of separately conducted jobs (Fig. 19c). The wall tops were capped by plaster, which dropped 0.33 m on either side of the rear doorway to form plastered lintel beds 0.72 m wide.

CONSTRUCTION STAGE 2

Both an exterior row of molding headers and an interior course of wall stretchers to support vaulting were installed on the wall-top plaster, presumably in this original stage rather than later when the medial wall was added (Figs. 19d, 22b, 73d). Molding headers were as long as 0.80 m and averaged 0.30 m high and 0.40 m wide. Vault stones measured 0.60 by 0.30 by 0.20 m and had parallel upper and lower surfaces and tapered sides. A crude vault backing of small untrimmed stones was unevenly plastered. Roofing between the four vault masses presumably comprised closely set beams and mortar. The central area of the room floor was not thoroughly searched for evidence of extra roof support, such as holes for wooden posts.

CONSTRUCTION STAGE 1

Upper zone construction began with a row of flat-laid stones which leveled the upper surface of the projecting molding (Figs. 19d, 22b). Four courses of a carved inset upper-zone panel, made entirely of stretchers, survived above the molding. The carving depicted a centered frontal face with open mouth, bifurcated tongue, scrolled fangs, glyphic medallions, and pendants (Figs. 21, 73a,b). The corners of the upper zone were also carved, perhaps with masks. Within the curve of the fang, a sky sign served to identify a sky monster (perhaps antecedent to "Chac" faces on later Yucatec upper zones). A fragment of a carved block fallen on the E stair also had front incisor teeth, proving that the central mask motif was repeated on the other sides of the building. A pyramidal 0.52 by 0.30 by 0.20 m block, smoothed and plastered on the front and the stepped sides, was discovered in debris E of the building. Identical in shape to *almenas* (merlons or rooftop elements) from Teotihuacan and other western Mesoamerican sites (Gendorp 1985:figs. 2, 4b, 5, 8a,b), the block was almost certainly one of a series of roof-edge ornaments (Fig. 22a).

ADDITIONS AND RENOVATIONS

Although not proven to be synchronous, the alterations that preceded full-scale modifications are treated as though they occurred together to comprise Str. 5D-43-B. *Unit 4* sealed the S (rear) doorway (Fig. 19b,d). The inner face was flush with the wall surface but the outer face was inset 0.10 m to retain the appearance of a rear doorway. It was not determined whether the original wooden lintels were buried in place. Probably at the same time, *Unit 13* filled the rear alley to the level of the substructural summit (Fig. 19d). Absence of wall masonry behind U. 13 proved that Str. 5E-97 was constructed with this platform. All three stair flights were clad by new masonry at this time. *Unit 1* encased the N stair with new steps and stair walls, which obscured large portions of the flanking decoration; *Unit 9* sheathed the W flight; and *Unit 8* covered the plaster treads and sockets of ripped-out E stair stones.

Following these modifications, the structure underwent a second and more striking change, termed Str. 5D-43-A. The large square room was subdivided by a *Unit 5* medial wall and vault mass, and by a higher *Unit 3* rear room floor. Both units extended through the side doorways to obliterate the lateral entries. Unlike the U. 4 closure, however, exterior door faces were flush with the walls so that side portals were no longer suggested by insets. Wall stones of U. 5 were like those of the primary structure, averaging 0.55 by 0.30 by 0.20 m. The vault mass differed from the original rear half vault, however, in having a short leveling course beneath the vault spring and lacking subvault plaster (Fig. 22b). The stones of the medial wall were distinguishable from those of the rear because they were the first to fall and differed only in having a slightly greater width. Two capstones within the rear-room debris, measuring 0.80 by 0.37 by 0.21 m and 0.75 by 0.38 by 0.23 m, were plastered on their underside before installation. A weathered 0.22 m central area on this plaster defined the width of the vault top. Height was reconstructed by combining this measurement with the 27° vault soffit angle (Figs. 19d, 22b).

In concert with the internal room changes described above, a flight of steps was built to the summit of the Central Acropolis behind the building (Figs. 19b, 73c,d). *Unit 10* buried the decorated facade of the SE corner and formed a new platform level from which the stair itself, *Unit 7*, ascended westward between the rear wall of the building and the Central Acropolis. The U. 7 fill was laid in two stages, first against the Central Acropolis wall, then against the structure (Fig. 19d). At the top, the upper-zone carving was kept in view by means of a V-shaped trench (Fig. 73b). The W wall of U. 7 merged with *Unit 14*, another stair to the Central Acropolis along the W side of the building. In conjunction with U. 7 and 10 all three substructural stairs were broadened to bury the carving completely (Figs. 19b, 72c). These new stairs were labeled *Unit 6*. A new Plat. 5D-2 plaster, U. 16, abutted the stair additions and feathered out onto the old U. 17 surface.

A minor alteration followed that of U. 7. The V-shaped trench or walkway along the rear upper zone was closed by Unit 15 fill, hiding the carving from view and allowing passage from the Central Acropolis summit onto the roof of the building, perhaps in order to view the ball game (Fig. 1).

OTHER FEATURES

Graffiti incised on the room walls (TR. 31:figs. 46, 47) show detailed scenes of activity including a profile of a ballcourt, which presumably is the East Plaza court seen from the S doorway. Two human figures are diving for the ball between them, two others stand back and watch, and a trumpeter sits on the edge of the court. The alley profile is that of Str. 5D-42 and 5E-31, as is the presence of a stair on the left-hand range. A temple fronted by a stela/altar pair is depicted to the left of the court, however, and these do not exist in the Plaza. Elsewhere, a figure dances on a drum or altar. Larger crude figures are superimposed. The scene demonstrates that the game was still played when the graffiti were incised. The graffiti were carved on secondary building walls belonging to 43-A and must pertain to that form of the structure or later.

RELATIONSHIP TO ADJACENT STRATIGRAPHY

Structure 5D-43-C was built on the unplastered surface of Plat. 5D-2:U. 19 before the U. 17 plaster was laid against it. A narrow trench extended to Str. 5E-31 was not able to prove that U. 17 was equivalent to the U. 1 floor abutting the ballcourt. Nevertheless, the floor sequences were identical and U. 19 and 17 are probably surfaces of Plat. 5D-2-1st-C. If so, the structure coincided in time with Str. 5D-42 and 5E-31. The structural alteration termed 43-B, which included the U. 4 doorway closure, U. 13 platform, and U. 1, 8, and 9 stair expansions, were coeval with Str. 5E-97, but not connected to any platform floor. The 43-A modifications, consisting of the U. 3 and 5 room division and U. 6, 7, 10, and 14 stairs, were accompanied by the U. 16 floor of Plat. 5D-2-1st-A.

ARCHITECTURE

Several of the unusual features of Str. 5D-43 occur elsewhere at Tikal. The radially symmetrical substructure that is missing its S stair only because of proximity to the Central Acropolis has a three-member profile, Tlaloc eyes, and Venus star signs, which are also found on Str. 5C-53 and 6E-144. Almost identical upper-zone faces were carved on Str. 6E-143 beside 6E-144. Tlaloc eyes and the Venus rays are now considered emblematic of warfare and sacrifice of war captives, based on associations within the murals at Cacaxtla, Tlaxcala, Mexico (Carlson 1991). Their presence on 5D-43-C might therefore identify the square room with four doorways as a *puzbal chaah*, or "Place of Ball Game Sacrifice," equivalent to the one mentioned in the Popol Vuh (Tedlock 1985:354–355). Although the edifice has been called "the Teotihuacan Building" since 1966 (Greene and Moholy-Nagy 1966), three-member profiles are not found at that site itself, but at Tajin and Xochicalco. Construction techniques of 5D-43 were characteristic of late Tikal structures as seen in the neighboring Gp. 5D-2 sequence, including the use of nuclear cores, wall stones laid on edge and dressed in place, leveling courses, unplastered wall-base surfaces, wall-top plaster, plastered lintel beds, mortared vault backs, preplastered capstones, and flat bas-relief facade sculptures (TR. 14:887–900). The postulated original beams and mortar roof had precedent in Str. 5D-Sub.1 (TR. 14:213), although the 4.45 m span here was wider, also exceeding that of Str. P-7 at Piedras Negras (Satterthwaite 1952:73–74). A square structure with four doorways has no known equivalent at Tikal, but appears later on the "Temple of the Dolls" at Dzibilchaltun (Coggins 1983), Str. A-3 at Seibal (Smith 1982:fig. 17), the High Priest's grave and Castillo at Chichen Itza, and the Castillo at Mayapan (Ruppert 1952:34; Marquina 1964:lám. 261, 275, apendice lm. 9).

The alterations that resulted in Str. 5D-43-B involved blocking the rear doorway, rebuilding the front and side stairs, and extending the rear substructure to the Central Acropolis facade. These might have already been necessary to buttress against collapse and did not severely alter the structural plan. In contrast, the Str. 5D-43-A modifications markedly changed the original aspect. The interior was divided into two parts, masonry vaulting was installed, side doorways were blocked, the expanded stairs covered all substructural carvings, and flanking stairs to the Central Acropolis summit incorporated the building completely into the Acropolis mass. Although the radial plan was largely obscured and the *Tlaloc* and Venus iconography thereby obliterated, nevertheless the continued exposure of upper-zone masks and three-member terrace corners recalled the original exotic appearance of the structure. For whatever reason, the changes appear to eliminate deliberately the symbolic aspects of the structure, that is, its radial room plan and *Tlaloc* and Venus symbols, even though the relationship to the ballcourt remained unchanged.

LOTS, GROUPING AND EVALUATION

INITIAL CONSTRUCTION

78P/40 from U. 2 in the axial trench, the only lot sealed within the inner nucleus, consisted mostly of Ik polychrome with one possible Imix sherd. 78P/39 from the U. 2 building platform, 78P/43 from substructural fill at the NE corner, and 78P/21 from within the front stair all had abundant Ik material with some possible early Imix sherds. These sealed collections, dominated by Ik ceramics with hints of Imix, date the structure to a time of Ik ceramic output at the earliest. As with Str. 5D-42 and 5E-31, Imix production is possible but not requisite.

SECONDARY CONSTRUCTION

78P/37 from the U. 13 platform had Manik and Imix sherds, demonstrating that 43-B was not built until Imix pottery was in full use. 78P/38 from U. 3, 78P/29 from U. 5, 78P/45 and 46 from U. 10, and 78P/18, 36, and 51 from U. 6 also included Imix sherds as the latest complex, showing that 43-A was finished during (or possibly after) a time of Imix Complex production.

OCCUPATION

78P/8 was derived from gray charcoal-flecked earth on the front-room floor and 78P/20 and 11 from the rear room floor; these included Eznab sherds among other ceramic complexes, along with human bones and teeth. 78P/12 from the N side of the W stair and 78P/16 from the foot of the E stair were rich in unweathered Eznab sherds. 78P/7, 10, 13, 17, 24, 35, and 42 from collapse debris on room floors, stairs, and surrounding plaza floors, as well as 78P/1–3 and 41 from the upper 0.30 m of the mound also included Ik, Imix, and Eznab sherds. Occupation of the building during a time of Eznab ceramics is indicated.

TIME SPANS

The staged development of Str. 5D-43 is outlined in Table 14. Assembly in TS. 9 accompanied several constructions in the East Plaza. Structure 5D-Sub.27, located at this spot almost from the beginning of the Plaza, was destroyed to make way for both the new structure and the Central Acropolis wall behind it. South-oriented 43-C was centered on the long axis of ballcourt Str. 5D-42 and 5E-31, and stratigraphy argues that the three were built together. As mentioned, the Tlaloc and Venus signs carved on substructural facades are symbols of war and human sacrifice and have firm associations with ball players elsewhere in Mesoamerica. The stratigraphic and positional relationship of the building to the court reinforces the connection between the game and the sacrifice. The large square four-portaled room seems ideal for ritual of some sort.

Initial alterations (TS. 7) were relatively minor, doing little to alter the plan or the outward appearance and obscuring almost nothing of the substructural carving. Structure 5D-97 was built beside it at this time, probably as an adjunct to an expanding complex of gallery marketplace buildings to the N and E. The second set of changes (TS. 5) were more radical. The substructural facade sculpture featuring Venus and *Tlaloc* motifs vanished behind widened stairs, although the front corners of the three-member profile remained visible. The side doors of the building were walled up, eliminating the radial layout as the formerly square room was converted into a standard two-room tandem arrangement. The rear of the building was encased by stairs leading to the Central Acropolis summit. Despite these changes, the structure continued to look down the ballcourt alley and to retain some radiality through the continued exposure of the lateral stairs and upper-zone sky-monster representations. Burial of the rear upper-zone sculptures in TS. 3, while having a minimal effect on this radial impression, did allow passage onto the roof and an outstanding view of ball games. Accumulation of Eznab sherds within ash-laden soils in and about the building defined a TS. 2 occupation period, and it is interesting that Eznab-rich trash was also sealed within the Str. 5D-42 and 5E-31 additions, which allowed continued ball play.

TABLE 14
Structure 5D-43: Time Spans

Time Span	Architectural Addition	Floor, Unit	Special Deposit	Lot	Other Data
1	—	—	—	78P/1,2,3,6,7,10, 13,17,24,35,41,42	Collapse
2	—	—	—	78P/8,11,12, 16,20,22	Use; Eznab ceramics
3	—	U. 15	—	—	Covering of rear upper-zone panel
4	—	—	—	—	Use
5	A	U. 3,5–7,10,14	—	78P/18,29,36, 38,45,46,51	Room and stair revisions, stairs behind building, with Plat. 5D-2-1st-A; Imix ceramics
6	—		—	—	Use
7	B	U. 1,4,8,9,13	—	78P/37	Rear extension, rear doorway closure, rebuilt stairs, with Plat. 5D-2-1st-B?; Imix ceramics
8	—		—	—	Use
9	C	U. 2,11,12	—	78P/21,39,40,43	Assembly (500 m^3) C; with Plat. 5D-2-1st-C; Ik (and Imix?) ceramics

STRUCTURE 5D-135

INTRODUCTION

Overlooked in the mapping for TR. 11, the small mound of Str. 5D-135 in the central area of the eastern part of the Plaza (Fig. 1) was discovered by Hellmuth in 1965 when the area was cleared of undergrowth. Excavation was by Jones and Orrego (Op. 78O). See Figs. 1, 25a,b, plan, section.

EXCAVATION DATA

CONSTRUCTION STAGES

Interior fill consisted of loose brown earth with tilted fill blocks apparently thrown down as dirt was piled up (Fig. 25b). Side walls were two courses high with some wall stones still in place and many dislodged or reduced to small pieces. One or two wall stones were identified as reused vault stones by the characteristic tapered sides and angled end surfaces. Mound height was 0.63 m, and a remnant of the summit floor body was seen at 0.60 m (two course heights). Blocks in the NW corner, which seemed to form an inset second step, were probably core walls instead (Fig. 25a). An irregularly shaped 0.30 m long stone protruding slightly from the center of the mound was perhaps set to imitate a stela, although it was not made of hard monument stone nor shaped in any way.

RELATIONSHIP TO ADJACENT STRATIGRAPHY

Unit 39 of Plat. 5D-2 (Fig. 25b) was a stratum of gravel laid against the base of the structure, a remnant of either the final U. 40 floor or, more likely, a local patching.

ARCHITECTURE

Structure 5D-135 probably never sustained a building. It was close in size and shape to other small masonry structures built within plazas on late or final floors (5D-92 and 136 in this report), as well as 5D-117, 132, and 133 on the Great Plaza and North Terrace (TR. 14:fig. 5). Volume amounted to 10 m³, area of trimmed wall surface to 10 m².

LOTS, GROUPING AND EVALUATION

CONSTRUCTION

78O/16 from within fill contained a tiny sample including Manik.

OCCUPATION

78O/15 on the surrounding floor included Eznab ceramics alone. Censer fragments, perhaps expected near an altar-like structure, were not noted.

TIME SPANS

Structure 5D-135 was built in TS. 3 (Table 15) as a low, straight-sided, nearly square platform. Its position on the axis of Str. 5D-41 was comparable to locations of 5D-117 in front of 5D-1-1st and 5D-132 and 133 in front of 5D-29 (TR. 14:585–586; 654–655, fig. 61). In form but not in location it resembles Str. 5E-92 (see below) and "kitchens" found in domestic groups (TR. 19; Haviland 1963:471–481). Platform U. 39 abutting the structure was probably a later patch. Eznab sherds indicated late activity nearby.

TABLE 15
Structure 5D-135: Time Spans

Time Span	Architectural Addition	Floor, Unit	Special Deposit	Lot	Other Data
1	—	—	—	—	Collapse
2	—	—	—	78O/15	Use, Eznab ceramics
3	—	—	—	78O/16	Assembly (10 m³) on U. 83 (of Plat. 5D-2-1st-A?)

STRUCTURE 5D-39

INTRODUCTION

Structure 5D-39 appears on the TR. 11 map as a low, rectangular mound in front of the broad stair, Plat. 5D-1:U. 72, that leads up to Str. 5D-38. Because it resembled a foundation for a perishable rectangular building, it was excavated for plan and stratigraphic association as well as for function. The 1965 investigation (Op. 78R) was directed by Hellmuth with supervision by the author. Hellmuth submitted a detailed preliminary report in 1966 (on file). See Figs. 1, 23a,b (plan, section), 27a,d, 75d.

EXCAVATION DATA

CONSTRUCTION STAGES

The retaining walls found within the substructure demonstrate a staged assembly. In the centerline trench (Figs. 23b, 75d), E and W nuclear walls were linked by an unplastered mortar layer, and a transverse wall defined the S side of this *Unit 1* primary core. A single-course alignment about 0.40 m from the N end of the structure may be the fourth side of this unit. *Unit 2* was then built over the rear of U. 1 and formed the W wall of the substructure. Units 1 and 2 created a two-level platform anticipating final structural form. *Unit 3*, also defined by crude retaining walls, extended the platform to nearly full length; upon it were constructed the final walls, front stairs, and a building platform distinguished by a front step, shallow lateral moldings (Fig. 27a,d), and a single-course west-facing rear step 1.30 m from the rear edge (Fig. 23a,b). Plaster floors were laid on all summit surfaces. Although a perishable pole-and-thatch building is implied by the presence of a building platform, no traces of postholes or masonry were found.

RELATIONSHIP TO ADJACENT STRATIGRAPHY

The rear wall of the substructure stood on the intermediate of three Plat. 5D-2 floors (U. 41, 92, and 91), which emerge from beneath the Plat. 5D-1:U. 72 stair just W of the structure (Fig. 23b). Severe erosion prior to construction must have eradicated platform floors U. 40 and 41 above U. 92 in this area because the N end of the structure clearly overlay U. 40 and was later than the stair (Fig. 27d). This stratigraphic interpretation was crucial to the analysis of Plat. 5D-2-1st-C, particularly the identification of U. 41 with Fl. 1.

ARCHITECTURE

A rectangular two-level substructure probably supported a perishable east-facing building typical of residences excavated elsewhere at Tikal (cf. TR. 19:fig. 41), which sometimes feature a two-level profile and a basal step narrower than those above it. An unusual feature is a rear terrace behind the building. Although a doorway possibly led out onto this terrace, stairs to the plaza were not found on the rear wall. The volume of fill and masonry for Str. 5D-39 was 250 m³ and the area of trimmed facing was 80 m².

LOTS, GROUPING AND EVALUATION

CONSTRUCTION

78R/36 from U. 1 contained Manik ceramics only, with no Ik or Imix material. The fill was perhaps obtained from a razed ancient entity. 78R/35 from within the substructure held Manik and Ik sherds, which are early for the probable date of the structure.

OCCUPATION

78R/31–34 from surrounding platform surfaces had Manik, Ik, and Imix sherds. 78R/26, 27, 39 from 0.10 m thick, ash-laden earth around the N end of the structure contained Eznab sherds also found in 78R/14 and 18 against the W side, as well as 78R/19 (with fragments of human skull and long bones) and 78R/46 at the S end. Imix sherds were present in all of these samples, but the ample Eznab deposits were probably undisturbed occupation debris.

TIME SPANS

This structure (assembled in Table 16:TS. 3) probably supported a single room facing E. In spite of contradictory stratigraphy, the structure was probably built on final floor U. 40 of Plat. 5D-2-1st-A as part of a large-scale construction effort in which other low rectangular structures (Str. 5D-39, 5D-134, 5E-92, and 5E-94) and small square structures were built in the plaza space (Str. 5D-135 and 136). Eznab pottery accumulated from occupation of the building during TS. 2.

TABLE 16
Structure 5D-39: Time Spans

Time Span	Architectural Addition	Floor, Unit	Special Deposit	Lot	Other Data
1	—	—	—	—	Collapse
2	—	—	—	78R/14,18,26, 27,39,46	Use; Eznab ceramics
3	—	U. 1–3	—	78R/31–36	Assembly (250 m³) on U. 40 of Plat. 5D-2-1st-A

STRUCTURE 5D-134

INTRODUCTION

On the TR. 11 map the mound of Str. 5D-134 is in the shape of a parapet extending between Str. 5D-37 and 39. It was investigated in 1965 by Hellmuth, who wrote a detailed preliminary report in 1966 (on file). The purpose of excavation was much like that of 5D-39, to understand why an apparent house-mound existed in the East Plaza (Fig. 1). See Figs. 1, 25c,d, 26 (plan), 27b–d (section), 75c.

EXCAVATION DATA

CONSTRUCTION STAGES

After this oblong mound was cleaned of undergrowth, narrow trenches were placed along the exposed walls and a centerline trench was dug to the basal floor level (Figs. 26, 27c,d, 75c). No fill-retaining walls or intermediate mortar layers were present to demonstrate a staged assembly. A line of vertically set east-facing blocks and lateral moldings marked the outline of a rear building platform (Fig. 27b,d). No trace of building wall masonry was seen, and no search for postholes was made on the summit. Masonry was like that of Str. 5D-40 and other late structures, consisting of standard-sized blocks with flat smooth faces and well-squared corners (0.55–0.60 by 0.30 by 0.15 m). There is no indication that blocks were reused from earlier constructions.

RELATIONSHIP TO ADJACENT STRATIGRAPHY

Fill was laid directly on Plat. 5D-2:U. 40, which was traced N to where it turned up to Str. 5D-37 and Plat. 5D-1:U. 72. Floor U. 42 between the structure and 5D-39 may be local rather than a widespread pavement.

ARCHITECTURE

A building platform distinguished by lateral moldings and a front step-up probably supported a perishable east-facing single-room building (Fig 24c,d, 25). The structure appears subsidiary to 5D-39 beside it, a pairing reflected in Str. 5E-98 and 94 across the Plaza. Approximately 45 m^3 of fill and masonry material and 25 m^2 of cut-stone surface area were required for assembly.

LOTS, GROUPING AND EVALUATION

OCCUPATION

78R/24–26, 38, and 39 from platform surfaces near the structure included Imix sherds and significant quantities of Eznab Ceramic Complex sherds from a final period of occupation.

TIME SPANS

The two-level oblong substructure probably once sustaining a perishable building was assembled in TS. 3 (Table 17) on the same U. 40 floor as Str. 5D-39 beside it (Fig. 1). The structure accompanied other low platforms in the Plaza (Str. 5D-135 and 136; 5E-92 and 94). Eznab trash located beside the structure and not in front suggests that the steps were kept clear during TS. 2 occupation. Disintegration of the abandoned building would presumably have been followed by weathering of the substructure. There was no evidence of subsequent disturbance.

TABLE 17
Structure 5D-134: Time Spans

Time Span	Architectural Addition	Floor, Unit	Special Deposit	Lot	Other Data
1	—	—	—	—	Collapse
2	—	—	—	78R/24–26,38,39	Use; Eznab ceramics
3	—	—	—	—	Assembly (45 m^3) on U. 40 (Plat. 5D-2-1st-A)

STRUCTURE 5D-136

INTRODUCTION

Undetected for the TR. 11 map, this small mound near the W end of Str. 5D-40 was distinguished in clearing of the plaza in 1965 (Fig. 1) and was excavated the same year by Jones and Orrego (Op. 78O). See Figs. 1, 24a,b (plan, section), 75b.

EXCAVATION DATA

CONSTRUCTION STAGES

Fill consisted of dark brown mud (Fig. 24b) resembling natural deposits in the ravine N of the East Plaza. Some fill blocks were clearly reused vault and cornice stones. A stair on the N side and a straight wall on the W were both certain, and the S and E sides possibly also had projecting steps (Figs. 24a, 75b). Structure height was ca. 0.65 m, although a summit floor was not found. Neither wall masonry nor postholes were found on the summit.

RELATIONSHIP TO ADJACENT STRATIGRAPHY

A Plat. 5D-2 floor preserved beneath the structure was assumed to be the latest plaza-wide pavement and labeled U. 40. It was not traced across to Str. 5D-40.

ARCHITECTURE

Enough masonry survived in place to delineate a small low platform with at least one projecting stair. In size and basic square plan the structure resembles Str. 5D-135 and 5D-92 of this report (Fig. 1) and Str. 5D-117, 132, and 133 on Plat. 5D-1 and 5D-4 (TR. 14). It is also reminiscent of postulated "kitchen" structures seen in Tikal domestic groups (TR. 19). Assembly utilized a mere 10 m^3 of material and 10 m^2 of cut stone surface.

LOTS, GROUPING AND EVALUATION

CONSTRUCTION

78O/14, from within fill, contained a small collection of Ik or Imix sherds.

TIME SPANS

Structure 5D-136 was erected in TS. 3 (Table 18) on the U. 40 floor of Plat. 5D-2-1st-A, roughly in front of Str. 5D-134 and beside the Maler Causeway. North orientation and location near the causeway are both suggestive of use as an entry marker to the Plaza or Causeway, perhaps as an altar. No trace of offerings was found, however.

TABLE 18
Structure 5D-136: Time Spans

Time Span	Architectural Addition	Floor, Unit	Special Deposit	Lot	Other Data
1	—	—	—	—	Collapse
2	—	—	—	—	Use
3	—	—	—	78O/14	Assembly (10 m^3) on U. 40 (Plat. 5D-2-1st-A)

STRUCTURE 5D-36

INTRODUCTION

The Str. 5D-36 mound appears on the TR. 11 map as a parapet between the Maler Causeway and the NE corner of Plat. 5D-1. Excavation revealed two platform levels N of that parapet. The N end of the structure was found by Broman in 1960 ceramic testings (Op. 22B, C). In 1965 Hellmuth dug several trenches into the structure and in 1966 submitted a preliminary report. See Figs. 1, 28a (plan), 28b–d, 29a, 30c.

EXCAVATION DATA

CONSTRUCTION STAGES

Unit 6 and *Unit 7* were nuclear fills and retaining walls covered by finished walls and floors (Fig. 28a,c,d). *Unit 1* on the S edge of the structure was a freestanding wall separating the Unit 2 level from the Plat. 5D-1:U. 77 landing and U. 74 stair leading to the Great Plaza. The U. 2 floor stretched N from the parapet to the summit of a terrace wall, from which the *Unit 3* floor extended at a lower level to its turndown over the *Unit 4* wall and stair. Units 2 and 3 were a unified construction effort as evidenced by wall-to-floor junctures in which the wall would have appeared unfinished without the floor. The U. 2 facing was vertical and constructed of standard-size stretchers and headers set on edge. A basal molding was 0.70 m above the floor. The U. 4 wall and stair were ca. 1.50 m high according to Broman's 1960 sketch plan and section. Unit 2 probably also had a central stair like that of U. 4 providing access to the upper level. Postholes or other indications of a building were not observed on either floor surface, but they were not systematically sought.

RELATIONSHIP TO ADJACENT STRATIGRAPHY

Platform 5D-1:U. 73, 75, 77, and 80 provided a set of stairs connecting the East Plaza with the Great Plaza between Str. 5D-37 and 36 (TR. 14:fig. 252a–d). The U. 77 landing was partially torn out for construction of the new U. 74 stair and Str. 5D-36 (Fig. 28c,d). Causeway Maler A-1st was built at the same time, which is demonstrated by the U. 3 floor abutment of the causeway parapet (Fig. 30c). The structure is thus contemporary with Plat. 5D-1-1st-A (U. 74) and 5D-2-1st-A (U. 40).

ARCHITECTURE

Structure 5D-36 consisted of two north-facing platform surfaces, one higher than the other. The upper one, backed by a parapet on the S. Entry, was by a central stair on the N; another stair probably communicated between the two levels (Fig.1, 28b, 29a). Both levels might have supported perishable buildings, but possibly were stands for viewing processions on the causeway. Assembly utilized 250 m^3 of material and 120 m^2 of dressed stone surface.

LOTS, GROUPING AND EVALUATION

CONSTRUCTION

12V/34, 42, and 54, sealed in fill, yielded Manik, and nothing postdates late Ik, even though Imix pottery was probably in production by this time.

OCCUPATION

12V/19, 20, 30–32, 40, 41, 43–45, and 55 from surface and collapse debris contained sherds of all periods; 12V/44 on the U. 1 floor against the causeway parapet held Imix sherds alone; and 12V/32 on floor U. 3 against Plat. 5D-1 had Eznab pottery, probably derived from late occupation.

TIME SPANS

Assembled in TS. 3 (Table 19) together with Plat. 5D-1:U. 74, Cswy. Maler A-1st, Plat. 5D-2-1st-A, and Str. 5D-40, the two paved levels were apparently the first construction at the base of the high Great Plaza corner and were accessible only from the N. Both floors afforded excellent views down the Maler Causeway.

TABLE 19
Structure 5D-36: Time Spans

Time Span	Architectural Addition	Floor, Unit	Special Deposit	Lot	Other Data
1	—	—	—	12V/20,30,31,40, 41,43–45,55	Collapse
2	—	—	—	12V/19,32	Use; Imix and Eznab ceramics
3	—	U. 1–7	—	12V/34,42,54	Assembly (250 m^3) with Cswy. Maler A-1st and Plat. 5D-2-1st-A:U. 40

CAUSEWAY MALER A-2ND

INTRODUCTION

The Tikal causeways can be divided for convenience of reporting. Segment A of the Maler Causeway encompasses the S end near Plat. 5D-2 (Fig. 1; TR. 11). The 1965 East Plaza excavations by Jones, Orrego, and Hellmuth took place at the juncture of causeway and platform. Other segments were excavated in 1960 by Luján, Broman, and others, and are not reported here (Op. 22; TR. 23H). Parapets and floors on the W side of the causeway were investigated by Hellmuth (Op. 78V) and on the E by Jones and Orrego (Op. 78Q). Both investigations uncovered evidence for an early causeway. See Figs. 28b, 29a,b, 30a–c.

EXCAVATION DATA

CONSTRUCTION STAGES

Evidence of an early causeway was seen in the trench through the E parapet just behind Str. 5D-40, where the lower of two floors, *Unit 4*, turned up to a 0.20 m high step, *Unit 7*, forming a 1.46 m wide summit landing that turned down over the top of a stair (Fig. 30a). It was first thought that the early causeway lacked a parapet because of its absence here, but in a trench 5 m to the N (Fig. 30b), a vertical *Unit 15* parapet face was seen ascending from the sloping side wall of the roadway. This parapet was ca. 1.25 m wide and at least 1.15 m high. On the W side of the roadway (Fig. 29b) the lower U. 4 floor ended against jagged bedrock, probably once fronted by masonry. In the next trench northward (Fig. 28b), U. 4 terminated against fill that was also most likely covered by a now-missing parapet facing. The *Unit 16* W face of the parapet, as well as a *Unit 14* basal floor, were preserved under Str. 5D-36. The early causeway was not reached in a third excavation even farther N (Fig. 30c). Unit 15 wall stones were on average shorter and thicker (under 0.30 m and over 0.20 m, respectively) than those of the later parapets.

RELATIONSHIP TO ADJACENT STRATIGRAPHY

The U. 4 floor was traced S on both sides of the causeway into the East Plaza where it became Plat. 5D-2:U. 41. The early causeway was thus coeval to the Plat. 5D-2-1st-C northward expansion of the East Plaza.

ARCHITECTURE

The early causeway anticipated the later one in having a paved roadbed, flanking parapet walls, exit gap, and stair near the S end.

LOTS, GROUPING AND EVALUATION

CONSTRUCTION

78Q/21 from within the U. 7 stair (Fig. 30a) contained Manik, Ik, and Imix sherds, and 12V/49 from U. 4 (Fig. 29b) contained Manik and a possible Ik or Imix body sherd. Imix ceramics appear to have been in vogue at the time of assembly.

TIME SPANS

A wide plaster-paved roadway above the general ground level was raised in TS. 2 (Table 20) in order to reduce a previously steep slope and cross the ravine. Raising the roadbed as it spanned the ravine created a reservoir. Presently unknown are whether a paved road had previously existed here and whether the causeway extended to the North Zone at this stage.

TABLE 20
Causeway Maler A-2nd: Time Spans

Time Span	Architectural Addition	Floor, Unit	Special Deposit	Lot	Other Data
1	—	—	—	—	Use
2	—	U. 4,7,13,15,16	—	12V/49; 78Q/21	Assembly with Plat. 5D-2:U. 41; Imix ceramics?

CAUSEWAY MALER A-1ST

INTRODUCTION

Five trenches exposed the causeway walls and floor in 1965. See Figs. 1, 28a,b, 29b, 30a–c, 31a,b.

EXCAVATION DATA

CONSTRUCTION STAGES

In the northernmost E side excavation (Fig. 30b) the *Unit 6* vertical parapet wall covered the earlier U. 15 face. A narrow ledge distinguished it from the sloping face of the causeway side below it. The W (inner) face of the parapet, *Unit 5*, was abutted by floor *Unit 3*. A similar profile was reconstructed on the W side of the causeway (Figs. 28a, 30c), where the exterior *Unit 1* face also rose from a narrow ledge at pavement level. Existence of the *Unit 2* bench in front of U. 1 was attested to by the fact that U. 1 commenced 0.50 m above floor level. In another excavation slightly S, the same U. 1 wall had a finished surface on its upper blocks, but not the lower ones (Fig. 28b), and in the southernmost excavation trench the bench profile had to be reconstructed (Fig. 29b). In all three W side sections and in one on the E side (Fig. 30b), the causeway floor concealed the unplastered base of the wall and must have been laid immediately. In contrast, where U. 3 turned down over stair *Unit 8* (Fig. 30a), it is clear that a gap existed in the causeway parapet.

ADDITIONS AND RENOVATIONS

Unit 9 blocked the gap in the E parapet, leaving a shallow alcove to be filled in later by *Unit 10* (Figs. 30a, 31a,b).

RELATIONSHIP TO ADJACENT STRATIGRAPHY

The U. 3 pavement became Plat. 5D-2:U. 40 where it entered the East Plaza. This places the causeway with Plat. 5D-2-1st-A and Str. 5D-40 in time.

ARCHITECTURE

New floor and parapets effected little change in causeway design, except for the appearance of benches on both sides of the roadway. Even the stair leading down from the N end of the E side was repeated in this version. The small ledge or molding that distinguishes the vertical parapet walls from the sloping causeway side walls is comparable to the ledge at the bases of Tikal building walls (Fig. 1).

LOTS, GROUPING AND EVALUATION

INITIAL CONSTRUCTION

12V/51–53 and 57 from within the W parapet contained Preclassic, Manik, and Imix sherds. Two lots from the E parapet, 12V/46 and 48, also held possible Imix sherds along with Ik and Manik. The causeway was probably assembled as late as the period of Imix ceramic production.

SECONDARY CONSTRUCTION

78Q/19, from U. 9 blocking the parapet gap, had Imix, Manik, and some probable Eznab sherds. The Eznab sherds might not have been sealed within the eroded wall, however. 78Q/17, within later U. 10, had Imix but no Eznab pottery.

OCCUPATION

12V/38 from an occupation deposit of black dirt, charcoal, and ash against the outside wall of the E side (Fig. 30b) contained Manik, Ik, and Imix sherds. Surface lots on and against the W parapet (12V/18, 23, 24, 40, 41, 44) and the E parapet (12V/36, 37, 39, 47; 78Q/20) contained Preclassic, Manik, Ik, and Imix sherds. 78Q/18 on stair U. 8 (Fig. 30a) contained many Eznab sherds.

TIME SPANS

Causeway Maler A-1st was assembled over A-2nd in TS. 7 (Fig. 1; Table 21). The only innovation was construction of benches on the interior faces of the parapets. A stair leading down from the causeway was rebuilt. The causeway is contemporary with Plat. 5D-2-1st-A, Str. 5D-36 and 40, as well as 5E-32-1st-A and the Mendez Causeway on the other side of the plaza. The stair gap was blocked in TS. 5, perhaps providing more privacy for the new structures (5D-39, 134, etc.) in the plaza above. Unit 10 further sealed the gap in TS. 3 in order to extend the side bench.

TABLE 21
Causeway Maler A-1st: Time Spans

Time Span	Architectural Addition	Floor, Unit	Special Deposit	Lot	Other Data
1	—	—	—	12V/18,23,24,37–41, 44,47; 78Q/18,20	Collapse
2	—	—	—	—	Use; Eznab ceramics
3	—	U. 10	—	78Q/19	Tertiary wall
4	—	—	—	—	Use
5	—	U. 9	—	78Q/17	Secondary wall; Eznab ceramics?
6	—	—	—	—	Use
7	—	U. 2,3,5,6,8,12	—	12V/46, 48,51–53,57	Assembly with Plat. 5D-2:U. 40; Imix ceramics

STRUCTURE 5D-40

INTRODUCTION

The mound on the N side of the East Plaza was correctly depicted as tall, oblong, and south-oriented by early investigations (Maler 1971; Tozzer 1911; and Morley 1938). The structure was not investigated after mapping (TR. 11) until excavated for basic design and stratigraphy by Jones and Orrego in 1965 (Op. 78Q). See Figs. 1, 31a,b, 32a–c (plan, section), 33, 34, 75a.

EXCAVATION DATA

CONSTRUCTION STAGES

CONSTRUCTION STAGE 3

Nuclear fill amassed on Plat. 5D-2:U. 41 included the irregular, untrimmed masonry of the *Unit 5* construction stair (Fig. 32c). Prior to stair construction, the Plat. 5D-2:U. 41 floor appears to have been cut by a large pit, *Unit 46*, which perhaps contains an unexcavated burial and was filled by a mixture of loose earth and stones protruding above floor level. The nucleus of the structure was also seen in *Unit 2*, a mortar layer 0.30 m beneath the room floor at the top of the mound. Core walls backing the facing were exposed in the E trench (Fig. 34).

CONSTRUCTION STAGE 2

Substructural facings were built 0.30–0.50 m in front of core walls, and stair stretchers 0.30 m high and 0.20 m thick overlay the U. 5 masons' stair (Figs. 32c, 34). Wall blocks were 0.34 m high and 0.45–0.53 m long. A corner stone of the basal molding measured 0.56 by 0.53 by 0.20 m, its sides angled to conform to the slope. A *Unit 1* mortar layer capped the substructure under the building walls on both sides of the central doorway (Fig. 32c).

CONSTRUCTION STAGE 1

Building walls were constructed of rubble core faced by dressed blocks which at ca. 0.50 by 0.35 by 0.18 m were higher and thinner than substructural blocks. A plaster coat could be seen on outer surfaces. The front wall was exposed from the central to the W doorway without encountering an intermediate door; thus only three front entries existed (Fig. 32b). The single gallery may have been subdivided into separate rooms and contained interior benches, although the SE corner of the room lacked any sign of a bench (Fig. 34). The room floor at both the center and E end were at the same 249.28 m elevation. The white plaster floor contained pink inclusions resulting from severe burning, and the underlying U. 1 mortar was blackened (Fig. 32c). Vault stones measuring 0.60 by 0.30 by 0.30 m with gray soffit plaster were found tumbled within the room. Evidently fires had been lit in the room before collapse. The front roof collapsed first as the lintels gave way, and the rear vault fell forward over the debris as the rear wall buckled outward.

OTHER FEATURES

A probable cord-holder socket 0.20 m deep and 0.22 m in diameter (without ceramic insert) was located on the interior surface of the front wall, 0.30 m W of the central doorjamb and 0.40 m above the floor. The walls were too destroyed for survival of the three other sockets. A smaller hole, 0.15 m deep and 0.13 m in diameter, was found on the E jamb of the central doorway 0.50 m from the inner edge and 0.30 m above the floor. The hole had small vertical rod sockets in its upper and lower surfaces once holding a wooden dowel, as seen in tie-holes elsewhere at Tikal. Finally, a third hole 0.20 m deep and 0.15 m in diameter was seen in the room floor 0.43 m back from the front wall in line with the W jamb (Fig. 32c). Its function or relationship to the others is unknown.

ADDITIONS AND RENOVATIONS

Secondary *Unit 6* facings were built on the U. 40 platform floor on both the S facade and the E stair wall (Fig. 32a,c). These new walls were abutted by U. 43 and then later dismantled to the level of that pavement. Loose interior fill behind them contained the gray ash and Eznab sherds that were found elsewhere against the structure. Unit 6 and the U. 43 floor thus seem to be very late and were perhaps designed to repair the corner of 5D-40 as well as to correct a plaza declivity by raising the plaza level 0.40 m.

RELATIONSHIP TO ADJACENT STRATIGRAPHY

A pair of floors, lying respectively beneath and against the NW corner of Str. 5D-40, were traced S to be seen as Maler Causeway floor U. 4 and 3, while on the other side of the road these were followed N to become Plat. 5D-2:U. 41 and 40. Therefore the pavements that bracketed the front stair were labeled U. 41 and U. 40 (Fig. 32c), and the first floor laid against the E end of the structure was also called U. 40 (Fig. 34). At all points U. 40 appeared to have been spread shortly after the structure was completed.

ARCHITECTURE

Excavation was sufficient for reconstruction of a three-step substructure, broad S stair, and single-galleried building with three widely separated doorways (Fig. 1, 32a, 33). A roofcomb is doubtful, given the paucity of collapse debris. Transverse walls might have divided the room; interior platforms were not seen either in the center or at the E end. Cord holders allowed curtaining of at least the central door. Masonry was similar in dimension and form to contemporary structures in the group including 5E-30 and 32-1st-A. Assembly utilized as much as 2,450 m^3 of fill material and 900 m^2 of surface dressing.

SPECIAL DEPOSITS

PROBLEMATICAL DEPOSIT 169

LOCATION

Found in loose dirt on the first terrace of the E side of Str. 5D-40 against the face of the second terrace (Fig. 34). 78Q/14.

CONTENT AND ARRANGEMENT

4 miniature pottery vessels (TR. 25A:fig. 148g:1–4) grouped with three upside down and one on its side.

DISCUSSION

The proximity to Eznab trash below suggests an association. Both deposits were on construction covered by loose earth and collapse debris.

SEQUENTIAL ARRANGEMENT

Unsealed PD. 169 probably pertained to TS. 2, the final period of occupation.

LOTS, GROUPING AND EVALUATION

CONSTRUCTION

78Q/8 from sealed stair fill contained sherds evaluated as either Ik or Imix.

OCCUPATION

78Q/5 from collapse debris within the room, and 78Q/6 and 20 from debris on the NW corner terraces, included Cauac, Manik, and Imix. 78Q/15 from accumulations against the E stair wall had Manik, Ik, Imix and Eznab sherds. 78Q/1, 2, 4, 7,

9–12, 16, and 22 from gray ash against building walls and basal terraces held rich deposits of Eznab sherds from reconstructible vessels. 78Q/2 from the E end of the substructure contained 17 lbs of Eznab sherds plus disarticulated bones of at least two adult humans including skull fragments, mandibles, leg, arm, ankle, and pelvic bones (Figs. 34, 75a). Notable were large fragments of Pabellon Modeled-Carved ware (MT. 351), Sahcaba Modeled-Carved ware (MT. 350), and an unnamed incised ware (MT. 145). This collection was the largest of the Eznab deposits from the East Plaza and is representative of those taken from plaza surfaces near Str. 5D-40, 39, 134–136, and 5E-30, 92, 94, and 98. 78Q/15 from the SE corner included a human mandible, three molars, and an incisor, plus crania and long bone fragments. Many bones were in excellent condition and bore signs of burning but were not worked. Similar disarticulated burned human bone appeared in 78Q/1 and 12 from the same area and in 78Q/7 from the W end of the substructure. Also within these deposits were flint and obsidian flakes and flake-blades, a flat crescent-shaped shell-mosaic piece, a fragment of *Dentalium* shell, land snails, and mano fragments. These trash heaps may have derived from the building above, where severe burning has been noted. They were clearly trash deposits from the final occupation of the western part of the East Plaza.

TIME SPANS

Assembly in TS. 5 (Table 22) involved standard core construction followed by finished masonry. Full expansion of Plat. 5D-2 had been accomplished by this time, first with U. 41, then U. 36 (Fig. 1). The base of the new structure was surrounded by the U. 40 floor, paving of most or all of the remainder of the platform, and completion of the long structures that fill the eastern half of the Plaza. Although Str. 5D-40 has three front doorways, cord holders, and considerable height like 5E-38 in this group and 5D-26 on the North Acropolis, it probably lacked a rear room and roofcomb. Residence and administration are probable functions, but the possible burial beneath its stair points to a commemorative meaning as well. It stands on the approximate centerline of the East Plaza space between the 5E-32 quadrangle and the Great Plaza. In TS. 3 part of the substructure was rebuilt with the new U. 43 floor, perhaps at a time when Str. 5D-39, 134 and others formed a domestic group within the Plaza. Gray ash and Eznab sherds accumulated on the platform outside the building and against the base of the substructure, implying that the structure was being used in TS. 2 as a domicile. Vault collapse occurred without evidence of masonry depredation (TS. 1).

TABLE 22
Structure 5D-40: Time Spans

Time Span	Architectural Addition	Floor, Unit	Special Deposit	Lot	Other Data
1	—	—	—	78Q/5,6,15,20	Collapse
2	—	—	PD. 169	78Q/1,2,4,7, 9–12,15,16,22	Use; Eznab ceramics, human bone, etc.
3	A	U. 6	—	—	Secondary construction with Plat. 5D-2:U. 43; Eznab ceramics
4	—	—	—	—	Use
5	B	U. 1–5	—	78Q/8	Assembly (2,450 m^3) with Plat. 5D-2:U. 40; Imix ceramics

STRUCTURE 5E-30

INTRODUCTION

The 5E-30 mound was described as parapet-like during the St. 17 investigations (TR. 8:153–154), but resembles a structure mound on the TR. 11 map. Excavation by Jones and Orrego in 1965 was confined to a transverse trench through the room and front corner probes. See Figs. 1, 32a,d (plan), 34, 35 (section).

EXCAVATION DATA

CONSTRUCTION STAGES

The nucleus of the structure was scarcely penetrated by excavation. A plastered floor beneath the U. 4 front substructural paving, *Unit 2*, is either core construction or original to the finished structure (Fig. 35). A sloped substructural face, vertical building platform wall, and one surviving course of the building wall were exposed by the W side trench (Fig. 34). Facing stones were 0.50–0.65 m long, 0.30 m high, and 0.18 m thick, set with their bedding planes horizontal. The terrace in front of the building platform was fronted by three wide steps (Fig. 32d).

Building walls were assembled on the unplastered substructure. Stones were 0.63–0.72 m long and 0.30–0.35 m high, slightly larger than those of the substructure. The *Unit 1* room floor abutted the walls and the *Unit 4* frontal platform floor turned up to the building platform. Parts of three doorways allowed the reconstruction by analogy of five for the S facade. The rear wall collapsed into the ravine, but its position was determined by a slight upturn in the U. 1 floor (Fig. 35). Vault stones in the debris were not measured.

RELATIONSHIP TO ADJACENT STRATIGRAPHY

The structure was erected on the U. 36 surface of Plat. 5D-2, and the abutting U. 35 floor was apparently laid shortly after, covering an unsightly gap at the base of the masonry (Figs. 34, 35). The structure was thus built at the same time as 5D-40 and Plat. 5D-2-1st-A.

ARCHITECTURE

Structure 5E-30 differed in significant ways from the structures to its E and S, such as 5E-29 and 32 (Fig. 1). Although the long building had several doorways, the substructure was higher, the front platform deeper, and doorways were separated by walls wider than themselves. These features appeared on 5D-40 to the N. Cord holders were not detected, but might have been present. Assembly consumed 500 m^3 of material and 570 m^2 of dressed surface.

LOTS, GROUPING AND EVALUATION

OCCUPATION

78Q/1, 2, 11, and 12 on floor surfaces W of the structure and 78T/1–3 from the E stair corner derived from deposits of Eznab sherds, ash, and scattered human bone. These lots contained at least 17 pieces of Pabellon Modeled-Carved ware, of which two fragments found in 78T/3 and 78Q/2 were probably from a single ring-base bowl. The deposits confirm that the structure was occupied in the Eznab ceramic period.

TIME SPANS

Structure 5E-30 was built in TS. 4 on the Plat. 5D-2-1st-B floor (U. 36), which expanded the Plaza N to its present limit (Table 23). Construction was completed with the U. 40/35 floor of Plat. 5D-2-1st-A, the Maler Causeway renewal, and Str. 5D-40. Although the greater height, deep front platform, and wide wall sections between doors distinguish it from the buildings to the E and S (Str. 5E-29, 32, etc.), the structure's function may be related to that complex rather than to the Plaza W of it. Deposits of ash, human bones, and Eznab sherds implied residential use during TS. 2, at a time when perishable structures such as 5E-98 and 92 in front of 30 may have transformed the plaza into a residential group. The roof and walls collapsed during TS. 1, dropping much of the debris into the ravine, as was the case with adjacent Str. 5D-40 and 5E-29.

TABLE 23
Structure 5E-30: Time Spans

Time Span	Architectural Addition	Floor, Unit	Special Deposit	Lot	Other Data
1	—	—	—	—	Collapse
2	—	—	—	78Q/1,2,11,12; 78T/1–3	Use; Eznab ceramics, human bone
3	—	—	—	—	Use
4	—	U. 1–4	—	—	Assembly (500 m^3) with Plat. 5D-2:U. 35

STRUCTURE 5E-98

INTRODUCTION

The low platform in front of 5E-30 was not noticed during Project mapping. When Orrego cleared the area in 1965, he saw wall alignments and traced a basic plan through narrow trenching. See Figs. 1, 36a (plan), 37b (section).

EXCAVATION DATA

The plan was suitable for a single-room thatched building (Fig. 36a). A step on the S side of the platform determined orientation. The unusual S projection on the W end might have supported an extra room or simply been a terrace. No attempt was made to locate postholes and plaster flooring on the mound. The two courses of standard 0.50 by 0.30 by 0.20 m wall blocks had no abutting platform floors (Fig. 37b).

ARCHITECTURE

The oblong substructure probably supported a single-room, south-facing pole-and-thatch building (Fig. 1). There were some unusual features, including an L-shaped plan and non-parallel sides. Assembly consumed 80 m³ of material and 35 m² of facial trimming.

TIME SPANS

Structure 5E-98 was constructed directly in front of older 5E-30 (Table 24: TS. 3), presumably to sustain a perishable building. The proximity of 5E-92 suggests that it was a related structure, perhaps a "kitchen" as in domestic groups at Tikal (TR. 19). Plan size matched that of structures described in TR. 19. This and other such structures in the Plaza were surrounded by Eznab-rich trash deposits made during TS. 2.

TABLE 24
Structure 5E-98: Time Spans

Time Span	Architectural Addition	Floor, Unit	Special Deposit	Lot	Other Data
1	—	—	—	—	Collapse
2	—	—	—	—	Use
3	—	—	—	—	Assembly (80 m³) on Plat. 5D-2:U. 35

STRUCTURE 5E-92

INTRODUCTION

Structure 5E-92 was discovered to be separate from 5E-98 in 1965. See Figs. 1, 36a (plan), 37a (section).

EXCAVATION DATA

Narrow excavations along the side walls showed that Str. 5E-92 was a square masonry platform only one course (0.30 m) high built on the same U. 40 floor as the larger 5E-98 platform it fronted (Fig. 1, 36a, 37a). The structural fill was not penetrated and ceramics were not collected.

ARCHITECTURE

Assembly of Str. 5E-92 utilized only 5 m³ of material and surface trimming of 5 m².

TIME SPANS

The platform was assembled in TS. 2 (Table 25) close to the front of Str. 5E-98 and on its centerline (Fig. 1). In its square shape and small size it is comparable to Str. 5D-135 and 136 in the same plaza, but also to structures that Haviland proposed as kitchens, such as Str. 4F-42 (TR. 19:120).

TABLE 25
Structure 5E-92: Time Spans

Time Span	Architectural Addition	Floor, Unit	Special Deposit	Lot	Other Data
1	—	—	—	—	Collapse
2	—	—	—	—	Use
3	—	—	—	—	Assembly (5 m^3) on Plat. 5D-2:U. 35

STRUCTURE 5E-29

INTRODUCTION

The slender parapet-like Str. 5E-29 mound on the N edge of the East Plaza was investigated by a single transverse trench by Jones in 1964 (Op. 78D). In the next year, Jones and Orrego briefly cleared the SW corner (Op. 78O). See Figs. 1, 36b (plan), 37c (section), 77a.

EXCAVATION DATA

CONSTRUCTION STAGES

50 centimeters beneath the structure lay a 0.10 m thick summit floor (U. 54) that might pertain to a buried structure or platform (Fig. 37c). The substructural fill assembled on unplastered Plat. 5D-2-1st-B stretched uninterrupted from the front step to under the building itself. Unusually high (0.40 m) frontal step stones intruded into the underlying fill and were abutted by the first floor capping this area of the platform (U. 36). One pier and the side of an adjacent pier were exposed E of centerline (Figs. 36b, 77a). The 2.07 m doorway width, 1.31 m pier width, and 0.87 m wall thickness conform to measurements on Str. 5E-32 and other nearby galleries. The rear wall fell into the ravine, but a floor turnup at the collapse line provided evidence for a room depth of 1.63 m. Vault stones were found in room debris, although most of the superstructure had fallen down the slope. Traces of red paint on the floor and interior front wall plaster were the only such surface modifications in the group.

ADDITIONS AND RENOVATIONS

Secondary flooring was spread both within the room (*Unit 1*) and on the frontal terrace (*Unit 2*), probably at the time of the final U. 35 floor platform (Fig. 37c).

RELATIONSHIP TO ADJACENT STRATIGRAPHY

Assembled on unplastered Plat. 5D-2:U. 36 and abutted by its plaster surface, Str. 5E-29 was undoubtedly coeval with Plat. 5D-2-1st-B and was earlier than 5E-30 beside it.

ARCHITECTURE

Structure 5E-29 was built along the N edge of the East Plaza as an extremely long yet scarcely elevated single gallery with closely spaced S doorways (Fig. 1). Although there were no interior transverse divider walls located, they might have existed. Eighteen doorways were estimated for the 33 m building length, although an even number of doorways would be unusual at Tikal. Interior red paint and secondary flooring are unusual for the East Plaza. Approximately 450 m^3 of material was used in construction and 300 m^2 of cut stone.

LOTS, GROUPING AND EVALUATION

OCCUPATION

78D/5 from collapse debris on top of room and frontal platform floors contained Preclassic, Manik,

Ik, and Imix sherds and was more likely derived from collapsed fill than occupation.

TIME SPANS

Built when the plaza was extended N to its present limit (Table 26:TS. 3), the structure framed the plaza along the edge of a sharp drop-off (Fig. 1). The long row of closely spaced doorways faced coeval and earlier structures of similar form, including 5E-95-2nd, 99-2nd, 32-1st-C, 32-1st-B, and 37, which formed the N limit of an expanded marketplace. Collapse (TS. 1) might have come early due to weaknesses in the many doors and narrow piers of the front wall and proximity to the ravine. Scarcity of fallen masonry suggests that most of the building collapsed down the slope.

TABLE 26
Structure 5E-29: Time Spans

Time Span	Architectural Addition	Floor, Unit	Special Deposit	Lot	Other Data
1	—	—	—	—	Collapse
2	—	—	—	78D/5	Use
3	—	—	—	—	Assembly (450 m^3) with Plat. 5D-2:U. 36

STRUCTURE 5E-94

INTRODUCTION

The low Str. 5E-94 platform on the NW corner of 5E-32 was not seen in mapping (TR. 11), and the 1964 excavation exposing its S side wall did not recognize it as a separate entity. Late in the 1965 season, Jones and Orrego noticed the shape and investigated it by means of a centerline trench and small probes. See Figs. 1, 39a (plan), b (section), 42a,b, 77d.

EXCAVATION DATA

The imposition of Str. 5E-94 on top of partially demolished 5E-32 is illustrated in Fig. 39b, wherein *Unit 1* structural fill covered the Plat. 5D-2 floor U. 35 and the diminished piers of 32-1st-A (see also Fig. 42a). The *Unit 3* rear wall and *Unit 2* room floor were based on U. 1 against the dismantled medial wall of 5E-32 (Figs. 39b, 77d). In the S side excavation the U. 3 lateral wall abutted the older U. 6 end wall of Str. 5E-32-2nd-A; U. 6 was incorporated into 32-1st-A (Figs. 39a, 42b). The masonry, which may have been robbed from 5E-32, did not seem different in shape or dimensions.

ARCHITECTURE

Two steps along the front of the substructure reached almost to the corners. The summit was divided into a front terrace and an elevated rear room (Fig. 39a). Side walls extended W only to the step between the two levels and did not turn to form a front wall. These lateral walls were unusually thin, and presumably wooden uprights along the front supported a roof made of perishable materials. Size and shape are comparable to contemporary Str. 5D-39 across the Plaza (see Figs. 1, 23a, 39a). Material required to erect Str. 5E-94 (over the remains of 5E-32) totaled 150 m^3 and the area of dressed wall surface 100 m^2.

LOTS, GROUPING AND EVALUATION

OCCUPATION

78U/1–2 on floor surfaces contained Ik or Imix sherds. 78U/3 from within the room had abundant Eznab material indicative of occupation during that period of ceramic production, like that of the structures to the W of it.

TIME SPANS

Structure 5E-94 was erected in TS. 3 on the partially demolished W piers of 5E-32-1st-A (Fig. 1; Table 27). It was not clear that 32 had previously suffered collapse, but ash deposits in the room suggest prior neglect. Design of the new building differed sharply from that of 32 in the absence of frontal piers and thinness of walls. These traits were seen earlier, however, in long-superseded 32-2nd-B and 95-2nd. The oblong two-level substructure resembled Str. 5D-39, 5D-134, and 5E-98 in the same plaza and was surely part of the group formed by those structures, facing away from the quadrangle. Eznab trash in the room reinforced the impression of late domestic occupation.

TABLE 27
Structure 5E-94: Time Spans

Time Span	Architectural Addition	Floor, Unit	Special Deposit	Lot	Other Data
1	—	—	—	—	Collapse
2	—	—	—	78U/1–3	Use; Eznab ceramics
3	—	—	—	—	Assembly (150 m³) on Plat. 5D-2:U. 35 and Str. 5E-32-1st-A

STRUCTURE 5E-32-2ND

INTRODUCTION

Structure 5E-32 was investigated by Jones in 1964 (Op. 78A, C, D) by trenching at the centers of the W and N sides, extensive excavation of the SW corner, and a small probe at the NE corner. In 1965 the NW corner was examined at several points by Jones and Orrego (Op. 78K, U). The E side was redesignated Str. 5E-99. Evidence was seen in 1964 of an early W building (2nd-B) and S building (2nd-A). For 2nd-B see Figs. 9, 38b (plan),c, 42b, 43b, 44, 45; for 2nd-A see Fig. 46.

EXCAVATION DATA

The *Unit 6* building platform was clear evidence of an early structure (2nd-B), its *Unit 15* summit floor extending beneath the W piers of 32-1st (Fig. 38c). Fill of U. 6 was layered earth and small stones with few large blocks and no interior core walls. Coursing on facing walls was inconsistent; there was, for instance, a tall and short course in one area (Fig. 44) and three shorter courses in another (Fig. 38c). The thin rear and side walls of the building (also called U. 6) rested on unplastered mortar and were abutted by the U. 15 room floor (Figs. 43b, 44, 45). Although most wall masonry had been removed along the U. 7 rip-out line, the original rear wall and plaster coating survived to a height of 1.08 m (Fig. 45). The wall could also be seen near the N end of the structure, badly deteriorated or patched. In a trench through the end wall (also U. 6), the floor beneath the later U. 5 stones is U. 15 (Fig. 42b). The 0.57 m wide rear wall and 0.40 m wide lateral wall were probably too thin to support vaulting. (The cornice stones in place on top of the wall were too long to fit on U. 6 and surely pertained to U. 5 of 32-1st.) The S and N building walls did not corner in front, hence a roof (thatch or beam and mortar?) might have been supported by frontal wooden posts (Fig. 38b). Unit 6 masonry was 0.30 to 0.70 m in length, 0.20–0.36 m in height, and 0.12–0.21 m in width. Coursing was irregular and large spalls were set between blocks. At least one stone was placed at an angle to compensate for a change in coursing height. This relatively unstandardized masonry resembles that of Str. 5D-42 and 5E-31.

Structure 5E-32-2nd-A was an early unattached south-facing version of the S wing, possibly of similar length to 2nd-B. The *Unit 14* floor beneath 5E-32-1st and the *Unit 12* steps were possible elements of 2nd-A (Fig. 46). The two preceding floors, *Unit 13* and *Unit 17*, may have been separate structures but remain uninvestigated.

RELATIONSHIP TO ADJACENT STRATIGRAPHY

The plaster surface of Plat. 5D-2:U. 5 on which 2nd-B is sited could not be followed W from beneath the structure (Figs. 9, 38c, 44). Its body, however, continued W within the final U. 35 paving and abutted 5E-31 as U. 1 (Fig. 9). Units 5 and 1 were surfaces of Plat. 5D-2-1st-C. No immediately abutting plaza floors were certain and the structure probably existed for some time before Plat. 5D-2-1st-B was built, represented by U. 24 abutting the E side (Fig. 38c), U. 34 at the S end (Fig. 44), and U. 50 against 32-2nd-A (Fig. 46).

ARCHITECTURE

Structure 5E-32-2nd-B has thin rear and lateral walls, no masonry front wall, probably no vaulting, and possibly thatch or beam-and-mortar roofing. With almost identical Str. 5E-95-2nd, the building type for the E side of the East Plaza was initiated: elongated rooms almost on plaza level, with open fronts and closed rears. Material for 32-2nd-B was ca. 140 m^3 and 310 m^2 of dressed surface; 2nd-A. is assumed to have an equivalent design, and thus similar volume and area.

LOTS, GROUPING AND EVALUATION

CONSTRUCTION

78A/10 from within the 2nd-B building platform contained Manik, Ik, and probable Imix pottery; 78C/23 from beneath the S end floor yielded a small sample of Manik sherds; 78C/18 and 19 were a large collection of well-preserved Ik or early Imix sherds from within floor U. 13 of 2nd-A. The sherds date the structures to Ik and possibly Imix ceramic production.

TIME SPANS

Structure 5E-32-2nd-B and A were built on U. 5 of Plat. 5D-2-1st-C (Table 28:TS. 2). Assembly was probably sometime later than the pavement that spread over the platform summit at the time of Str. 5E-31, 5D-42, 5D-43, and 5E-95-2nd, and the Central Acropolis and Plat. 5D-1:U. 73 terrace faces. The unusually thin building walls have the erratic coursing seen in 5D-42, 5D-43, and 5E-31. Thin walls were seen on Str. 5E-Sub.2 and 3 in Gp. 5E-11, also dated by sealed Imix ceramics (Larios and Orrego 1983).

TABLE 28
Structure 5E-32-2nd: Time Spans

Time Span	Architectural Addition	Floor, Unit	Special Deposit	Lot	Other Data
1	—	—	—	—	Use
2	A, B	U. 6,12–15,17	—	78A/10; 78C/18,19,23	Assembly of 2nd-A (140 m^3?) and 2nd-B (140 m^3) on Plat. 5D-2-1st-C; Ik or Imix ceramics

STRUCTURE 5E-32-1ST

INTRODUCTION

The 1964 and 1965 excavations of Str. 5E-32 are described above with 32-2nd. See Figs. 1, 38a–c, 39a,b, 40, 41, 42a–c, 43a,b, 44–46, 47a,b, 48b, 76a–d, 77b,d.

EXCAVATION DATA

CONSTRUCTION STAGES

Structure 5E-32-1st is treated here as a single architectural entity because final 1st-A incorporated C and B without burying them. The final manifestation of Str. 5E-32 began with 32-1st-C, an almost complete rebuilding of 2nd-B. The thin U. 6 walls were torn down to rip-out line *Unit 7* and a *Unit 5* masonry liner wall was erected against the interior surfaces to create support for a vaulted roof (Figs. 44, 45, 76b–d). Although the facing of this new room bonded only weakly to U. 6, some blocks of U. 5 stayed in position, especially where supported by the U. 3 interior platform at the S end. Cornice stones survived where held in place by later additions (Figs. 44, 45, 76b).

Room floor U. 16 ran through the centerline doorway in the medial wall and was apparently laid later with 1st-A (Fig. 38c). Front piers, standing on floor U. 15 and abutted by U. 16, pertained to the 1st-C structure discussed here rather than to prior 2nd-B or later 1st-A (Fig. 45, 47). Shallow excavations at the N end of the structure showed these same floor-wall relationships (Figs. 42b, 43b).

Unit 5 stretchers averaged 0.60 by 0.30 by 0.15 m, thin and long compared to earlier blocks of U. 6. Height varied considerably and irregularities occurred, such as two stones making up a single course and corners removed to fit. Wall-top cornice stones were 0.71 by 0.33 by 0.24 m, tapered back to a butt width of 0.15 m and with a front angle of ca. 7°.

The new room was vaulted. A fallen 0.70 by 0.30 by 0.22 m vault stone with 35° soffit angle allowed reconstruction of a 2.06 m chamber height (Fig. 45). Two upper-zone courses still in place above the cornice at the corner probably framed an inset panel as on other Tikal buildings.

ADDITIONS AND RENOVATIONS

Unit 1 was a structural addition of uncertain form built against the rear or E side of the building platform (Fig. 38c). The sole surviving feature was a bench facing W behind 1st-C. It was faced with well-shaped masonry and topped by plaster that turned down over the W edge in a smooth curve. A fill wall beneath the E end of the plaster probably once supported a room wall. Unit 1 extended S for at least 6 m from the axial trench and an altogether separate room attached to the back wall of 32-1st. No entries or other features were discovered.

Unit 11 was a posthole 0.20 m in diameter and 0.44 m in depth penetrating the Plat. 5D-2:U. 34 floor against the SW corner of 32-1st-C (Figs. 38b, 44). Although depicted on the plan of 2nd-B (Fig. 38b), it should pertain rather to 1st-C and the U. 34 floor. The post might have supported a roof or awning of another auxiliary room. The hole was sealed by 32-1st-B.

Structure 5E-32-1st-B, a stratigraphically distinct development, consisted of a south-facing gallery attached at a right angle to the S end of 1st-C (Figs. 40, 41, 76b). Its Unit 8 rear wall was built against U. 5 of 1st-C (Fig. 44). The substructural fill of compact earth without large blocks covered the U. 12 steps and U. 14 floor of 2nd-A (Fig. 46), which did not extend as far W as 1st-B (Fig. 44). Unit 8 had even courses, few headers, and blocks 0.55–0.63 m long, 0.32–0.40 m high, and 0.17 m thick. Course heights were generally greater than on either 2nd-B or 1st-C. Thin mortar lines between interior and exterior faces indicated that the wall was built course by course, a phenomenon not seen in earlier stages of 32. An in situ cornice stone measured 0.72 by 0.44 by 0.22 m and had a 7° front angle and markedly tapered sides. Cornice stones of an upper zone lay fallen in front of the building. Vault stones fallen within the room averaged 0.60 by 0.30 by 0.25 m and had a 32° soffit angle. One had a severe side taper to 0.12 m and

another had none. Two successive room floors turned up to the rear wall and over the front step. The lower floor was probably the original, with the upper one laid at the time of the 1st-A revision.

Unit 4 was built against the juncture of 1st-C and 1st-B as a secondary stair to the roof (Figs. 41, 45, 76d). Two steps survived under 1st-A fill, the other steps and the stair wall having been torn out along the *Unit 9* rip-out line. Stones were stretchers averaging 0.50 by 0.30 by 0.20 m. A stair riser measured 0.31 m and the tread was 0.34 m deep. Since the buried U. 8 wall and cornice were relatively unweathered, construction of the flight may have closely followed completion of 1st-B.

Structure 5E-32-1st-A, the final and most ambitious expansion of Str. 5E-32, added additional galleries onto the back walls of 1st-C and 1st-B and completed the quadrangular enclosure with the double-galleried N wing and Str. 5E-99-1st on the E side (Figs. 1, 81a,b). Examining first the W end of the S wing (Figs. 45, 46), the *Unit 18* building platform and rear wall of the addition can be seen to bury the wall and partially dismantled stair U. 8 and 4 of 1st-B. Two floors were laid in the room, the lower one perhaps merely a preparation floor. The *Unit 16* floor extended through the central medial door of the W wing, which must have been built to mark the centerline of the new 1st-A (Fig. 47b). Another new feature was *Unit 10*, a step aligned with the W doorway of the centerline passageway (Fig. 38c). The *Unit 3* platform against the interior S wall of 1st-C was probably also built at the time of 1st-A, because the U. 16 floor abutting it covered a gap at its base (Figs. 44, 45, 76c). Its rough, uneven surface and 1.20 m height are uncharacteristic of interior platforms designed for sitting or lying, and a buttressing role is therefore likely. The rear (E) wall of 1st-C was heavily damaged and crudely patched prior to construction of the 1st-A gallery against it (Fig. 43b). Beyond the N end of old 1st-C, both galleries and the medial wall were assembled together (Fig. 39b).

The N wing of 32-1st-A was exposed by three trenches located at the NW corner (Figs. 38a, 42a), the centerline (Figs. 42c, 43a), and at the E end (Fig. 48b). Building platform fill was a uniform dark brown earth containing roughly cut blocks (Fig. 42c). Walls were erected on a thin mortar layer and were abutted by a single room floor. A step on the N side of the structure inexplicably increased in depth from 0.70 m at centerline to 1.40 m at the W end.

Units 21a and *b* were transverse walls built on both sides of the passageway through the W wing (Figs. 38a, 47b, 76a). Overlying the U. 16 room floor, they must be considered additions to 1st-A. The S walls were the only ones excavated, but similar N ones can be assumed. Block faces were uneven in dimensions, although generally of less height than those of 1st-A. The walls are comparable to those that line the passageway through Str. 5E-37.

RELATIONSHIP TO ADJACENT STRATIGRAPHY

Stratigraphy was complicated by the fact that 32-1st-C utilized the building platform of preceding 2nd-B (Figs. 38c, 44). Hence the 1st-C building did not touch floors of Plat. 5D-2. Platform 5D-2-1st-C (U. 5) supported 2nd-B and U. 25 turned up to it, perhaps when the building was renovated into 1st-C. Structure 5E-32-1st-B was built against the S end of 1st-C on the U. 34 floor equivalent to U. 25 (Figs. 44, 46). Structure 5E-32-1st-A abutted the rear walls of 1st-C and 1st-B and buried the U. 4 stair, which is interpreted as part of Plat. 5D-2-1st-B (Figs. 38c, 39b, 42a–c, 43b, 45, 46, 77d). The new 1st-A incorporating C and B was immediately abutted by a final floor called U. 35 on the W and N, U. 24 within the quadrangle, and U. 37 on the S. In several trenches this widespread Plat. 5D-2-1st-A pavement could be seen to follow the 1st-A construction immediately.

ARCHITECTURE

Exterior dimensions of 32-1st-C are the same as those of 32-2nd-B (2.95 by 55.5 m) and room size was reduced by the U. 5 liner wall (Figs. 38a, 41). Closely spaced doorways lined the W facade; the northernmost doorjamb was flush with the side wall. The building had a makeshift quality as seen in the use of an old building platform, shoddy liner walls, and patchwork masonry. Most importantly, the thin-walled thatched building was changed into the earliest of the full-fledged vaulted collonades of the Plaza. If, as suspected, 32-1st-B extended all the way E to the later quadrangle corner, it was also 55 m length! It appears to have been a continuation of the original design, creating an L-shaped building with closely spaced outward-facing doorways and blank interior faces. Final 32-1st-A continued to expand the gallery concept, again fashioning a single building by merging the accretions. One significant innovation was a passageway through the center of the W side, which also marked the center of the U-shaped structure. Material for constructing 1st-C amounted to 450 m^3 (not including the existing 2nd-B building platform); the area of dressed surface was 750 m^2. Comparable quantities for 1st-B were 400 m^3 and 1,150 m^2, and for 1st-A, 1,900 m^3 and 2,450 m^2.

LOTS, GROUPING AND EVALUATION

INITIAL CONSTRUCTION

78C/14 from beneath the room floor of 1st-B contained Ik and mostly Imix polychrome (as well as a fragment of a shell "tinkler"), and 78C/17 from within the rear wall had Manik and nothing later than Ik. Judging by the first lot, Imix ceramics were in vogue. 78A/12 from within the U. 1 bench behind 1st-C had Manik, Ik, and probable Imix. 78A/3, 8; 78C/2 from collapsed vault and wall fill produced Cauac, Manik, Ik, and Imix sherds.

SECONDARY CONSTRUCTION

78A/5, 11, 15; 78C/1, 9, 16; 78D/2 from within 1st-A building platform and walls contained Imix as the latest ceramic complex (78A/15 specifically had Imix Zacatel Cream Polychrome, Red Bar variety). 78C/11 from the U. 3 interior platform also had Imix sherds (and another fragment of a shell tinkler). 78A/16 from within the U. 21 transverse walls lining the central passageway of the W wing produced an intact Imix Zacatel Cream Polychrome plate.

OCCUPATION

78A/2, 9, 17; 78C/3, 4, 7, 8, 12 from the surface of 1st-A room floors had many large sherds of (unspecified) Ik or Imix ceramics. 78A/2 on the platform floor in front of the central passageway contained as latest sherds both late Imix and early Eznab. 78A/1, 4; 78C/5, 6; 78D/1 from the top 0.20 m of the mound contained sherds of all periods including Eznab.

TIME SPANS

The lengthy structural history of 5E-32 is outlined in Table 29. Structure 5E-32-1st-C of TS. 13 consisted of the existing building platform plus a new building with thicker walls, frontal masonry piers, and vaulted roof. The in situ cornice and upper-zone courses allowed a confident reconstruction of roof profiles. Erected at the time of or slightly before the Plat. 5D-2-1st-B northward expansion of the East Plaza, the construction initiated a shift toward the use of vaulting in the galleries of the eastern part of the Plaza. Wall openings occurred only on the W side of the building, and the room floor was usually only one step up from plaza level. In TS. 11, Str. 5E-32-1st-B was attached at a right angle to the S end of 1st-C, resulting in a single L-shaped building with a solid back wall and multiple front doorways facing W and S. With the contemporaneous construction of similar 5E-29, 37, 95-2nd, and 99-2nd, an outer ring of E, N, and S streets came into existence, lined on both sides by doorways. Enigmatic U. 1, built against the rear of 1st-C around the time of 1st-B, was perhaps an additional room with an interior platform, though end walls and doorways remain undiscovered. In TS. 9, stair U. 4 against the inside rear corner of the L-shaped 1st-C, 1st-B building provided access to the roof. In what appears to have been a unified TS. 7 construction project, the single-galleried 1st-C and 1st-B buildings were incorporated into a larger double-galleried U-shaped 1st-A. This now formed the N, W, and S sides of a quadrangle with 5E-99-1st forming the E side. The new rooms were added to the S and W wings without dismantling the old walls or upper zones, and the W wing was extended N to the corner. Four structures inside the square formed an interior open-cornered quadrangle (5E-33 to 36). A hypothetical eighth-century (TS. 6) marketplace use of this finished design, replete with people and market goods, was depicted in two reconstruction drawings by Peter Spier based on 1975 consultations with Jones (Hall and Spier 1975:799–801, 808–809). The theory of a marketplace function depends primarily on their unusual and consistent plan (Fig. 1), which seems suited for such a use rather than for residence, administration, or staging of ceremonies. In addition, the structures are located in a large centrally placed plaza at the ends of at least two major entrance roads into the city. A deep deposit of Imix ceramic sherds, worked bone, and worked shell collected in a test trench at the base of the Plat. 5D-2 N wall (Op. 22O; see Plat. 5D-2-1st) is likely to have derived from use of the structures in this time span. A religious or educational cloister also comes to mind, but would be less likely to have had both inward- and outward-facing doorways.

In TS. 5, four transverse walls (U. 21) blocked passageway into adjacent rooms from the axial W entrance of the quadrangle. The NW corner of 5E-32 was destroyed in TS. 3 by construction of 5E-94 over the stubs of demolished piers (Fig. 39a). Built with Str. 5E-98, 92, 5D-39 and 134, this was part of what appears to be a group of thatch-roofed domestic structures intruded into the formerly open western half of the platform. Collapse of gallery roofs possibly began in TS. 3. Imix and Eznab pottery lay on some floors under fallen vault stones, but for the most part rooms were clean at collapse.

TABLE 29
Structure 5E-32-1st: Time Spans

Time Span	Architectural Addition	Floor, Unit	Special Deposit	Lot	Other Data
1	—	—	—	78A/1,3,4,8; 78C/2,5,6; 78D/1	Collapse
2	—	—	—	78A/2,9,17; 78C/3,4,7,8,12	Use
3	—	—	—	—	Str. 5E-94
4	—	—	—	—	Use
5	—	U. 21	—	78A/16	Interior walls
6	—	—	—	—	Use
7	A	U. 3,16,18	—	78A/5,11,15; 78C/1,9,16; 78D/2	Quadrangle complete (1,900 m^3), with Plat. 5D-2-1st-A; Imix ceramics
8	—	—	—	—	Use
9	—	U. 4	—	—	Stair addition
10	—	—	—	—	Use
11	B	U. 1,8	—	78C/12,14,17	S wing and U. 1 (400 m^3), on Plat. 5D-2-1st-B; Imix ceramics
12	—	—	—	—	Use
13	C	U. 2,5,10,11,14	—	—	Assembly of W wing (450 m^3) on Plat. 5D-2-1st-C with 1st-B; Imix ceramics

STRUCTURE 5E-99-2ND

INTRODUCTION

The large quadrangle in the E sector of the East Plaza, labeled Str. 5E-32 on the TR. 11 map, was shown to have a separate E structure when in 1964 Jones placed a short trench near the centerline (Op. 78G) and cleared the NW corner (Op. 78D). See Fig. 48c.

EXCAVATION DATA

An early 99-2nd structure was detected because the Plat. 5D-2:U. 74 floor turned up to a minuscule *Unit 1* wall stub (Fig. 48c). The plan is virtually unknown, although the building platform was probably long and low like its 99-1st successor, and contemporary and slightly later structures nearby (5E-95-2nd, 32-2nd-A and 32-1st-C and B) all had single-galleries. Platform 5D-2 floors underneath, against, and on top of U. 1 (Fig. 48c) were labeled U. 73, 74, and 75 by their analogous positions to floors in nearby 5E-95 (Fig. 53a).

RELATIONSHIP TO ADJACENT STRATIGRAPHY

Unit 74 turned up to 99-2nd and was part of Plat. 5D-2-1st-B, laid with Str. 5E-29, 32-1st-C, and 37.

ARCHITECTURE

Assuming that 99-2nd was a 45 m long single-gallery building like 32-1st-C to the W, its assembly would have required 100 m^3 of material and 200 m^2 of dressed surface.

TIME SPANS

The location and orientation of the wall stub are suitable for an antecedent of 99-1st, perhaps differing only in having a single gallery with doors facing outward, in keeping with contemporary Str. 5E-32-1st-C.

TABLE 30
Structure 5E-99-2nd: Time Spans

Time Span	Architectural Addition	Floor, Unit	Special Deposit	Lot	Other Data
1	—	—	—	—	Use
2	—	—	—	—	Assembly (100 m^3) with Plat. 5D-2-1st-B

STRUCTURE 5E-99-1ST

INTRODUCTION

Structure 5E-99-1st, which forms the E wing of the 5E-32 quadrangle, was briefly excavated at its N end (Op. 78D) and centerline area in 1964 (Op. 78G). See Figs. 1, 48b,c, 52a, 77b,c, 81a,b.

EXCAVATION DATA

CONSTRUCTION STAGES

The axial excavation, which cut into the E side of the mound without transversing it (Figs. 48c, 52a, 77c), revealed that the building platform and single frontal step were erected over the *Unit 2* rip-out of 99-2nd. Building platform fill at the N end of the structure was composed of small angular stones and a few large blocks (Figs. 48b, 77b). The outer corners of a 2.10 m wide, axial E side doorway (Fig. 52a) and one jamb of the northernmost W doorway (Fig. 48b) sufficed to reconstruct a double-galleried plan like that of 32-1st-A (Fig. 1). Thin underlying mortar ran beneath the walls and a room floor abutted the doorjambs. Vault stones were not identified, but probably existed in collapse debris. Structural fills were not penetrated for a sampling of sherds and artifacts.

RELATIONSHIP TO ADJACENT STRATIGRAPHY

Platform 5D-2:U. 75 was installed upon completion of 99-1st (Fig. 48c), and the same floor, labeled U. 24 in the N end excavation (Fig. 48b), turned up against 32-1st-A to position the structure stratigraphically with Plat. 5D-2-1st-A.

ARCHITECTURE

Structure 5E-99-1st conformed to 32-1st-A in having a two-gallery plan with multiple doorways on both long sides, a step on the outer side, absence of substructure under the building platform, use of 0.50 by 0.30 by 0.20 m blocks, and absence of a plaster floor under building walls. A search was not made for an axial passage through the medial wall like that found in the W wing. The 67 m long structure utilized ca. 930 m^3 of materials and 1,450 m^2 of trimmed wall surface.

TIME SPANS

Structure 5E-99-1st was built in TS. 3 (Table 31), probably as a complete double-galleried building with doorways facing both E and W, (Fig, 1, 81a,b). The structure matched U-shaped 32-1st-A in its long parallel double galleries, closely set doorways, low floor elevation, and masonry. The two structures formed a nearly square quadrangle that enclosed four interior buildings and was ringed by outer galleries.

TABLE 31
Structure 5E-99-1st: Time Spans

Time Span	Architectural Addition	Floor, Unit	Special Deposit	Lot	Other Data
1	—	—	—	—	Collapse
2	—	—	—	—	Use
3	—	—	—	—	Assembly (930 m^3) with Plat. 5D-2:U. 24,75

STRUCTURE 5E-34

INTRODUCTION

Of the four rectangular mounds enclosed within Str. 5E-32 and 99, 5E-34 and 36 on the E and S were excavated (by Jones) in 1964 while 5E-33 and 35 were not. See Figs. 1, 38c, 39c, 48a.

EXCAVATION DATA

CONSTRUCTION STAGES

There was no evidence of earlier construction in the area. The hard-packed fill and facing of the building platform were placed directly on the surface of Plat. 5D-2:U. 25 (Figs. 38c, 48a). Large blocks were intermixed with the fill, including a vault stone salvaged from a prior structure. The medial wall was raised on the building platform without intervening plaster (Fig. 38c). A 0.15 m molding defined the building platform summit on the exterior (Figs. 38c, 48a). The plan (Fig. 39c) was that of a double-galleried building having an unbroken medial wall and five doorways separated by piers on the N and S sides. No curtain-holder sockets were detected on the interior surfaces of piers. Wall stones averaged 0.50 by 0.35 by 0.20 m. Vault stones found fallen within the room measured 0.50 by 0.30 m and had 54° soffit angles identical to those of 32-1st-A.

RELATIONSHIP TO ADJACENT STRATIGRAPHY

Structure 5E-34 was built on Plat. 5D-2:U. 25 of 1st-B and flanked soon afterward by floor U. 24 pertaining to Plat. 5D-2-1st-A. The axial trench traced the lower of these two floors to 32-1st and demonstrated that they bracketed both structures, making them contemporaries (Fig. 38c). Another trench extending S to Str. 5E-36 showed an identical relationship of floor to structure (Fig. 48a).

ARCHITECTURE

The only structure within the enclosure excavated for plan, 5E-34 stands as a model for the other three (Fig. 1). Dimensions of E and W piers and portals were identical to those of 5E-32. As with the interior facades of the quadrangle, only one step led from the plaza level into the rooms. Clearly the structure conforms to type. Assembly required 290 m^3 of material and 400 m^2 of dressed stone surface.

LOTS, GROUPING AND EVALUATION

CONSTRUCTION

78B/5 from within the W room floor contained Manik, Ik, and Imix pottery, indicating that construction occurred while Imix ceramics were in vogue.

TIME SPANS

The structure was almost certainly built entirely in TS. 3 (Table 32), and floor connections between 5E-34, 36, and 32-1st-A show that the three were built together. There is no evidence of an earlier structure.

TABLE 32
Structure 5E-34: Time Spans

Time Span	Architectural Addition	Floor, Unit	Special Deposit	Lot	Other Data
1	—	—	—	78B/2,3	Collapse
2	—	—	—	—	Use
3	—	—	—	78B/5	Assembly (290 m^3) with Plat. 5D-2-1st-A; Imix ceramics

STRUCTURE 5E-36

INTRODUCTION

Structure 5E-36, the S mound of four within the quadrangle, was barely touched by excavation in 1964 (Op. 78B). See Figs. 1, 39c, 48a.

EXCAVATION DATA

A narrow trench from Str. 5E-34 into the front of the 5E-36 mound near the NW corner exposed a one-course high building platform and two courses of the front wall (Figs. 39c, 48a). One jamb of the end door was seen. Masonry was identical to that of 34. Two Plat. 5D-2 floors, U. 25 and 24, bracketed the structure as they did 32-1st and 34. The upper U. 24 floor turned against the unplastered wall base and seemed to have been installed at completion of the structure.

ARCHITECTURE

Masonry dimensions, low floor elevation, and the close proximity of a doorway to the corner of the facade are like those of 5E-32 and 34. The plan in Fig. 1 is based on analogy with 5E-34. The mound is almost twice as long, however, suitable for nine or ten doorways on the side. With a 32 m building length, 580 m^3 of material and 800 m^2 of dressed surface were required by the builders.

TIME SPANS

Floor connections in addition to similarities of plan and masonry confirm that Str. 5E-36 and 34 were built at virtually the same time as 32-1st-A (Table 33). Thus the complex of enclosing galleries and four inner structures was completed as a single project.

TABLE 33
Structure 5E-36: Time Spans

Time Span	Architectural Addition	Floor, Unit	Special Deposit	Lot	Other Data
1	—	—	—	—	Collapse
2	—	—	—	—	Use
3	—	—	—	—	Assembly (580 m^3) with Plat. 5D-2-1st-A

STRUCTURE 5E-95-2ND

INTRODUCTION

Undetected during mapping, Str. 5E-95 was discovered during the 1964 excavations of Plat. 5E-1 by Jones. The earlier version, 95-2nd, was seen both on centerline (Op. 78G) and at the S end (Op. 78L). See Figs. 52b, 53a,b, 54a,b.

EXCAVATION DATA

CONSTRUCTION STAGES

Preparation for this long west-facing building involved extensive demolition of the front of Plat. 5E-1 (Fig. 53a). All that remained of the U. 6 platform stair was a basal course and a thin layer of interior fill with the Plat. 5D-2:U. 47 floor turning up to the W face. The line of demolition, *Unit 11*, extends back to an old fill-retaining wall. Either large amounts of fill had been replaced in this razing of the platform or this demolition line has been drawn too far E.

In the S trench (Fig. 53b) the sculptured facade of Plat. 5E-1 was partially demolished (rip-out line *Unit 18*) and buried by *Unit 17* and *Unit 12* fill as well as by the *Unit 15* stair, all of which appear to have been installed in preparation for 95-2nd. It is possible, however, that U. 12 and 17, thickly covering the sculptured masks, were put in place in advance of planning for the structure, in which case they should be treated as an addition to the platform. The plaster floor of U. 17 and curving steps of U. 15 (Fig. 53b) are evidence of an attempt at stabilizing the corner of the platform.

Unit 4 fills of the 5E-95-2nd substructure were laid over the ripped-out stair (U. 6) and facade (U. 3) of Plat. 5E-1 (Fig. 53a,b). The fill differs from one excavation to the other, having relatively fewer blocks at centerline. The centerline section shows a two-course front wall on U. 4 where steps should occur.

The *Unit 1* rear wall of the front room and the floor of *Unit 4* were placed directly on the fill of the substructure without intervening plaster or mortar (Fig. 53b). The wall seems too thin (0.60 m) to have supported a vault. At the S end of the building, an extra room behind the U. 1 wall featured *Unit 2* as its side wall and *Unit 10* as its floor (Fig. 54a,b). The base of U. 2 has a most unusual *talud-tablero* profile. A masonry front wall could not be detected even where the U. 4 floor was intact (Fig. 53b). Wooden posts possibly supported a roof, although postholes were not noted. Wall stones were set on their sides in contrast to the flat-set masonry of Plat. 5E-1. The 0.28 by 0.32 m cross section is thicker and shorter than those of 95-1st.

ADDITIONS AND RENOVATIONS

A *Unit 6* step was placed against the front of the substructure at centerline (Fig. 53a). *Unit 3* in the S end excavation (Fig. 53b) might be contemporary to U. 6, serving as a front terrace wall rather than a step.

RELATIONSHIP TO ADJACENT STRATIGRAPHY

The Plat. 5D-2:U. 47 floor supported the structure, and U. 73 turned up to it shortly after construction (Fig. 52b). These belong respectively to Plat. 5D-2-2nd-B and 1st-C. Identifications of these features make the structure earliest among the long gallery type. The edifice cut deeply into the U. 6 front stair of Plat. 5E-1 and covered its frontal facade. The later U. 6 step was built in conjunction with the U. 74 floor of Plat. 5D-2-1st-B.

ARCHITECTURE

Like those of Str. 5E-32-2nd-B, the building walls were exceedingly thin, with no trace of a front wall. Hence it was probably not vaulted and might have been roofed with thatch or beam and mortar. A small room (U. 10, 2) occupied the S end of the space behind the front room (and presumably the northern end as well). Extending across the full 90 m face of the platform, the structure required a total 520 m^3 of material and 440 m^2 of dressed masonry surface.

LOTS, GROUPING AND EVALUATION

CONSTRUCTION

78L/23 from beneath the S end rear room floor contained Manik, Ik, and Imix sherds. 78G/5 and 16 from the central trench had mostly Ik or early Imix material. The structure appears to have been built as late as the time of Imix ceramic production.

TIME SPANS

Assembly of Str. 5E-95-2nd (Table 34:TS. 4) marked the demise of Plat. 5E-1 with destruction of the sole stair and sculptural masks. The huge platform possibly fell into ruin above and behind the new building lining the E edge of the East Plaza. The many doorways of 5E-95-2nd faced the back of a similar, long, perishably roofed building across the Plaza, 5E-32-2nd-A. The front step and terrace added in TS. 2 were built in conjunction with the Plat. 5D-2-1st-B expansion and neighboring Str. 5E-29.

TABLE 34
Structure 5E-95-2nd: Time Spans

Time Span	Architectural Addition	Floor, Unit	Special Deposit	Lot	Other Data
1	—	—	—	—	Use
2	—	U. 3,6	—	—	Front step, with Plat. 5D-2-1st-B
3	—	—	—	—	Use
4	—	U. 1,2,4,10, 15,17,18	—	78L/23; 78G/5,16	Assembly (520 m^3) with Plat. 5D-2-1st-C; Imix ceramics

STRUCTURE 5E-95-1ST

INTRODUCTION

Structure 5E-95 remained undetected within the talus of Plat. 5E-1 until its centerline was excavated by Jones in 1964 (Op. 78G) and the S end by Orrego and Jones in 1965 (Op. 78L). See Figs. 1, 52a,b (plan), 53a,b (section), 59a,c, 60b, 78.

EXCAVATION DATA

CONSTRUCTION STAGES

The first step in construction was an almost total razing of Str. 5E-95-2nd (Fig. 53a,b, 54a,b). The *Unit 8* rip-out line on both sections marks the probable extent of this demolition. The new substructure was apparently assembled as a unit with no break in the fill to distinguish the building platform. No plaster floor caps the substructure beneath the *Unit 5* rear wall, although the S wall was built on a recognizable mortar layer (Figs. 53a,b, 78). One complete frontal pier and adjacent doorway were excavated in the centerline area (Fig. 52a) and another pier and door near the S end (Fig. 52b). The 2.00 m wide doorways and 1.25 m wide piers match those on Str. 5E-32-1st, 5E-34, and other structures nearby (Fig. 1). Rear wall stones averaged 0.55 by 0.35 by 0.25 m, and were laid in a 2:1 bond (two stretchers to a header); exposed surfaces were trimmed smooth after installation. Curtain-holder sockets were not detected on the piers, but may have existed above the preserved interior wall faces. Vault stones with beveled soffit ends were found in the room debris, confirming that the gallery was vaulted.

Behind the building in the centerline section (Fig. 53a) the plaster surface of *Unit 5* created a narrow walkway between the rear upper zone and Plat. 5E-1. At the S end of the building (Fig. 53b) the *Unit 17* steps of Str. 5E-95-2nd were abutted by this same U. 5 fill at the level of the building cornice.

A *Unit 16* wall was built from the rear S corner of Str. 5E-95-1st, extending with no breaks in masonry along the W facade of the old Plat. 5D-1 and around the corner to its S side (Figs. 52b, 54a, 59a,c, 60b). The wall is vertical and built with the same dimensions and type of masonry as that of the structure itself. The wall is abutted by the U. 29 floor of Plat. 5D-2-1st-A. Its purpose was clearly to clean up the deteriorating base of the old Plat. 5E-1 and the approach to the causeway.

ADDITIONS AND RENOVATIONS

At centerline (Fig. 53a) the raised platform behind the building (U. 5) was buried by roof-level *Unit 9* fill and a plaster floor, which were not seen at the S end (Fig. 53b). *Unit 14*, a stair with at least two steps, led upward from U. 9 and possibly ran S to join the older U. 11 steps, providing access to the summit of Plat. 5E-1. Yet undiscovered is a stair leading up to U. 9 and 14 from plaza level.

RELATIONSHIP TO ADJACENT STRATIGRAPHY

The upper floor of Plat. 5D-2, U. 75, appears to have been laid soon after assembly of 95-1st, and as the first pavement to follow construction at the S end, U. 29 was presumably equivalent. There, however, it raised the platform around 0.60 m, perhaps in order to join a higher causeway surface (Figs. 53a, 54b). Units 75 and 29 pertain to Plat. 5D-2-1st-A and serve to link 95-1st with Str. 5E-99-1st and 32-1st-A and the completion of the full quadrangle. Although the Mendez Causeway was not investigated, the U. 16 wall beside 95-1st as well as the Plat. 5D-2:U. 29 floor suggest that the roadway itself underwent improvements at this time.

ARCHITECTURE

Structure 5D-95-1st improved on 2nd with its sturdy walls, frontal piers, and vaulted roof (Fig. 1). The back room on the S end was filled in and eliminated. Room and doorway dimensions matched those of 32-1st and 99-1st. The structure and the U. 5 terrace behind it required 1,200 m³ of material and 970 m² of surface dressing. Secondary U. 9 and 14 used 170 m³ of fill and 20 m² of facing.

LOTS, GROUPING AND EVALUATION

CONSTRUCTION

78G/8 from under the building floor and 78G/19 from U. 5 fill behind the building contained an abundance of Imix sherds, providing a date no earlier than Imix ceramic production.

OCCUPATION

78G/1 from over the front platform surface, 78G/9 on the room floor, and 78G/13 from collapse debris within the room contained unweathered Imix sherds, probably from structure fills though possibly resulting from occupation activity. 78L/9 from the room interior had mixed Imix and Manik material. It is interesting that no Eznab sherds were found inside the building, even though some turned up beyond the S end (78L/13, 18, 19).

TIME SPANS

The substructure, the building itself, and the terrace behind were assembled in a single project (Table 35:TS. 5). Unity of structural plan from the central area to the S end provides a basis for asserting that U. 75 and 29 turning up to the base were a single platform floor. Given the minimal exposure of interior space, the long room possibly had transverse dividers, benches, and even cord holders, although none were seen in this or in any of the gallery buildings of the area. The level behind the building was secondarily raised to roof level at the centerline and new steps climbed Plat. 5E-1 from this surface. Absence of Eznab sherds within the building suggests that collapse (TS. 1) occurred before this pottery was made.

TABLE 35
Structure 5E-95-1st: Time Spans

Time Span	Architectural Addition	Floor, Unit	Special Deposit	Lot	Other Data
1	—	—	—	—	Collapse
2	—	—	—	78G/1,9,13; 78L/9 13,18,19	Use
3	—	U. 9,14	—	—	Rear roof-level terrace and stair
4	—	—	—	—	Use
5	—	U. 5,7,16	—	78G/8,19	Assembly (1,200 m³) with Plat. 5D-2-1st-A; Imix ceramics

STRUCTURE 5E-38

INTRODUCTION

Maler called this large structure the "Three-storied Palace with Three Chambers in the Top Story" (1911:25–26, pl. 7, 2). Subsequently it was designated Structure 27 by Tozzer (1911:110–111, figs. 20, 21) and finally Str. 5E-38 in TR. 11. In 1964 Hug and Nagy excavated small basal trenches at the front and rear (Op. 92A) and an axial profile was drawn (Fig. 49c). In 1967 Loten recorded details of standing architecture with no operation or lots defined. Both investigations were primarily intended to record extant architectural evidence, and although digging went beyond that goal, it did not penetrate the structure. Clearing and consolidation by Larios and Orrego of the *Instituto de Antropología y Historia de Guatemala* followed in the 1970s. See Figs. 1, 49a–c, 50a–c, 51a–c, 79a–d.

EXCAVATION DATA

CONSTRUCTION STAGES

CONSTRUCTION STAGE 4

The step stones of the Str. 5E-38 stair rose directly from the surface of Plat. 5D-2 floor U. 59 (Figs. 51b, 79a,c). The stair was not penetrated for a glimpse of possible earlier structures, caches, or burials. Masonry consisted of vertically faced, tapered headers averaging 0.55 by 0.40 by 0.20 m (Fig. 51a–c). A diminutive stair chamber stood on the centerline near the level of the first terrace top (Fig. 49b). A narrow front landing extended to ascending stairs at the sides of the chamber (Figs. 49c, 50c). Interior walls and vault were intact, and the surviving exterior wall stubs allow reconstruction of plan. A small niche spanned by stone lintels was in the rear wall opposite the doorway. Wall stones 0.26–0.35 m high were laid on their larger surfaces like those of the building above. Two rounded beam holes at the tops of the doorjambs once held lintel beams 0.13 m in diameter. Wall-top plaster was not evident beneath the two courses of 0.64 m long plaster-faced vault stones. Excavation proved that the chamber was integral to the structure and not a later addition.

CONSTRUCTION STAGE 3

Standing walls within the rear rooms and at the N end and center of the front rooms were sufficient to reconstruct the plan, although the front gallery was perhaps not divided into three rooms as shown (Fig. 49a). Wall blocks were laid flat on larger surfaces like those of the small room on the stair. The 2.18 m high back wall was built with an unusual 10° incline (Fig. 49c). It was not determined whether or not the walls rose from plaster surfaces.

CONSTRUCTION STAGE 2

Rear room vaults were exposed by collapse on the N side (Fig. 50b, 79c). The first course of the vaulting and the projecting bottom course of the upper zone were both laid on wall-top plaster. One cornice stone measured 0.81 m long and 0.25 m high. Vault soffits were stepped at coursing levels 0.30 m apart, and coursing levels could be seen as mortar layers within the vault mass. The vault stones were ca. 0.60 m long with tapered sides and top. The rough plaster vault-top surface apparently stepped down from the rear to a lower-front level.

Beam holes 0.08 m in diameter and 0.34–0.50 m deep were spaced ca. 1.0 m apart in three rows on the five-course vault (Fig. 50b). A staggered pattern was apparent: middle row beams are equidistant between those in the upper and lower rows.

CONSTRUCTION STAGE 1

An upper zone was constructed against the roughly plastered vault back. As below, the 0.42–0.50 m long and 0.28 m high blocks were installed on their larger surfaces rather than on edge (Fig. 50b). A smooth plaster cap roofed the building. Maler's photograph shows 3.5 m wide decorative panels on the three sections of the rear upper zone (1911:pl. 7, 2). These were not drawn and illustrated

ADDITIONS AND RENOVATIONS

Rear rooms of the building were packed to the vault spring line with mud mortar and salvaged masonry slabs, presumably to reinforce the building for construction of the roofcomb. The plaster flooring on the building summit was further evidence that the roofcomb was installed secondarily (Fig. 50b, 79b). As on the Great Temples of Tikal, the lower and upper roofcomb chambers were sealed shut, serving only to reduce weight on the building below (Fig. 49c). Tozzer's profile mistakenly portrayed these roofcomb chambers with doorways (1911:fig. 21). In the lower set of chambers, vault-beam holes ca. 0.10 m in diameter and 0.70 m deep were aligned in rows 1.50 and 3.00 m above the spring. In Maler's photograph the rear wall of the roofcomb was divided in three parts by vertical grooves (1911:pl. 7, 2).

RELATIONSHIP TO ADJACENT STRATIGRAPHY

Although at least four Plat. 5D-2 floors were encountered in an excavation at the base of the front stair, bedrock was not reached (Fig. 51b). The two lower floors (U. 59 and 60) ran beneath the structure, and the upper ones (U. 58 and 57) turned up against it with U. 58 probably coeval. In the rear axial excavation (Fig. 50a), U. 63 and 62 duplicated the two upper floors in turning up to the structure. These turn down over separate Plat. 5D-2 facings behind the building. The closest plaza excavation across the Mendez Causeway also uncovered two floors, U. 76 of Plat. 5D-2-1st-C and U. 29 of 1st-A (Fig. 53a). If U. 58 and 63 were built to finish the structure and are equivalent to U. 76, as seems likely, the structure is coeval with Plat. 5D-2-1st-C and the ballcourt complex, Str. 5D-42, 5D-43, and 5E-31.

ARCHITECTURE

The three front doorways and lateral and rear outsets of the building have precedents in all eight of the final summit buildings of the North Acropolis (Fig. 1; TR. 14:fig. 61). Mortared vault-backs are also found on these structures. Plastered wall tops, on the other hand, are late in Gp. 5D-2. The roofcomb further links the structure to the North Acropolis buildings and to the later "Great Temples." The roofcomb of Str. 6F-27, "The Temple of the Inscriptions," might also have been secondary as this one apparently was. The flat-laid large block masonry of 5E-38 might be typologically intermediate between the smaller flat-set stones of Plat. 5E-1, Str. 5E-Sub.1, 5D-Sub.16, and the full-size, edge-laid blocks of Str. 5E-31, 5D-42, 5D-43, and other later structures. The total volume of material used in assembly, including the roofcomb, was ca. 7,200 m^3 and 1,370 m^2 of dressed facing.

SPECIAL DEPOSITS

PROBLEMATICAL DEPOSITS 260 AND 261

LOCATION

Two human skulls were found in separate pits at the base of the stair under the first step. They were sealed by Plat. 5D-2 floor U. 58 and 57, which turned up against the structure (Fig. 51a,c, 79d).

DISCUSSION

Trenching on the stair centerline in 1964 uncovered two round cuts in the floor under the stair (Fig. 51a,c, 79d). One of the holes was partially under the step and contained PD. 260, which consisted of an upside-down human skull. The second small pit to the S in front of the step contained PD. 261. Cranium, jaw bone, lower teeth, and axis vertebra of PD. 260 were in anatomical position indicating that the flesh had not decayed before deposition. Haviland noted in 1968 that the individual was male, aged 30 to 40, with frontal-occipital cranial deformation, and without tooth modification. The PD. 261 pit held fragments of at least one skull, adult, sex unspecified. Teeth included 15 molars from more than one individual. An upper canine was notched in one corner.

SEQUENTIAL POSITION

The position of the PD. 260 pit partially beneath the first step implies that the structure was completed when the problematical deposits were placed. Both repositories were cut into the 5D-2:U. 59 pavement that supported the stair. The next floor, U. 58, covered a stone slab over PD. 260 and sealed both holes as it turned up to the stair base. Therefore the deposits were likely coeval with this floor, which was laid either immediately or long after assembly of the structure. Though not traced across the plaza, U. 58 is likely part of Plat. 5D-2-1st-C.

LOTS, GROUPING AND EVALUATION

CONSTRUCTION

92A/3 and 4 from the problematical deposit pits contained Manik, Ik, and Imix sherds. 92A/2 from within the U. 58 floor included fragments of a "late" type hollow-torso flanged censer showing signs of burning. Fragments of this censer type were found in the pits themselves and apparently censers were smashed during the deposition of the skulls.

OCCUPATION

92A/1 from debris on the front steps and plaza floors had Classic Period sherds.

TIME SPANS

Structure 5E-38 may have existed for a time without a roofcomb (Table 36:TS. 5), and the roofcomb along with its supportive fill was added in TS. 3 within the rooms below. Alternatively, the roofcomb may have been primary and only the room fill secondary. The first abutting floor, U. 58 in front and U. 63 at the rear, is probably the finishing pavement for the structure, but may also have been laid considerably later. Unit 58 is tentatively identified as Plat. 5D-2-1st-C, which means that the structure is either contemporary with Str. 5D-43, 5D-42, and 5E-31 or earlier with the flooring of Plat. 5D-2-2nd-A.

Structure 5E-38, with its tall substructure, tandemly arranged rooms, triple front doorways and roofcomb, resembles "temples" such as Str. 5D-22-1st on the North Acropolis, and 6F-27, the "Temple of the Inscriptions." The latter, built at the far end of the same causeway that begins at the side of 5E-38, might even have taken over its function as the eastern entrance marker for Tikal. Another possibility is that the building served as an eastern "burial shrine" structure in an elaborate domestic group consisting primarily of "palatial" Str. 5D-46 before construction of Str. 5D-45, the huge Central Acropolis facade behind Str. 5D-43. If so, burials and earlier structures would be expected beneath it.

TABLE 36
Structure 5E-38: Time Spans

Time Span	Architectural Addition	Floor, Unit	Special Deposit	Lot	Other Data
1	—	—	—	—	Use
2	—	—	—	92A/1	Collapse
3	A	—	—	—	Roofcomb(?) and filled rear rooms
4	—	—	—	—	Use
5	B	—	PD. 260,261	92A/2–4	Assembly (7,200 m^3) with or before Plat. 5D-2-1st-C

STRUCTURE 5E-37

INTRODUCTION

This long low mound stretching from the NE base of the Central Acropolis almost to the NW corner of 5E-38 (TR. 11) was excavated in 1964 and 1965 by Jones and Orrego (Op. 78E and 78H). Only the W end was investigated. See Figs. 1, 19b,d, 51, 55, 56a,b.

EXCAVATION DATA

CONSTRUCTION STAGES

The only penetration into the original 5E-37-B structure was a short trench into the N side near the W end (Fig. 55). The substructure was erected on leveled bedrock without the underlying floors seen in front of Str. 5E-38 to the E and 5D-43 to the W (Figs. 54a,b, 19d, 47c). Either the immediate area had never been paved or earlier pavements had been stripped away. The light brown compact substructural fill was capped by soft mortar and faced with masonry. A 1.20 m deep step lined the N side. A slight difference in fill distinguished a separately assembled building platform.

Front and medial building walls were built without underlying plaster. Mound breadth indicated that the building consisted of two parallel galleries (Fig. 1). Even if added secondarily, as in the case of Str. 5E-32-1st-A, the S gallery preceded 37-A (Fig. 56b). Wall stones measured roughly 0.50–0.60 by 0.30 by 0.17 m. A greater regularity in block size and coursing was discerned on the medial wall than on the front piers, where occasional small filler blocks were used and one block was installed on end. Fallen upper zone molding blocks measured ca. 0.86 by 0.50 by 0.15 m and had sides tapered to 0.30 m and a slight frontal batter. Vault stones ca. 0.58 by 0.30 by 0.23 m were also tapered on the sides.

ADDITIONS AND RENOVATIONS

The gap between the structure and the Central Acropolis was closed by a double-galleried addition that extended the doorway facades and generated Str. 5E-37-A (Fig. 19b). The addition was fronted by a slightly deeper N step than on the original structure. The N end of Str. 5E-96 appears to have been removed and its rear wall and vault possibly incorporated into the addition, considering that the vault stones in place on this extreme W wall have more side taper than those from the other vaults. A rip-out line was not seen in excavation, however. The medial wall was broken by a doorway that aligned with doorways in the N and S walls to create a passage through the building identical to one through the center of the W wing of Str. 5E-32-1st-A (Fig. 38a). The thin E jambs of these doors were built against the end wall of Str. 5E-37-B and, though only 0.34 m in width, were evidently sufficient to support the lintel beams and vault (Figs. 19b, 56b). The possibility of a N-S corbeled archway was considered during excavation, but these skimpy end piers and the originally open entry into the side rooms do not allow for it. Wall stones measured 0.50–0.60 by 0.35 by 0.18 m, vault stones 0.45–0.60 by 0.32 by 0.20–0.25 m.

Transverse wall *Units 1 and 2* were installed within the rooms at a later time in order to separate W end rooms of the addition from the passageway (Fig. 19b). Built directly on the room floor, U. 1 survived to a height of 2.16 m and probably once extended to the capstones. Masonry differed little from that of the original building. Unit 2 was considerably thicker, 0.90 as opposed to 0.50 m, and could have been built separately (Fig. 56a).

Collapse of SW room vaulting tumbled earth and stones onto the floor and against U. 2. Consequently the transverse door into the adjacent Str. 5E-96 gallery was sealed by *Unit 3*. Although the S face of this wall was made of dressed masonry, the N face was composed of small stones laid against the collapse debris.

RELATIONSHIP TO ADJACENT STRATIGRAPHY

Two Plat. 5D-2 floors overlaid bedrock at the W end of the structure (Fig. 55). The lower one, U. 50, abutted 37-B and the upper one, U. 37, turned up against 37-A. These unit designations were carried across from the Str. 5E-32 excavation to the N (Fig. 46). Structure 5E-37-A was bracketed by these two floors and was therefore likely built with Plat. 5D-2-1st-A.

ARCHITECTURE

Structure 5E-37-B was the first double-galleried structure of the plaza. Vaulting, room size, floor height, doorway dimensions, and masonry did not differ from the later structures of this plan (Fig. 1). For construction of the 52.4 m long structure, approximately 1,270 m^3 of material and 1,270 m^2 of surface dressing were required.

LOTS, GROUPING AND EVALUATION

CONSTRUCTION

78E/6 and 7 from within the 37-B substructure contained Manik, Ik, and Imix Complex sherds.

INITIAL OCCUPATION

78E/1, 2, and 5 from within the room and in front of the original building also contained Manik, Ik, and Imix sherds.

SECONDARY OCCUPATION

78H/7 on the floor of the SW room had Imix material and much Eznab. 78H/1 and 2 on top of collapse in the SW room also contained Eznab pottery, burned, disarticulated, and scattered human cranial, mandibular, and long bone fragments from one or more individuals, and long bone fragments, probably deer, with cut marks to remove extremities. This material perhaps fell from the edges of the Central Acropolis summit, rather than resulting from encampments within 37-A itself after the roof collapse.

TIME SPANS

Assembly of freestanding Str. 5E-37-B in TS. 7 was made complete with the U. 50 floor against it, a pavement believed to be Plat. 5D-2-1st-B (Table 37). The low room floor and the position of the doorway near the corner are characteristic of 5E-32 and other buildings in the area. The structure separated the SE sector from the rest of the East Plaza, yet S doorways identical to those facing N imply that the two sides of the building had similar functions. These were clearly the same uses as those of Str. 5E-32 and the other structures to the N.

Structure 5D-37-A (TS. 5) was a westward prolongation of the building that merged with the N end of preexisting Str. 5E-96. The gap between the structures was closed by this addition, but a passageway between Plaza sectors was maintained through a set of aligned doorways. Assembly was completed with the laying of the U. 37 floor pertaining to Plat. 5D-2-1st-A. In TS. 3 the passageway was lined by transverse side walls similar to those placed beside the passageway through 32-1st-A. The small rooms W of these walls may have been storage chambers. At a later date (TS. 2) the doorway from Str. 5E-96 was sealed against vault collapse by wall U. 3. Eznab sherds found within the SW room of the addition were indications of late occupation.

TABLE 37
Structure 5E-37: Time Spans

Time Span	Architectural Addition	Floor, Unit	Special Deposit	Lot	Other Data
1	—	—	—	—	Collapse
2	—	U. 3	—	78H/1,2,7	Use; Eznab ceramics
3	—	U. 1,2	—	—	Transverse walls
4	—	—	—	—	Use
5	A	—	—	—	W extension, with Plat. 5D-2-1st-A
6	—	—	—	78E/1,2,5	Use; Ik or Imix ceramics
7	B	—	—	78E/6,7	Assembly (1,270 m^3) with Plat. 5D-2-1st-B; Imix ceramics

STRUCTURE 5D-97

INTRODUCTION

Hidden beneath Central Acropolis talus, Str. 5D-97 was not discovered until the investigation of adjacent 5D-43 by Orrego and Jones in 1965 (Op. 78P). See Figs. 1, 19b 74c,d.

EXCAVATION DATA

Upon discovery of the NW corner, the N and E facades were cleared by narrow trenches (Fig. 19b, 74c,d). Like nearby Str. 5E-37 and 32, walls were inset slightly from the edges of the 0.30 m high building platform. The two N doorways, exterior corners of the E doorway, and an inside wall surface were recorded. Fill behind the room wall rested against the same Central Acropolis face that was exposed in the tunnel behind Str. 5D-43 (Fig. 19d). The distance from the facade to the Central Acropolis wall was like that behind 5E-93 (Fig. 57), and space was not available for a second gallery. Wall stones measuring 0.55 by 0.35 by 0.20 m were set on edge with occasional headers. Vault stones were in the debris. The edifice was contemporary with Str. 5D-43-B as demonstrated by the merging of wall masonry with the 5D-43:U. 13 platform. The rear corner of the E end touched Str. 5E-96, suggesting contemporaneity.

ARCHITECTURE

The structure is unusual among the edifices of the E half of the East Plaza for its small size and the presence of an end doorway (Fig. 1). It is standard, however, in its low room elevation and size of doorways and piers. Construction required ca. 80 m^3 of material and 140 m^2 of surface dressing.

LOTS, GROUPING AND EVALUATION

OCCUPATION

78P/24, 25, 52, and 53 from all levels of debris in front of the structure had Imix and Eznab sherds deriving from fill or occupation of the building itself or the Central Acropolis above. A ceramic curtain-holder insert, otherwise unknown in buildings of the type, probably came from Str. 5D-45 of the Central Acropolis, where such features were common.

TIME SPANS

Construction (TS. 3) of a small single-room structure against the corner of the Central Acropolis occurred when the first revisions were undertaken on Str. 5D-43, and probably when 5E-96 and 93 were built along the W side of the Acropolis (Table 38). As one of the smallest buildings of the area, it and similar Str. 5E-40 possibly served to control access into the complex from the S and W as guardhouses or official's shelters.

TABLE 38
Structure 5D-97: Time Spans

Time Span	Architectural Addition	Floor, Unit	Special Deposit	Lot	Other Data
1	—	—	—	—	Collapse
2	—	—	—	78P/24,25,52,53	Use; Eznab
3	—	—	—	—	Assembly (80 m^3) with Str. 5D-43-B

STRUCTURE 5E-96

INTRODUCTION

This structure was not detected under the Central Acropolis talus and therefore does not appear on the TR. 11 map. It was excavated in 1965 by Jones and Orrego (Op. 78P) and reexamined by Orrego in 1967. See Figs. 1, 19b.

EXCAVATION DATA

CONSTRUCTION STAGES

Structure 5E-96 was hardly touched by excavation. The long gallery was not cleared, nor was the platform floor exposed in front. The W wall and vault of what is now 5E-37-A might originally have been the extended rear wall of 5E-96. Although only two doorways were excavated, it is clear that the facade had piers of the same size as 5E-37 (Fig. 19b).

ADDITIONS AND RENOVATIONS

Construction of Str. 5E-37-A apparently brought about demolition of the N end of 5E-96 to accommodate the new rooms. This sequence of events was not investigated in the field and therefore can only be suggested as an explanation for the difference between the W vault masonry and that of other walls in 5E-37-A.

RELATIONSHIP TO ADJACENT STRATIGRAPHY

Structure 5E-96 was roughly coeval with 5E-97 and 37. It was modified by 37-A. Platform floors were not exposed at its base.

ARCHITECTURE

The long single gallery resembled other nearby structures in its piers, low substructure, and exterior molding at room floor level. It apears that the SE sector of the Plaza became an extension of the eastern sector, lined with doorways on the N and W sides. Prior to Str. 5E-37-A the structure may have extended to the corner of 97. As such, the facade would have possessed 13 doorways, though it now has 12 (Figs. 1, 19b). The 41.5 m length required 650 m^3 of material and 720 m^2 of wall dressing.

TIME SPANS

Extending from the central stair to the corner of the Central Acropolis, Str. 5E-96 was probably built as a single entity (Table 39:TS. 5). Rooms of Str. 5E-37-A were attached later (TS. 3) to its N end, and the continuity of rear vaulting argues that 96 was partially dismantled and assimilated into the addition.

TABLE 39
Structure 5E-96: Time Spans

Time Span	Architectural Addition	Floor, Unit	Special Deposit	Lot	Other Data
1	—	—	—	—	Collapse
2	—	—	—	—	Use
3	—	—	—	—	Partial demolition with addition of Str. 5E-37-A
4	—	—	—	—	Use
5	—	—	—	—	Assembly (650 m^3)

STRUCTURE 5E-93

INTRODUCTION

Structure 5E-93 was concealed under the debris slope of the Central Acropolis S of the E side stair. It was discovered and investigated in an axial trench and N end probe by Orrego and Harrison in 1964, 1965, and 1967 (Op. 107B and 133B). See Figs. 1 and 57.

EXCAVATION DATA

CONSTRUCTION STAGES

In the centerline excavation a single Plat. 5D-2:U. 45 floor covered level bedrock and turned up to the front step (Fig. 57). Thus earlier floors either never existed or had been destroyed. Vault stones were found in the room debris. The N exterior wall of the building was abutted by a final Central Acropolis stair (Fig. 1).

ADDITIONS AND RENOVATIONS

Unit 3 was a secondary interior platform or bench against the rear wall opposite the central doorway, and *Unit 2* was a floor turning up to its base. Bench length was not determined.

RELATIONSHIP TO ADJACENT STRATIGRAPHY

The sloping Central Acropolis face behind the N end of the structure (not illustrated) was probably of the same construction as that exposed behind Str. 5D-43, 5E-97, and 96. Unit 45 of Plat. 5D-2 abutted the structure and was not traced to other locations. As the upper floor, nevertheless, it is presumably the same as U. 37.

ARCHITECTURE

The low building platform and narrow room were identical to those of Str. 5E-96 beside it (Fig. 1). Piers were not demonstrated realities but were assumed on the basis of their presence on 96. The estimated 22.75 m length required 240 m^3 of construction material and 270 m^2 of dressed surface.

TIME SPANS

As far as is known 5E-93 was constructed in TS. 5 as (Table 40) a long building against the Central Acropolis and a twin to 5E-96 on the other side of the central stair (Fig. 1). Although floors prior to the structure were not detected, several were seen on the other side of the plaza in front of Str. 5E-38. An interior platform (U. 3) and room floor (U. 2) altered the building in TS. 3. Such features were not found in other gallery structures of the group. The closely set doors and narrow room suggest that function was originally the same as that for 5E-96 beside it as well as for 5E-37 and other buildings to the N. Perhaps the use changed with addition of the interior platform.

TABLE 40
Structure 5E-93: Time Spans

Time Span	Architectural Addition	Floor, Unit	Special Deposit	Lot	Other Data
1	—	—	—	—	Collapse
2	—	—	—	—	Use
3	—	U. 2,3	—	—	Interior platform and secondary room floor
4	—	—	—	—	Use
5	—	U. 1	—	—	Assembly (240 m^3) with Plat. 5D-2:U. 45

STRUCTURE 5E-40

This small mound off the SE corner of the Central Acropolis was excavated by Miguel Orrego in 1967 (Op. 107B and 133B). A front right doorjamb, room corner, and step-up from plaza level were seen. The E end of the mound was not penetrated, however. The reconstructed plan as given (Fig. 1) is Orrego's. The existence of two front doors recalls Str. 5E-97, and consequently there may also have been an E doorway.

IV

Platform 5E-1

PLATFORM 5E-1

INTRODUCTION

The imposing mass set upon the E end of the East Plaza is comparable in proportions and size to both the North and the South Acropolis. When Hazard mapped the area in 1958, he stated in field notes that the platform would be called "The East Acropolis" but it was not so named on the TR. 11 map. Remains of facing were still visible on terrace flanks. In spite of his comment that "the top is not very level but has no distinct mounds or ruins, only low indefinite platforms," six features on the summit were designated and drawn as structures on the TR. 11 map sheet. Following brief 1964 excavations that cast doubt on their authenticity, these were omitted from the maps and structure counts in TR. 13 (p. 45, fig. 2a).

In 1963, Sisson dug two ceramic test pits (Op. 71J and K), one on Str. 5E-28 and the other W of Str. 5E-25. In 1964, a 0.50 m interval contour plot of the platform summit was made by Jones and Orrego, trenches were placed into Str. 5E-23, 25, and 27 by Jones and Bates (Op. 78F), and a trench and tunnel penetrated the W base of the platform at centerline (Op. 78G). Finally, in 1965, Jones and Orrego exposed basal elements of the SW corner via trenches and a tunnel (Op. 78L).

Discovery of west-facing architectural facade sculpture and an inset corner demonstrated that a finished, formal platform had once existed here. Furthermore, masonry and sealed pottery suggest that the construction was early rather than late. Nevertheless, excavations on the summit could not prove either that the separate mounds were residues of structures or represented a partially demolished or never completed upper stage of the platform itself. Brief descriptions of the excavations appeared in Coe 1965a:380, Coe 1967:72–73, and Lowe 1966:461. See Figs. 1, 52b,c, 53a,b, 58a,b, 59a–c, 60a,b, 61, 62, 63a,b, 78a.

EXCAVATION DATA

SEQUENCE AND COMPOSITION

Deep within the centerline W side trench (Fig. 53a) a row of thin stones, *Unit 6*, possibly represents the first course of a Plat. 5E-1 stair. The rest of the presumably long, broad flight was demolished by the construction of Str. 5E-95-2nd. The line of horizontally set stretchers, 0.25 m wide and 0.15 m high, stands 6 m W of the platform wall line (U. 3) at the corner, hence in correct position for a projecting stair (see Fig. 53a,b). Prior to the existence of U. 6, portions of the Plat. 5D-2:U. 72 floor beneath were weathered through to the prior surface, U. 71. Both these underlying floors continued E beyond the reach of the tunnel, either to turn over a platform edge or turn up to an unseen early version of Plat. 5E-1. Initial Plat. 5E-1 fill behind the stair course was a thick stratum of dark brown soil, in turn supporting a crudely built fill retaining wall, *Unit 2*, behind which lay brown-and-white lensed earth below and brown dirt with rough blocks above. A south-facing retaining wall was exposed on the N side of the tunnel. The earth overlaying U. 6 continued all the way to U. 2, so apparently the rip-out for Str. 5E-95-2nd (U. 11) penetrated deeper than required.

The *Unit 3* facade was exposed in the SW corner excavations (Figs. 52c, 53b, 58a,b, 59a–c). Severely destroyed but unmistakable remains of large architectural sculpture (Fig. 58a,b) faced W between the unlocated S edge of the stair and the corner. The sculptures were supported by a plain sloping basal element 1.30 m high, rose to a second terrace level 3.35 m above the plaza, and were flanked on the S by a 1.06 m wide inclined border element. Although not well understood, at least two separate faces were exposed, each possessing an oval eye and round apron-like cheek line. Both faces seem to be original, but the left one was later rebuilt with new masonry and stucco (U. 10). South of the sculptured area and its border element, a 6.30 m wide inset facing featured a basal molding at a height of 1.00 m and an apron molding at 2.52 m (Fig. 59a). Still farther S a second inset wall with a basal molding also at 1.00 m and a lower apron molding at 1.82 m extended 4 m to the corner (Figs. 52c, 59c, 60b). In these facades blocks were generally 0.30–0.50 m long, 0.10–0.20 m high, and 0.25 m wide and were installed flat on their largest surfaces with headers more common than stretchers. (Although labeled U. 12 of Plat. 5E-1 [Figs. 62, 63b], a facing on the E side of the platform stood 3 m lower in elevation, was of lesser height [1.80 m], had no molding, and was more likely a part of supporting Plat. 5D-2.)

A plaster surface, perhaps a summit floor of Plat. 5E-1, was exposed as *Unit 15* at the W base of Str. 5E-25 (Fig. 61), *Unit 13* beneath the N side of 5E-27 (Fig. 63a), and a floor in a ceramic test pit 8 m W of 25 (Op. 71K; unillustrated). At an elevation of 249 m, these exposures were 7.50 m higher than the U. 6 base of the theorized W stair. Hence the 3.35 m basal terrace height at the SW corner is approximately half the 7.50 m to this floor.

A meter-wide trench (Fig. 61) was dug on a slight diagonal into the W side of the central mound (5E-25), its western limit beginning about a meter S of the centerline of a then ostensible cardinally oriented structure. The U. 15 floor at the bottom of the trench consisted of a slightly sloping 0.10 m thick mortar on a fill of marly brown earth and large stones. A vertical west-facing wall, *Unit 16*, and a conjoined south-facing wall N of the section both rest on 3 cm of mortar overlying the floor. The uneven wall blocks were laid flat like those of fill-retaining walls in Str. 5E-Sub.1 and 5D-Sub.16 (see Fig. 9). Layers of earth against the inside corner of these walls are either occupation debris or construction fill. East of the walls, the section cuts into centerline nuclear fill. A rough mortar layer, common in core construction, ran E from the wall to the base of a retaining wall forming a second stage of the nuclear mass, *Unit 17*. The face of U. 17 was covered in turn by hard-packed earth and stone fill. A mortar surface extended E from the top of U. 17 for at least 4 m and was covered by *Unit 18*, a third stratum of fill 0.80 m deep. The flat summit of the mound showed no protruding blocks to indicate a masonry building.

Contour mapping in half-meter intervals in 1964 (unillustrated) confirmed the rectilinear plan of the mound as it had been rectified in the TR. 11 map. The retaining walls found in excavation appear to be nuclear construction.

A shallow trench into the centerline of Str. 5E-27 on the N edge of the platform summit uncovered a plaster floor designated *Unit 13* (Fig. 63a). Rising from this hard smooth mortar surface was a vertical N face, *Unit 20*, built of variably sized blocks laid flat and similar to those of U. 16. A plaster coat was noted, though both the verticality of U. 20 and the construction fill lying against it argue for its identification as core construction. The upper fill of the mound lacked recognizable walls or floors, and the trench did not extend far enough to define a S face.

A 1.5 m square ceramic test pit near the center of Str. 5E-28 penetrated to a depth of 1.5 m. The tops of two N-S retaining walls and a connecting E-W wall were encountered at 0.80 m, signaling that a change in fill had occurred at that depth, as in Str. 5E-25. The flat rectilinear surface of the mound was at the same level as that of 5E-25. Walls and fallen masonry blocks were not present.

Finally, a shallow trench into the S side of 5E-23 near its centerline (Fig. 60a) uncovered a south-facing nuclear retaining wall fronted by a tumble of earth and stones. The section shows a flat mound surface uncluttered by masonry. Contour mapping confirmed the gradual and indistinct frontal slope.

ADDITIONS AND RENOVATIONS

Unit 10 is a masonry resurfacing of the architectural sculpture (Figs. 53b, 58a,b) in which the left-hand mask was covered by a slightly larger masonry face and the right-hand mask by new plaster. The renovations indicate that the facade was exposed for a long time.

At a later date, Str. 5E-95-2nd built across the entire facade of the platform resulted in the destruction of the U. 6 stair and burial of the mostly destroyed architectural sculpture (Figs. 52b, 53b, 54a,b).

RELATIONSHIP TO ADJACENT STRATIGRAPHY

The base of Plat. 5E-1 was abutted immediately by Plat. 5D-2 floor U. 47 on the centerline and U. 32 in the SW corner area (Figs. 53a, 59a,c, 60b). As the second "smell floor," this pavement is thought to correspond to Plat. 5D-2-2nd-A (Fl. 2). The stair and W facade of the platform was destroyed for construction of Str. 5E-95-2nd against its front, when U. 73 of Plat. 5D-2-1st-C (Fl. 1) was laid.

ARCHITECTURE

The large architectural sculpture and inset corner facings demonstrate convincingly that Plat. 5E-1 was once a huge finished entity that approximated the present planar dimensions of the mound. Masonry and ceramics support a construction date within a period of Manik ceramic production. Details of insets, moldings, and sculptured facade were most like those of Plat. 5D-4-3rd of the North Acropolis, which may have served as a model (TR. 14:fig. 6j).

Unit 6 is interpreted as the sole surviving course of a single projecting W stair, probably quite broad, and extending from the East Plaza to the summit. Projecting rear and side stairs can probably be ruled out, given the configuration of the platform.

Yet unresolved is the nature of the highly uneven top of the platform. Unfortunately, our excavations neither proved nor disproved the presence of structures. The six mounded features mapped by Hazzard for TR. 11 were surveyed anew in 1964 via 0.50 m contour lines. This, however, added little information to the rectified lines seen in TR. 11 and thus were not used in the drafting of Figure 1. The mapping revealed that summit heights of 5E-25, 28, and 23 are at 253 m, while 5E-27 is at 252 m, and 5E-24 and 26 are lower at 251 m.

These enigmatic features can be interpreted in at least three ways. The mounds might belong to the upper stage of the platform itself, founded on a plastered floor of the prior construction stage. The mounds, whose summits are at the same level could either be remnants of partial demolition or the results of an abandoned building project. Points in favor of either interpretation are that finished walls were not found, the floor slopes beneath the central mound, and the platform summit is not level around the "structures." This summit construction could have begun long after the base of the platform was built and demolition could have occurred at any time.

The third and more likely possibility is that at least a few of the mounds are the remains of authentic structures. Four of them (5E-23, 25, 27, 28) "read" well as substructures of demolished or perishable buildings, and are remarkably similar, in both location and shape, to the four principal structures atop the South Acropolis. Because the other two are not as high, they can be dismissed as debris resulting from the razing of buildings. The earth piled on floor U. 15 at an elevation of 250 m might also be demolition debris (Fig. 61). In sum, even though excavation did not find finished structural facades, some of the mounds look like the remains of substructures. Superimposed buildings, if they once existed, were either of perishable materials or were totally demolished.

The 110 by 120 m planar dimensions and 7.5 m frontal height of Plat. 5E-1 required 90,500 m^3 of building material and 3,450 m^2 of dressed masonry surface. These estimates include possible earlier constructions but not separate figures for summit mounds: 2,160 m^3 and 310m^2 for 5E-23, 680 m^3 and 170 m^2 for 5E-25, 880 m^3 and 250 m^2 for 5E-27, 1,800 m^3 and 300 m^2 for 5E-28.

LOTS, GROUPING AND EVALUATION

CONSTRUCTION

78G/18, from within the W side tunnel, contained 29 lbs of Manik sherds with traces of Cauac but no subsequent material. 71J/2-6, from the five lower levels of the ceramic test pit on 5E-28 (from undisturbed structural fill), contained mostly Manik ceramics and some Preclassic sherds. 78F/8, from within the U. 15 floor, had only Manik material, except for one dubious Ik or Imix sherd. 78F/2-4, from fills of 5E-25, had large samples of Manik sherds and some Preclassic.

78F/7, from the layered fills or occupation deposits against the base of the 5E-25 wall, had no sherds later than Manik (as did 71K/1-8 from the ceramic test pit into the platform top). These lots strongly indicate that the platform was built during the time when Manik ceramics were manufactured.

TABLE 41
Platform 5E-1: Time Spans

Time Span	Architectural Addition	Floor, Unit	Special Deposit	Lot	Other Data
1	—	—	—	—	Collapse after construction of Str. 5E-95-2nd
2	—	—	—	78F/1,5,6;71J/1	Use
3	—	U. 10	—	—	Repair of sculptures
4	—	—	—	—	Use
5	—	U. 2,3,6,8, 12,13,15	—	71J/2-6; 78F/2-4,7,8; 78G/18	Construction (90,500 m^3) with Plat. 5D-2-2nd-A; Manik ceramics

OCCUPATION

Surface lots 78F/1 from the top of 5E-25, 78F/5 from the surface of 5E-27, 71J/1 from 5E-28, and 78F/6 from 5E-23 contained mostly Manik pottery, although Ik and Imix sherds in all lots speak of later occupation or activity.

TIME SPANS

Platform 5E-1 time spans are outlined in Table 41. Construction of the basal W facade (TS. 5) was concurrent with Plat. 5D-2-2nd-A, Str. 5D-Sub.16, and 5E-Sub.1, consequently with Plat. 5D-1-2nd-B and 5D-4-2nd of Gp. 5D-2, which date to ca. A.D. 475 (TR. 14:179 and chart 1). Given the early masonry techniques and absence of late sherds within large collections of Manik ceramics from fills at the base and on top, it is almost certain that the platform was a completed Early Classic entity rather than an unfinished one of Terminal Classic date. At least some of the summit mounds may have been substructures of separate buildings.

The sculptures beside the central stair were renovated by U. 10 masonry and plaster in TS. 3. In TS. 1 the drastic intrusion of Str. 5E-95-2nd must have prevented further use of the platform by eliminating use of the sole platform stair and thus of the summit. This seeming abandonment coincided with the building of the first of the gallery structures that increasingly came to dominate the E half of the Plaza in front of the platform.

V

Structure 5E-22

STRUCTURE 5E-22

INTRODUCTION

The Tikal map (TR. 11) depicts Str. 5E-22 as a small square mound between the rear of Plat. 5E-1 and the wide esplanade leading from the Mendez Causeway to Str. 5E-1 (Morley's Group F). The 1964 excavation by Jones (Op. 78J) was part of the East Plaza investigations. Backfilling was delayed at the request of the Tikal National Park, and the exposed masonry was later consolidated so that the structure is presently open to view. See Figs. 1, 62 (plan), 63b, 64a–d, 80a–d.

EXCAVATION DATA

CONSTRUCTION STAGES

CONSTRUCTION STAGE 1

Structure 5E-22 was built either directly on the flat bedrock surface or on a thin stratum of earth (Fig. 63b). The area might have been undeveloped at the time. Building walls atypically rise from plaza level with no supporting substructure. Within the single room, 0.75 m high lateral platforms (benches) fill most of the space and form the sides of a central plaza-level alleyway between them. Benches and walls were built as a unit with interior wall faces starting just below the bench top, utilizing the same type of blocks. Bench-top plaster turned up to the walls (Fig. 64c). Floor *Unit 4* was confined to the narrow aisle between the lateral benches, sloping from the firepit wall to act as a drain leading out the front door and perhaps continuing E as the single platform floor in front of the building. The firepit was part of the original building (Fig. 80b,d). It was separated from the central aisle by *Unit 2*, a single course of blocks blackened by burning on their interior surfaces and worn down at least 0.10 m from use (Fig. 64b). The rest of the firepit lining was constructed of hard yellow limestone pebbles 0.15–0.20 m long and 0.10 m high. The exposed surfaces of these stones were deeply charred and occasionally disintegrated by heat. Plaster flooring lined the bottom of the pit.

Exterior wall blocks measuring 0.45–0.60 by 0.35–0.44 by 0.20 m included few headers (Figs. 64d, 80b). Corbel vaulting remained in place over the front doorway (Fig. 80c). Courses were shorter than those of the walls and the blocks were laid on larger faces rather than on their sides. The doorway was only 0.76 m wide. The vault spring was 1.12 m above the floor and the level bedding for a capstone was 0.43 m above that. The vault spring of the room itself was 2.15 m above front floor level and 1.40 m above the bench top at the rear (Fig. 63b). A low subspring course supported the vault stones, for which a soffit angle of 22° was estimated from fallen pieces (Figs. 64a, 80a). The 2.75 m span from front to back wall would have required a most unlikely nine-vault course. It seems more likely that 1.05 m high vaults were spanned by wooden beams instead. Vault stones measuring 0.50–0.60 by 0.30 by 0.25–0.30 m were parallel-sided or tapered (Fig. 64a). Some had a parallel top and bottom, others showed a noticeable upper taper or even a concave upper surface approaching that of the boot-shaped vault stones of Puuc Maya architecture (Pollock 1980:575–577).

A hole in the bedrock 0.15 m deep and 0.25 m in diameter with a shallow NW extension was found 1.25 m E of the SE corner, aligned with the S wall of the building (Fig. 62). This feature may have held a supporting post for a supplementary roof.

OTHER FEATURES

Intense, prolonged heat from fires charred and blackened the sides and floor of the firepit. The floor and lateral walls of the central aisle to the doorway were also darkened. This burning probably resulted from use of the room as a sweathouse. Large jar sherds and ash filled the firepit and aisle to a depth of 0.50 m (Fig. 63b). Within the pit itself, the lower 0.15 m of ash was light brown and white. Above this and within the passageway was a thick stratum of dark brown ash with small charred stones and more large sherds. Similar deposits were found in front of and behind the building, probably derived from repeated cleaning of the firepit. A 5 cm layer of white earth covered this ash stratum in the aisle, perhaps from wall plaster or the burning of wooden ceiling beams. Vault collapse (Fig. 63b) began with back wall vault stones falling directly on this white layer, then 0.30 m of unshaped blocks and rounded gravel falling from the roof itself, and finally the failure of the S vault stones. Both the front and back walls fell outward.

RELATIONSHIP TO ADJACENT STRATIGRAPHY

A single plaza floor abutted Str. 5E-22 and the Plat. 5D-2:U. 97 terrace wall behind it. The structure and U. 97 are probably contemporaries, as both were unfinished without this abutting floor at their bases.

ARCHITECTURE

Structure 5E-22 was unusual in its lack of building platform or substructure, diminutive corbel-vaulted front doorway with low vault spring, large benches filling most of the room space, and charred firepit (Figs. 1, 62). These features conform to the sweathouses at Piedras Negras (Satterthwaite 1952) and Chichen Itza (Ruppert 1952:56, 82–83, figs. 50, 127). Table 42 compares dimensions of Str. 5E-22 with two Piedras Negras sweathouses.

Room size was intermediate between the two Piedras Negras examples. Semivaults and wooden beam ceilings were probably present at both sites. Door width was identical, the greater Tikal height narrowed at the top by corbeling. The benches that filled most of the room were constructed so that participants would be closer to the ceiling. The central aisle drained out the doorway as at Piedras Negras. An interior firepit (Satterthwaite's fire box) was present and heavily charred by use. A sill separated the fire from the aisle. Use of the room might have involved dry heat only, but the draining of the aisle and the presence of jar sherds implies the use of water as well. Assembly required only ca. 70 m^3 of masonry and 150 m^2 of surface dressing.

TABLE 42
Comparative Measurements of 5E-22 with Piedras Negras Sweatbaths

Dimension	Tikal Str. 5E-22	Piedras Negras Str. P-7-1st-B	Piedras Negras Str. N-1-1st-B
Room Length (m)	5.14	3.30	4.80
Room Width (m)	2.75	2.20	3.25
Room Height (m)	2.40	2.70	—
Room Area (m^2)	14.14	7.26	15.60
Doorway Width (m)	0.76	0.77	0.77
Doorway Height (m)	1.55	1.10	1.00

LOTS, GROUPING AND EVALUATION

OCCUPATION

78J/1,2 on the plaza floor in front of the building, 78J/3–5 from inside the room, and 78J/6,7 from behind the structure, contained many large body sherds from coarse-ware round-bottomed water jars. These were evaluated as intermediate Imix and Eznab and probably reflect the period of use.

TIME SPANS

Assembly of this sweathouse in TS. 3 (Table 43) dated to or followed construction of the Plat. 5D-2 facing behind it that belonged either to Plat. 5D-2-1st-B or to 1st-A. Two Plat. 5D-2 pavements reaching the NE corner of the East Plaza (U. 36 and 35) were quite possibly the first to extend around the base of Plat. 5E-1 to the U. 97 terrace wall at its rear (Fig. 1). The building was probably used for a long time (TS. 2) before ash and broken Imix or Eznab water jars were dumped behind it, against the front, and within the room itself. Collapse in TS. 1 began with flaking plaster and possibly burned roof beams, and it continued with the failure of the roof vault and the outward buckling of the walls.

TABLE 43
Structure 5E-22: Time Spans

Time Span	Architectural Addition	Floor, Unit	Special Deposit	Lot	Other Data
1	—	—	—	78J/1,5,6	Collapse
2	—	—	—	78J/2-4,	Use; Imix or Eznab ceramics
3	—	—	—	—	Assembly (70 m^3) with Plat. 5D-2:U. 97?

VI

Group 5D-3 Time Spans

INTRODUCTION

This segment of the report provides a concise history of Gp. 5D-3. Internal stratigraphic connections among structures and platforms are expressed in Fig. 65 and Chart 1, which emulate fig. 8 and chart 1 of TR. 14. Of special interest are integration, function, and chronological relationship to adjacent Gp. 5D-2 (TR. 14).

TIME SPAN 9

Construction activities prior to TS. 9 were not detected within the group. A slightly earlier facing wall of Plat. 5D-1-4th B stood high to the W but did not descend to the East Plaza level. As was the case with subsequent floors, the lowermost pavements above bedrock in several trenches across the East Plaza mark the beginning of the paved platform. They were, however, treated as separate units (in this case U. 8, 71, and 78) in order to stress that they were not linked to each other by means of trenching.

The eastern edge of the platform was raised at least a meter over undisturbed sloping ground (Figs. 2b, 53a). It is not known whether summit pavement turned up to an early version of Plat. 5E-1 or down over a terrace wall or stair. In the center, the pavement covered lensed earthen fill on bedrock (Fig. 9), and on the W and S sides bedrock was probably leveled before the floor was laid (Figs. 2b, 19d; TR. 14:fig. 254). Excavation did not reach bedrock in front of Str. 5E-38, and thus it is not known if the SE sector was paved this early (Fig. 51c). The N edge of the platform probably fell where the N side of 5E-32 was later positioned (Fig. 42c).

Two constructions were erected on the body of Fl. 5 and abutted by its final surface plaster. These are Plat. 5D-2:U. 17 on the W (TR. 14:fig. 254) and Str. 5D-Sub.27 on the S (Fig. 19d). Although U. 17 has been considered a terrace facing (TR. 14:821), a stair can alternatively be proposed on the basis of almost identical stair masonry on Str. 5D-Sub.9 (TR. 14:figs. 29a, 30c). Certainly less demolition would have been needed later to destroy such a stair rather than a terrace wall. Structure 5D-Sub.27 was probably a north-facing structure, perhaps anticipating 5D-43 in form.

Sometime during TS. 9, Str. 5D-Sub.28 and 29 were assembled on U. 78 (Fig. 9). These low wall stubs or steps may be either remains of structures with twin-facing stairs or walls or simply fill-retaining walls. Their relative positions anticipate those of both the twin pyramids of TS. 6 and the ballcourt of TS. 5. Unfortunately, they were considered as possible structures only after excavation had closed and were not further explored.

Contemporaneity of Fl. 5 to U. 17 of Plat. 5D-1-4th-A and thereby to Fl. 4A in the Great Plaza allowed placement of TS. 9 within the parameters of Gp. 5D-2:TS. 11 (TR. 14:820–824), which by radiocarbon dating is thought to have begun ca. 0 A.D. (ibid.:chart 2). Floor 4A is less than halfway through the suggested 75 years of TS. 11 (ibid.:chart 1); therefore TS. 9 of Gp. 5D-3 should date roughly to A.D. 30.

With the exception of Str. 5D-Sub.10-2nd on the Acropolis summit, building activity in Gp. 5D-2 at this time concentrated on the E side of the Great Plaza adjacent to the East Plaza. Shortly before, however, Fl. 4B initiated the Great Plaza itself as a paved expanse (ibid.:820–821), the West Plaza probably received its first paving, Str. 5D-Sub.20 and 25 were erected in the Great Plaza, the N Terrace was rebuilt, Str. 5D-Sub.3 was renovated, and Sub.11 was erected over Bu. 166, the first of several interments to contain Cauac ceramics (ibid.:figs. 33–35). The paving programs creating the Great Plaza and West Plaza, and then the East Plaza provided an expanded setting for the North Acropolis and N Terrace. Shortly after the East Plaza paving, a male was buried in the center of the Acropolis summit (Bu. 85), perhaps the first ruler to be interred in Gp. 5D-2 (TR. 14:820, 859). Replacement of Chuen ceramics by Cauac in the burials might reflect a change in leadership. Following that time, the Acropolis was clearly a focus of dynastic ritual and commemoration as expressed in further rich burials and stone monuments. The paving projects perhaps took place within the reign of the man in Bu. 85.

Quantities of construction material and areas of trimmed stone surface for the structures and platforms of this time span (Table 44) were culled from individual reports. Volume includes all fill and facing materials; Area is the amount of upright dressed surface in terrace walls, stairs, interior and exterior walls, upper zones, and vault soffits. Group 5D-3 used up 170,800 m³ of construction materials and 27,660 m² of dressed masonry in all.

TABLE 44
Volumes and Dressed Surface Areas, Time Span 9

Construction	Volume (m³)	Area (m²)
Plat. 5D-2-3rd-B	6,540	420
Str. 5D-Sub.27,28,29	?	?
Total	6,540	420

TIME SPAN 8

The second paving of the East Plaza (Plat. 5D-2-3rd-A) might have been initiated in order to reduce a pronounced central dip. Floor 4 was first identified as the second-to-bottom surface at the W end of the platform (TR. 14:fig 254) and subsequently in comparable positions in the center and E end (U. 10, 72, 78; Figs. 9, 19 d, 48c, 53a). The pavement contained soft white inclusions like the preceding floor, rather than the "flinty" gravel of those immediately overlying them. On the E and W sides of the Plaza the floor was thin, but in the center it covered thick lensed fill like that under early floors of Plat. 5D-4 (see TR. 14:fig. 10).

The only known activities in the Plaza were demolition of Str. 5D-Sub.28 and 29 in the center (Fig. 9) and erection of Str. 5D-Sub.26 in front of Sub.27 (Fig. 19d). Floor 4 was the second pavement to abut Plat. 5D-1:U. 17 and hence could have been built with Great Plaza Fl. 3B (Gp. 5D-2:TS. 11). These floors of the East Plaza and Great Plaza, in addition to Fl. 11 of the North Acropolis, share a common thickness and soft stone inclusions. They seem to be for the purpose of repaving and do not accompany changes in group composition. At a later time within TS. 8, U. 4 was laid as a thin floor restricted to the central area (Fig. 9). The quantity of material employed in these platforms was not great (Table 45).

TABLE 45
Volumes and Dressed Surface Areas, Time Span 8

Construction	Volume (m³)	Area (m²)
Plat. 5D-2-3rd-A	2,180	?
Str. 5D-Sub.26	?	?
Plat. 5D-2:U. 4	100	?
Total	2,280	?

TIME SPAN 7

As known through several exposures, the summit surface of Plat. 5D-2-2nd-B consisted of a thick 0.30 m of hard-packed fill capped by smoothly surfaced flint-graveled plaster. This was variously labeled Fl. 3 at the W end of the Plaza (TR. 14:fig. 254), U. 80 and 92 in the central area (Figs. 9, 19d), and U. 49 and 60 at the E end (Figs. 48c, 51c, 53a). The floor was recognized by its hard flint chips that "exude an ozone odor when trowelled" (TR. 14:833), and its greater thickness than Fl. 2 above or Fl. 4 below.

New constructions did not accompany the paving, which turned up to existing faces of Plat. 5D-1:U. 17

on the W and Str. 5D-Sub.27 on the S, while covering the stub of Sub.26 in front of 27. As the third floor to abut Plat. 5D-1:U. 17, it was laid at or near the time of Great Plaza Fl. 2B at the beginning of Gp. 5D-3:TS. 7, dated ca. A.D. 325 (TR. 14:832–834). A span of 250 years thus lay between Fl. 4 and Fl. 3; this comprises the later part of Gp. 5D-2:TS. 11 and all of TS. 10, 9, and 8. During that long interval, construction in Gp. 5D-2 was confined for the most part to the North Acropolis and N Terrace, with little work within the Great Plaza itself. The Acropolis was enlarged and raised significantly, successively paved by Fl. 9, 8, 7, and provided with a single front stair, massive round-cornered walls, and a broadly staired N Terrace. The summit structures, 5D-22, 23, 24, and 26, were rebuilt several times (TR. 14:824–826). This focus on the Acropolis was finally broken by the Great Plaza paving project (Fl 2B) which was accompanied by pyramidal Str. 5D-1-2nd and 2-2nd on the E and W sides of the Great Plaza and ballcourt Str. 5D-74-2nd in the SE corner. Hence, the substantial East Plaza paving was undertaken within the context of a renewed interest in redesigning the approaches to the N Terrace and North Acropolis. Volumes of material increased (Table 46)

TABLE 46
Volumes and Dressed Surface Areas, Time Span 7

Construction	Volume (m³)	Area (m²)
Plat. 5D-2-2nd-B	5,450	?
Total	5,450	?

TIME SPAN 6

Identification of a plaza-wide Fl. 2 was critical to the placement of major Gp. 5D-3 constructions in TS. 6. Floor 2 and the U. 83, 18, 59, and 47 equivalents were generally the thinner and uppermost of two flint-laden floors (Figs. 9, 19d, 48c, 53a). On the W side of the Plaza, Plat. 5D-1:U. 18 replaced ancient U. 17 (TR. 14:fig. 254). This was probably a massive rebuilding of the Great Plaza facade with a new stair or terrace. Twin pyramids Str. 5D-Sub.16 and 5E-Sub.1 were erected in the Plaza center (Figs. 4, 5, 6a), and the great facade of Plat. 5E-1 (Fig. 58) rose at the same time on the E. The rest of the Plaza possibly remained free of structures.

Floor 2 was laid immediately upon completion of Plat. 5D-1:U. 18, as demonstrated by the fact that the floor covers unsightly remains of prior U. 17 (TR. 14:fig. 254). Unit 18 can be identified as a part of the Fl. 2A refurbishment of the Great Plaza at the commencement of Gp. 5D-2:TS. 6, dated to ca. A.D. 475 (TR. 14:838–840). Hence it appears that this East Plaza flooring and its constructions were accompanied by simultaneous paving projects to the W: Fl. 2A of the Great Plaza, U. 25 of the Terrace, Fl. 3 of the Acropolis, and perhaps a West Plaza floor as well. Furthermore, the U. 288 platform supporting Str. 5D-29, 30, and 31 was built on the E edge of the N Terrace. This may have had a broad rear stair (Str. 5D-38:U. 8) descending to the East Plaza (TR. 14:661-663).

Because the N edge of Fl. 2 and the subsequent East Plaza (TS. 5) lay considerably S of the present location, the twin pyramids would have occupied the approximate center of the Plaza space (Fig. 1). Their radial stairs, five plain terraces, and E-W alignment are identical to those of later Tikal twin pyramids, although they are positioned closer to one another and do not have a verifiable E monument row, S nine-doorway building, and N enclosure. Stelae 30, 16, 22, and 19 in Twin-Pyramid Groups dating after A.D. 692 are dedicated to Katun endings and portray a named ruler holding a segmented staff and bag. Likewise, katun-ending monuments from around A.D. 475 display named dynastic figures holding segmented staffs and bags. The ruler Kan Boar is on St. 9 at 9.2.0.0.0 (A.D. 475) and Jaguar Paw Skull on St. 7, 15, and 27 at 9.3.0.0.0 (A.D. 495). Perhaps the actions or events portrayed on these monuments took place first in the East Plaza and then in the other successively built groups.

Although excavation of Plat. 5E-1 was overly brief, some facts were determined. The W facade showed the surviving features of one or more large faces near the S corner, including two eye sockets and a sloping cheek line. Existence of an axial W stair is demonstrated by forward location of a surviving basal course of stones appropriate to a step. Finally, several trenches at the SW corner exposed a series of inset and aproned corner walls that could only belong to a large platform like the North Acropolis. Some details, such as the double corner insets and the mask and flanking sloping element raised on a plain terrace (Figs. 58a,b, 59a,c, 60b), recall the slightly earlier and better-known U. 56 facade of Plat. 5D-4 (TR. 14:figs. 6j, 11b). Trenching of Plat. 5E-1 summit mounds exposed facade or core walls on plaster floors of consistent elevation. Distinctive mound outlines and flat summits were confirmed by contour mapping (Figs. 63a, 61). Hence these protrusions might still be remnants of substructures, rather than merely the results of interrupted dismantling or of construction of the platform top. Four of the mounds (Str. 5E-23, 25, 27, and 28) are analogous in plan and position to Str. 5D-100, 102 (composed of two structures), and 104 on the South Acropolis (Fig. 1 and TR. 11). Except for a few Imix sherds on the top, the huge ceramic samples from platform fills and summit surfaces are almost all Manik with a scattering of earlier material. In sum, Plat. 5E-1 appears once to have been, or at least planned as, an Acropolis comparable to the North Acropolis and South Acropolis. At the time it was constructed, the North Acropolis was already partially obscured behind Str. 5D-32-2nd, 33-2nd, and 34, and therefore perhaps needed a replacement. Finally, it may be of interest to point out that, for reasons unknown, the central structures on these three platforms, Str. 5D-26, 5D-104, and 5E-25, form a right triangle with two equal sides.

Within TS. 6, Str. 5D-Sub.16 and 5E-Sub.1 were extensively reconditioned by U. 1 and 6 on the former and U. 1 on the latter (Figs. 6a,b, 9). Whether or not these stair additions covered the entire pyramids or only reached the height shown, dedicatory caches within them demonstrate that they were significant. With these, the pyramids probably functioned longer than the one or two katuns postulated for later Twin-Pyramid Groups (Jones 1969:130). Minor repairs were also conducted on the Plat. 5E-1 masks (U. 10:Fig. 58a,b). Structure 5E-38 possibly was built at this time, before laying the plaza floor around it. These mid-TS. 6 events should correspond roughly in time to Gp. 5D-2:TS. 6, in which Str. 5D-22-1st was assembled (TR. 14:839–840). The twin-pyramid stair revisions resemble 22-1st in masonry (Fig. 9; TR. 14:figs. 9a, 107b). The bulk of Plat. 5E-1 far exceeded that of any other project within the group (Table 47).

TABLE 47
Volumes and Dressed Surface Areas, Time Span 6

Construction	Volume (m³)	Area (m²)
TS. 6B		
Plat. 5D-2-2nd-A	3,270	330
Plat. 5E-1	90,560	3,450
Str. 5D-Sub.16-B	610	200
Str. 5E-Sub.1-B	610	200
Str. 5E-23	2,160	310
Str. 5E-24	670	140
Str. 5E-25	680	170
Str. 5E-27	880	250
Str. 5E-28	1,800	300
Total	101,240	5,350
TS. 6A		
Str. 5D-Sub.16-A	380	310
Str. 5E-Sub.1-A	380	310
Str. 5E-38	7,150	1,370
Total	7,910	1,990

TIME SPAN 5

Floor 1 and equivalent U. 1, 5, 7, 19, 20, 26, 33, 41, 58, 68, and 73 are thought to represent a single plaza-wide Plat. 5D-2-1st-C surface. Connectives between these separate appearances, where not traced physically, were inferred on the basis of position in a sequence or typology. The floor contained soft white chunks, in contrast to the flint chips in the two prior pavements.

Major changes occurred on the edges of the platform in TS. 5. On the W side of the East Plaza, U. 8, 20, and 71 of Plat. 5D-1-1st-E replaced the U. 18 facade (TR. 14:figs. 7, 248, 254). Unit 8 consisted of at least two upper terrace levels, below which U. 20 was an enigmatic sloping floor that might be core construction. Unit 71 is a better-documented two-stage set of terrace faces on the northern part of the Plat. 5D-1 facade. On the other side of the East Plaza, Str. 5E-95-2nd covered the only known stair of Plat. 5E-1, thus rendering unusable its front and probably its summit as well. On the S rose the new terrace facings of the Central Acropolis, identical in profile to those of U. 71 (Figs. 2c, 19d). These facades ascended ca. 8 m in two stages to form an impressive backdrop for the centrally placed ballcourt. As the earliest surviving pavement on the NW corner of the Plaza, U. 41 provided a broad terminus for the Maler Causeway, in turn paved by a continuation of the floor. The E and N edges of Plat. 5D-2 (as seen in terrace wall U. 44, Maler Causeway stair U. 8, and stair U. 53) dropped into presumably unimproved terrain (Figs. 30a, 42a,c). This early causeway had a parapet wall, but may have lacked the later parapet benches (Figs. 28b, 30c). A Mendez Causeway probably also existed at this time.

The transformation of the group, which was completed by this widespread flooring, was profound. Structures 5D-Sub.27, 5D-Sub.16, and 5E-Sub.1 disappeared beneath the masonry of Str. 5D-43, 5D-42, and 5E-31 (as may be seen in Fig. 1 by removing all other structures and using the Fig. 8a and 19a plans). These three new structures have unusual and unique features. The vertical sides of the ballcourt ranges are divided into visually separate front and rear sections, each with upper and lower zones as if they were the outer walls of rooms (Fig. 8b,d,e). The lower zone panels might be analogous to those on ballcourt Str. 5D-74 in Gp. 5D-2 (TR. 14:fig. 286). Cylindrical door columns are unique at Tikal and perhaps for the Classic Maya. The hieroglyphic panels could be the earliest facade texts at Tikal, with 1 Ahau possibly marking the katun end 9.10.0.0.0 (A.D. 633). Striking features of Str. 5D-43 are the radial stairways, three-member moldings, Tlaloc eye and Venus star decorations, and flat-relief upper-zone masks (Figs. 19a, 22a). These also appear in Tikal on Str. 6E-143 and 144 as well as on Str. 5D-53. Similar though not identical three-part profiles can be seen on substructures in Xochicalco, Monte Alban, and Tajin (Marquina 1964:lám. 290). Stepped merlons are also common on radial structures in Central Mexico (Gendorp 1985). As discussed, the three structures form a unit suited to Taladoire's Type I, Variety I ballcourt: "Open Courts Without Benches, One Axial Structure" (1981:147–150, 161). Taladoire mistakenly placed the court in his Type II because he thought it possessed a sloping bench front and back wall. Ballcourts of Type I, Variety I are listed from Balakbal, Becan, Copan, Naachtun, and Sayil (ibid.:150, pls. 30, 31). The most similar ballcourt is that formed by Str. A-19 and A-13 at Seibal, Guatemala, which dates to A.D. 830–930 on the basis of Bayal pottery and a C-14 sample (Smith 1982:59–63, 77–82, map 2; Willey 1990:199–200). The 12.4 by 39 m Seibal court is larger than the one in the East Plaza of Tikal (8.4 by 24.7 m), but has the same bench profile and approximately 1:3 planar proportion. Its end structure (A-13) stands 32 m E of the alley (26 m at Tikal) and four radial stairs. Furthermore, disarticulated, fragmentary bones of 11 or 12 individuals, most if not all young males, found buried in a shallow pit beneath the center of the structure summit (Burial 4), were cited as evidence of ball-game sacrifice by Tourtellot (1990:90–91). Similar burials were not found in Tikal Str. 5D-43, but the Tlaloc eyes and Venus sign decorations on the substructure, as well as the stepped merlons on the roof, also help to define it as a place of sacrifice (Carlson 1991:figs. 13a, 13i). In Late or Terminal Classic Maya sites of Quiche and Huehuetenango, Guatemala, and Chiapas, Mexico, Taladoire's Type IV ballcourts, "Courts Open to a Plaza with Altar" (1981:190–195, 242–244, pls. 41–44, 58), also have an axial structure, usually square or radial in plan. This later highland Maya design may have derived from the earlier Tikal-Seibal models, providing yet another link between the Classic Maya sites and the Postclassic highland Maya legends of ballcourt sacrifice and burial in the *Popol Vuh*.

The starting point of TS. 5 probably coincided with that of Gp. 5D-2:TS. 5. The upper surface of the U. 8 terraces corresponds in level with Fl. 1 of the Great Plaza and is linked stratigraphically with U. 23 and U. 71 to the N (TR. 14:240–242, fig. 248). Furthermore, U. 8, U. 71, the Central Acropolis wall, and Str. 5D-42, 5E-31, and 5D-43 were all constructed with ca. 0.20 by 0.30 by 0.50 m blocks laid on their edges as stretchers and headers. Great Plaza Fl. 1 was the first to abut the Plat. 5D-4:U. 209A stair of the North Terrace, and therefore equates with Plat. 5D-4:U. 25 and Str. 5D-32-1st.

These connectives should place East Plaza Fl. 1 at the time of sealing Bu. 195 beneath 32-1st (TR. 14:240–241; Jones 1991:115–117). On the other hand, the wall blocks of Str. 5D-32-1st are installed on their largest surfaces like those of earlier Plat. 5E-1, Str. 5D-Sub.16, and 5E-Sub.1; in contrast the stones of Str. 5D-33-1st stand on-edge like those of Plat. 5D-1:U. 8 and 71, Str. 5D-42, 5D-43, and 5E-31 (Figs. 14d,e,g, 20; TR. 14:figs. 190d–g; 200b,f). Only 50 years or so, from A.D. 600 to 650, separate 32-1st from 33-1st (TR. 14:842, chart 1), but dynastic contexts are beginning to emerge for the period, and it would be valuable to know whether or not the East Plaza ballcourt, the Tlaloc-Venus building, Central Acropolis terraces, and the earliest marketplace galleries and causeways were erected around the time of Bu. 195 when the ruler Animal Skull was laid to rest, or at the time of Str. 5D-33-1st and its Bu. 23 and 24.

The victory by Ruler A over Jaguar Paw of Calakmul in A.D. 695, commemorated on Lintel 3 of Str. 5D-1, would be a suitable event to be celebrated by such expensive sacrifice-related construction as seen in the East Plaza. Although the stratigraphy as outlined here and in TR. 14 indicates that the project took place at the time of 32-1st before Ruler A's reign, that is, during that of his father, Shield Skull, the match between the masonry of 5D-33-1st and the East Plaza construction advances the guess date toward the second half of the 6th century. That triumphant Ruler A was the instigator of Gp. 5D-3:TS. 5 is not an impossibility.

During the course of TS. 5, Str. 5E-32-2nd-B and A were constructed on the East Plaza floor (Fig. 38b,c). These structures, the former a long unvaulted gallery facing W, continued the growth of this unique colonnade type of building on the E half of the Plaza.

TABLE 48
Volumes and Dressed Surface Areas, Time Span 5

Construction	Volume (m^3)	Area (m^2)
TS. 5B:		
Plat. 5D-2-1st-C	8,440	760
Str. 5D-42-D	1,150	730
Str. 5E-31-C	1,000	680
Str. 5D-43-C	510	520
Str. 5E-95-2nd	520	440
Total	11,620	3,130
TS. 5A:		
Str. 5E-32-2nd-B	140	310
Str. 5E-32-2nd-A	180	310
Total	320	620

TIME SPAN 4

A plaster floor variously labeled U. 25, 34, 36, 58, or 74 initiated TS. 4. It was spread over the northeastern surface of the East Plaza, and the platform edge was extended N to line up with the prior northern limit. New paving was not seen in the W part of the Plaza, however. The floor is penultimate in the sequences and can often be traced between appearances by its similar relationship to opposite ends of long structures. Several structures were built and immediately abutted by the floor in a major expansion of the gallery complex (Fig. 1). Structure 5E-29 was erected along the N edge of the expanded surface, 5E-37 faced it far to the S, 5E-95-2nd and 99-2nd were built on the E, 5E-32-1st-C on the W, and 5E-96 and 93 were placed in the SE sector against the side of the Central Acropolis. Two small structures of almost identical plan, 5E-97 and 40, were constructed near entrances to the eastern part of the Plaza. The complex attained its maximum dimensions with these buildings, although more would be inserted later. Structures 5E-96, 93, 40 and the first known double gallery, 5E-37, incorporate the SW sector of the Plaza into the growing marketplace plan.

Stratigraphic relationships in the W part of the East Plaza are unknown for lack of flooring. Structure 5D-37 and the attached stair U. 72 of Plat. 5D-1 rose on prior floor U. 41 of TS. 5 and stood for some time before being abutted by the next floor, U. 40 of TS. 3 (TR. 14:figs. 247–250). Hence these constructions might have been built in TS. 4. Structure

5D-41-2nd, which stands on the TS. 5 floor and never had an abutting floor prior to its replacement by 41-1st (Fig. 16d), might also belong to TS. 4.

A sequence of four events on the Great Plaza has indirect stratigraphic connections to the East Plaza (TR. 14:846–850). First, a Plat. 5D-1-1st-D floor (Gp. 5D-2:TS. 4B) was laid in the W portion of the Great Plaza around Str. 5D-2. Second, floor U. 31 and 22B (of Plat. 5D-1-1st-C) were laid against both Str. 5D-1-2nd and Str. 5D-38:U. 1, a platform or substructure under 5D-38. A third development, Plat. 5D-1-1st-B (TS. 4A), is represented by U. 30, a floor that abuts the base of Str. 5D-1-1st yet underlies its stair wall. Unit 30 is surely the pavement at the summit of the U. 16 stair rising from the East Plaza and is probably the U. 22A floor that abuts the N end of Str. 5D-38 (TR. 14:855–856, figs. 243, 244c). The fourth stage is Str. 5D-37, which stands on U. 22A. All of these four episodes succeed U. 41 of Plat. 5D-2-1st-C (TS. 5) and precede U. 40 of 5D-2-1st-A (TS. 3). Therefore, even though Bu. 116 is important in marking a transition between the reigns of Ruler A and Ruler B around A.D. 732, there is no direct stratigraphy to fix the event in the context of Gp. 5D-3 constructions, and we cannot be sure whether TS. 4 occurred during the long reign of Ruler A or in the years of his son, Ruler B.

TABLE 49
Volumes and Dressed Surface Areas, Time Span 4

Construction	Volume (m^3)	Area (m^2)
TS. 4B:		
Plat. 5D-2-1st-B	17,980	900
Str. 5E-29	460	300
Str. 5E-32-1st-C	450	750
Str. 5E-99-2nd	100	200
Str. 5E-95-2nd-A	170	20
Str. 5D-41-2nd	280	150
Str. 5E-37	1,270	1,270
Total	20,710	3,590
TS. 4A:		
Str. 5D-43-B	40	70
Str. 5E-97	80	140
Str. 5E-96	650	720
Str. 5E-93	240	270
Str. 5E-40	80	140
Str. 5E-32-1st-C	450	750
Str. 5E-32-1st-B	390	1,150
Total	1,930	3,240

TIME SPAN 3

Although the uppermost Plat. 5D-2-1st floor survived on the extreme W side of the Plaza only as U. 94, this a gravel layer abutting the U. 16 stair (TR. 14:fig. 254), it was well preserved as U. 35 around Str. 5D-41, 42, and 5E-31, U. 24 inside the Str. 5E-32 quadrangle, U. 37 on the S, U. 75 and 29 on the E, and U. 40 on the W (see Plat. 5D-2-1st).

The group plan (Figs. 1, 81a,b) illustrates the Plaza in TS. 3 if one first removes Str. 5D-39, 134, 135, and 136 along with 5E-92, 94, and 98 and then restores the NW corner of 32-1st to its original state (Fig. 38a). The gallery structures in the E half of the Plaza were completed in this time span by a fresh floor surface sealing the bases of walls and steps. Structures 5E-32-1st-A and 99-1st formed a completely enclosing quadrangle for the first time, with known entries only at two of the corners and the center of the W wing. Four double-galleried structures, 5E-33 through 36, formed a smaller open-cornered court within. Structures 5D-95-1st and 5E-29 and 37 lined the outer edges of "streets" running along the N, E, and S sides. The formerly open passageway into the SE sector was cut off by an extension of 5E-37 that joined 5E-96. Structure 5D-43 was transformed into a two-room building with single door, encased by stairs leading behind and beside it to the Central Acropolis. Structures 5D-40 and 5E-30 lined the N edge of the Plaza. The Maler and perhaps the Mendez Causeway were rebuilt at this time.

Time Span 3 probably follows the final events in Gp. 5D-2:TS. 4A, in which Str. 5D-37 and the U. 72 stair were erected (TR. 14:194,table 28). The U. 74 stair on the N side of 5D-37 is one of the few constructions thought to pertain to TS. 3 of that group. It is interesting that the enormous construction projects of Gp. 5D-3:TS. 3 may have taken place with little coeval activity in Gp. 5D-2.

Minor changes occurred during the course of TS. 3. Interior transverse walls were erected along the passageways through the W side of Str. 5E-32-1st (Fig. 38a) and the W end of 5E-37 (Fig. 19b), and a wall blocked the stair descending from the E side of the Maler Causeway (Fig. 31b).

The gallery structures in the eastern part of the Plaza (Figs. 1, 81a,b), with their long narrow rooms, piers between doorways, and low building platforms, are entirely distinct from the range-type structures of the Central Acropolis and elsewhere. They do not possess substructures below the building platform, wide wall sections between doorways, room divisions, medial doorways, upper-zone carving, bench-like interior platforms, or cord holders.

Marketplaces have been suggested in several archaeological sites in Mesoamerica. At Seibal, the north half of the central plaza of Group A was thought to have housed a possible marketplace (Smith 1982:106, 108, 232; Willey 1990:202–203). The square is edged on the N and W by long, low platform mounds which may have supported buildings (Str. A-52, 56, 57) and has at least three small low, square platforms within it (Str. A-53, 54, 55). Structures A-54 and A-56 are probably Bayal (Terminal Classic) in date. As at Tikal, to the S stands a ballcourt (A-19) and radial platform (A-13).

A close analogy to the East Plaza market can be seen in the map of Yaxha by Miguel Orrego and Nicholas Hellmuth (Hellmuth 1971a, 1971b). Like the East Plaza at Tikal, Plaza J stands E of the main plaza at the end of a SE causeway (the Lincoln Sacbe). Three structures, ca. 4 m. wide and 18 m to 23 m long, face an open center and are encased by an almost unbroken quadrangle of long mounds measuring ca. 50 by 80 m. This in turn is surrounded by Vias 2, 3, and 4 on the N, E, and S, the outer edges of which are edged by additional long mounds. The complete complex is 80 by 100 m. A visit to Yaxha in 1995 confirmed that the mounds differ little from those in the East Plaza of Tikal. Given that Hellmuth and Orrego mapped a perfect Tikal style Twin-Pyramid Complex at Yaxha beside Plaza J, it is not surprising that the marketplaces of the two centers also share similar design. The Yaxha structures have not been excavated to verify room and doorway plan.

At Chichen Itza the Court of the Thousand Columns has also been suggested as a marketplace (Ruppert 1924:269–70; 1952:72–74; Tozzer 1957:73–74, fig. 57). This is centrally located, has colonnaded galleries on three sides, and is adjacent to ballcourt Str. 3D-2, 4, and 9. Within the plaza as many as 58 low platforms of many shapes and sizes are aligned in rows like market stalls. These were built with stones robbed from other buildings and therefore probably postdate the nearby structures.

At Teotihuacan, the Great Compound at the juncture of the axial causeways of the site has been cited as a possible marketplace by Millon (1973:57). The plaza itself is apparently void of structures, but the surrounding raised platforms supported buildings and limited excavation revealed obsidian workshop debris.

Perhaps the best-known marketplace in Mesoamerica is that of Tlatelolco in Tenochtitlan, described in full operation by Cortés (1962:87–89) and by Díaz (1956:156–157). Several architectural features are mentioned in those eyewitness accounts: peripheral arcades under which cocheneal, herbs, and many other goods were sold, a building where judges sat and magistrates gathered to inspect the merchandise, a central announcement stand next to which criminals were executed, and streets devoted to particular items of sale. An early colonial plan of the market, recently published and analyzed by Feldman (1978), shows a square plaza surrounded by long arcade-like structures with portals and only six entry points. The center is occupied by a raised platform, a square platform stands at one corner, and a small building at the opposite corner. Feldman was able to ascertain the locations of different market functions. Importers, *pochteca* (traveling merchants), and wholesalers in cotton cloth were clustered, for example, near the corner platform, which might have been the judge's hall, whereas craftsmen and producers dominated the larger, more distant sections.

Historical references make it clear that marketplaces were present in most areas of Mesoamerica before the European arrival. This is true of the Aztec (Durán 1971:275; Brundage 1972:53), the Zapotec and Mixtec (Spores 1965:972), the Huastec (Stresser-Péan 1971:594), the Yucatec Maya (Landa and Oviedo, in Tozzer 1941:96), and the Highland Maya (Ximenez, in Blom 1932:545).Oviedo mentioned large market plazas in Yucatan, but their architectural features have not been described. Several sources state, nevertheless, that ballcourts were located at or next to the market (Stern 1950:51).

The eastern half of the East Plaza has many of the characteristics of Mesoamerican marketplaces. It is located at the juncture of entry roads, the Maler and Mendez Causeways, is near the principal ceremonial area (Gp. 5D-2) and a ballcourt (Str. 5D-42 and 5E-

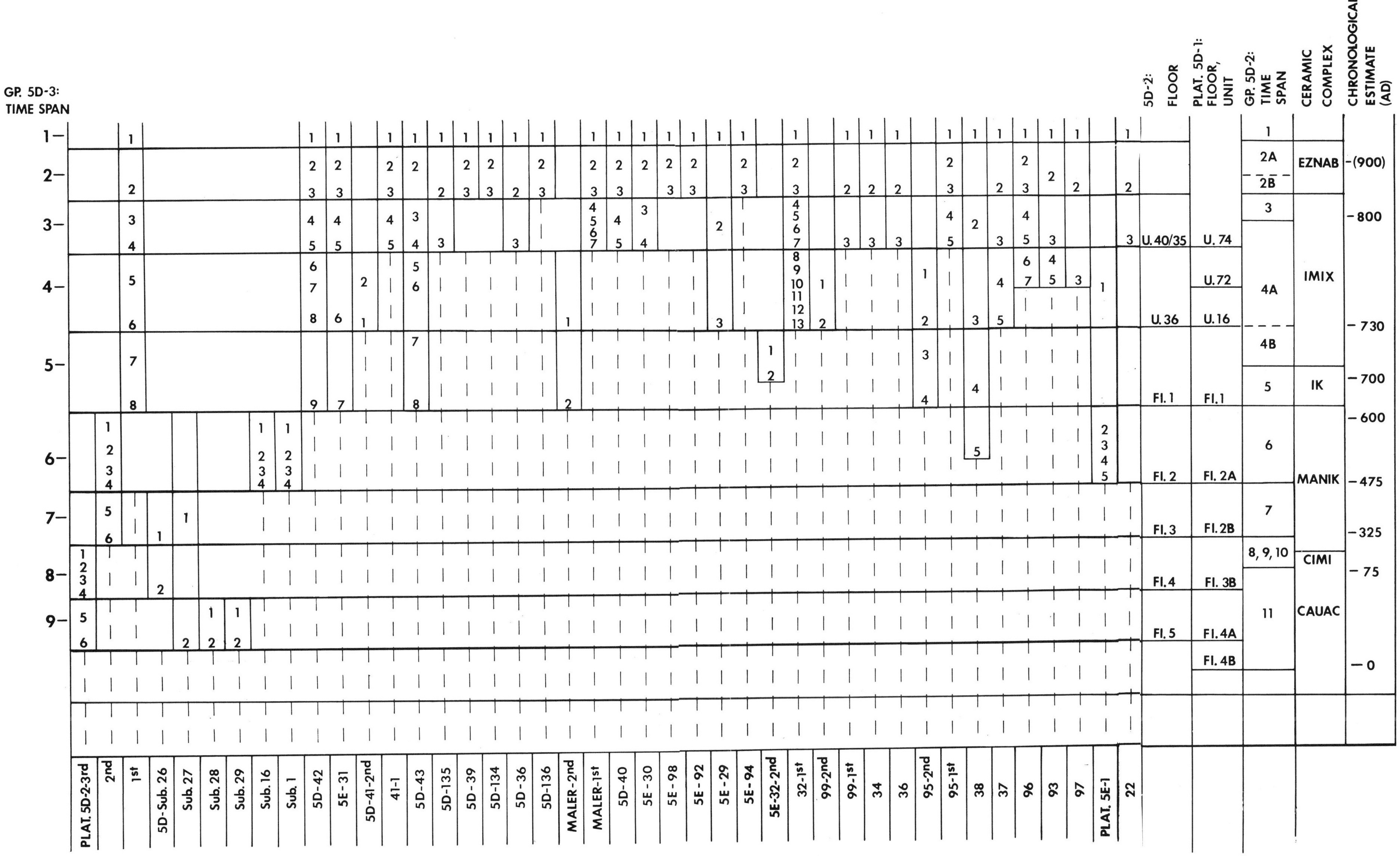

Chart 1. Group 5D-3 Time Spans.

31), has arcades or roofed galleries (Str. 5E-29, 95, and 37), a design of streets and stalls around an open center (Str. 5E-32-36 and 99), and distinctive separate buildings at corners (Str. 5E-30, 40, and 97). Furthermore, the doorways that open onto outer streets are identical to those within the enclosing quadrangle, arguing for identical interior and exterior functions, and making it less likely that the complex was cloistered or restricted. Workshop debris was not found in limited clearing of room floors, but may have been sampled in the trench off the N edge of the platform between Str. 5E-30 and 29 (see Plat. 5D-2-1st text), the most accessible dumping site to Str. 5E-32. Ceramics found there are almost exclusively Imix, with few earlier or later pieces. Polychrome wares, large plain jars, fragments of cut and polished bone and shell, figurine heads, and censer fragments were plentiful.

TABLE 50
Volumes and Dressed Surface Areas, Time Span 3

Construction	Volume (m^3)	Area (m^2)
Plat. 5D-2-1st-A	1,320	?
Str. 5D-42-C	190	130
Str. 5D-42-B	100	70
Str. 5E-31-B	80	60
Str. 5D-41-1st	1,000	420
Str. 5D-43-A	5000	160
Str. 5D-36	250	120
Str. 5D-40	2,450	900
Str. 5E-30	500	570
Str. 5E-32-1st-A	1,930	2,440
Str. 5E-99-1st	930	1,450
Str. 5E-34	290	400
Str. 5E-36	580	470
Str. 5E-35	290	400
Str. 5E-33	580	470
Str. 5E-95-1st	1,200	970
Total	12,190	9,030

TIME SPAN 2

The transition to TS. 2 is marked by a shift in architecture, in the appearance of Str. 5E-92, 94, and 98 and 5D-39, 134, 135, and 136 in the NW sector of the Plaza (Fig. 1). Some stratigraphic control is provided in the superimposition of Str. 5E-94 over 5E-32-1st (Fig. 39a) and of Str. 5D-39 and 134 over the U. 40 floor that abuts 5D-37 (Figs. 23a, 26). Also of this time were the ambitious, perhaps unfinished stair U. 8 on the E side of Str. 5D-37 (TR. 14:657); a new U. 6 facade on the substructure of Str. 5D-40 (Fig. 32a); the U. 43 floor in front of it (Figs. 32c, 34); and the U. 42 floor between Str. 5D-39 and 134 (Fig. 27d).

The largest of the new structures, 5D-39 and 5E-94, face each other across a wide area, and the slightly smaller 5D-134 and 5E-98 stand beside them in subsidiary positions. Structure 5E-92 appears to be an annex to 5E-98, perhaps a kitchen or an altar. Perishable buildings presumably stood on the four house-sized substructures, though neither postholes nor wall stubs were found. Building platforms ranged from 17 to 24.5 m in length and from 3.5 to 4.5 m in width, comparable to the average size of structures that are postulated for domestic use elsewhere at Tikal (see Figs. 23a, 26, 36a, 39a; TR. 19:figs. 9, 10, 19, 20, 26). Structures 5D-39, 5D-134, 5E-94, and 5E-98 have an estimated total of 363 m^2 of interior space (not counting front "porches"). With a nuclear family housed in each, the inhabitants would have numbered around 20. The more-elevated Str. 5D-37, 38, 40, 41, and 44 were also possibly domestic, as suggested by the presence of cord holders and burning in Str. 5D-40. Adding these room areas (68 m^2 for 5D-37, 210 m^2 for 5D-38, 100 m^2 for 5D-40, 56 m^2 for 5D-41, and 120 m^2 for the N room of 5D-44), a total of

917 m² would have been available, with space for at least five more families, or 25 more occupants. Contemporary habitation is attested to within intact buildings of the Central Acropolis (Harrison 1970).

Two square structures in the W half of the Plaza, 5D-135 and 5D-136, straddle the N-S centerline of the open area between Str. 5D-41 and 5D-39. One is near the causeway entrance and the other axial to 5D-41. In size and shape (Figs. 24a, 25a) they are analogous to Str. 5D-132, 133, and 177 on the Great Plaza and N Terrace, which may have been masonry altars within the setting of carved monuments and "temples" (TR. 14:figs. 6l, 205a,b, 244a,c).

The structures listed above are probably all late, as they are on what is thought to be the Plat. 5D-2-1st-A floor and, furthermore, are strewn with Eznab potsherds in loose ash-laden dirt. Pertinent lot numbers are seen in the time-span charts of Str. 5D-36, 37, 40, 41, 42, and 134 as well as 5E-30, 31, 37, 94, and 97. Also to be included in a TS. 2 inventory are lots around and within Str. 5D-38 (TR. 14:665–667). The deposits were usually beside and behind structures rather than on their stairways. Besides the distinctive and plentiful Sahcaba and Pabellon Modelled-Carved bowls and drinking cups, there were also many pieces of larger jars, flint and obsidian flakes and flake-blades, pieces of mano and metate, and human bone. The largest and most typical collection is 78Q/2 from the alleyway between Str. 5D-40 and 5E-30 (see Fig. 75a photo). Listed are pieces of 11 reconstructible Modeled-Carved ceramic vessels, including examples of MT. 350 (Sahcaba Text 2), MT. 351 (Pabellon Text 1) and MT. 145 (unnamed incised), plus 9 flint and obsidian flakes and flake-blades, and 2 mano fragments. An interesting aspect of the deposit is the more than 20 fragments of burned, disarticulated human bone. These were clearly part of the general trash and hint strongly of cannibalism.

Although the structures might have been built before manufacture of the Eznab Ceramic Complex (Eznab pieces were not found sealed within them), it is logical that the shift in plaza architecture from public to domestic would correlate with a change in pottery complexes. Coe placed the Eznab-laden deposits of Str. 5D-38 within Gp. 5D-2:TS. 2A and estimated a tenth-century date (TR. 14:873). Although production of Eznab ceramics has been timed by Culbert (1973:89) as early as 10.0.0.0.0 (A.D. 830), Coe is reluctant to allow its presence (at least in the central area of Tikal) until sometime after Stela 11 and Altar 11 were erected in the Great Plaza at 10.2.0.0.0 (A.D. 869) (TR. 14:861–873).

In recent excavations at the site of Dos Pilas, Guatemala, Modeled-Carved sherds corresponding to those in the Eznab deposits at Tikal were part of the trash around similar Terminal Classic house-sized structures within the main plaza (Demarest 1993). Crude defensive walls surrounded the group of structures. The occupants at Dos Pilas were interpreted as longtime residents trying to defend themselves, rather than newcomers.

Other constructions within Gp. 5D-3 can be assigned by sealed ceramics to the production period of the Eznab Ceramic Complex, thus correlating with occupation of the domestic structures if not with their assembly. The alley between Str. 5D-42 and 41 became littered by as much as a meter of ash-laden dirt, charcoal, Eznab sherds, human bone fragments, even a mano fragment, all of which recall the deposits described above. The alley was then filled to the top with rubble intermixed with Eznab sherds and masonry derived from the apparently collapsed building on Str. 5D-42. The fill was sealed by well-built floors, walls, and stairs, which allowed continued play on the end zone of the ballcourt. On the S side of the court, another low masonry retaining wall (Str. 5E-31:U. 3)

TABLE 51
Volumes and Dressed Surface Areas, Time Span 2

Construction	Volume (m³)	Other Data (m²)
Str. 5D-135	9	9
Str. 5D-39	250	80
Str. 5D-134	50	20
Str. 5D-136	4	9
Str. 5E-98	80	30
Str. 5E-92	5	5
Str. 5E-94	150	110
Str. 5D-42-A	50	20
Str. 5E-31-A	7	9
Total	610	440

sealing Eznab sherds extended in the direction of Str. 5D-43 (Figs. 10, 13b) and may have been a defensive wall comparable to the one at Dos Pilas.

Time Span 2 thus is thought to include the assembly of domestic structures within the Plaza, the accumulation of Eznab ceramics and domestic trash around them, and repairs to the ballcourt. It probably corresponds in years to TS. 3, 2B, and 2A of Gp. 5D-2, which span the "rats and bats" occupation of North Acropolis rooms, the looting of burials and caches, and minor paving and repairing. Strangely, there occurred almost no deposition of Eznab pottery in Gp. 5D-2, except for the above-mentioned Str. 5D-38 deposits on the edge of the East Plaza.

TIME SPAN 1

Time Span 1 comprises the many centuries following desertion of the East Plaza by the producers of Eznab ceramics. Abandonment may have been sudden or gradual. Some structures, such as thatched buildings, probably lasted only a few years after abandonment, whereas vaulted rooms might have remained intact much longer. In general, however, even the vaulted buildings in the East Plaza had greater structural weakness than those on the Central Acropolis, many of which survived intact to the present. There is evidence that the ballcourt rooms collapsed early. Buildings with multiple doorways in the eastern part of the Plaza would also have failed quickly, and those on the N side of the platform fell backward when the edge collapsed. Structures seem to have disintegrated mostly through natural forces, as there is little evidence of human interference such as removal of stones. No fragments of the Caban Ceramic Complex or of the Xnuc Censer Complex were found in the group as evidence of the "post-abandonment" visits documented in adjacent Str. 5D-1-1st, 5D-2-1st, and 5D-33-1st of Gp. 5D-2 (TR. 14:873–874).

VII

Concluding Remarks

Even though renewed excavation in Gp. 5D-3 may reveal that several stratigraphic and architectural conclusions presented here are in error, the existence of the following basic components is not in question: five successive plaza floors; twin pyramids; the W-facing East Acropolis; the Str. 5E-38 "temple"; the ballcourt; the Venus-Tlaloc structure; an inner and outer quadrangle of long colonnaded galleries; the open area and lofty structures on the W half of the plaza; and, finally, the late, intrusive domestic structures. The profound transformations in form and function that took place over time in Gp. 5D-3 contrast strongly with neighboring Gp. 5D-2, where a certain constancy of form was maintained (TR. 14:947).

The East Plaza apparently served large crowds. Long causeways from the northern and eastern outskirts led into the Plaza without obstruction, and broad stairs descended from the Great Plaza and ascended from the roadway across the southern ravine. Wide streets allowed easy passage around all sides of the huge Str. 5E-32 quadrangle. Vaulted rooms as arrayed in the eastern half of the Plaza, here interpreted as the principal marketplace of Tikal, probably were used both for exchange of staples and marketing of imported and manufactured items. Large crowds can also be imagined in Gp. 5D-2, where most of the leaders of Tikal were probably buried (TR. 14:846–66) and which would therefore have been the focus of communal and individual rites directed toward ancestral dynastic figures. In turn, Harrison has proposed a "royal" residential and administrative purpose for equally adjacent Gp. 5D-11, the Central Acropolis (1970). The very central area of Tikal therefore seems to have been made up of three contiguous groups reflecting the major divisions of society: the religious, the governmental, and the economic.

It is clear, however, that a marketplace would not have been the exclusive function of Gp. 5D-3. The ballcourt and shrine in the center of the Plaza provided other diversions, and, prior to that, the twin pyramid group in the same spot would also have attracted large audiences to its presumed ceremonies of katun and tun-ending celebration. Furthermore, if Plat. 5E-1 served at least throughout TS. 6 (A.D. 475–600) as a west-facing Acropolis with functioning summit structures, then the East Plaza was the frontal approach to it. The plaza to the S of Str. 5D-37, an area not bordered by market galleries until late in its history, may originally have been dedicated to Str. 5E-38 or its possible predecessors. This structure once faced without interruption Str. 5D-45 (the "Early Classic Palace") and hence may have been the eastern component of a Plaza Plan 2 layout, that is, a burial place of the principal personages of an extended-family residence (Becker 1971). Because the western half of the plaza revealed no intrusion of long gallery buildings, it may never have had any direct connection with the market to the E. It can be envisioned as a gathering or staging area from which one prepared to enter the Great Plaza. It seems more analogous to the West Plaza in its juxtaposition to the Great Plaza, its placement at the end of a causeway that enters the community from a cardinal direction, and in the heights of surrounding edifices (TR. 11). Structure 5D-15 is especially similar to 5D-40 in plan and orientation. The two plazas (although the western one was slightly earlier) were probably perceived originally as balancing entities and continued to serve as entries to the Great Plaza throughout their nearly 1,000-year history. The twin pyramids, ballcourt, and market may have been complementary to this key role, adding drawing powers to that of the heart of the community, the even more centralized Gp. 5D-2.

It is to be hoped that Gp. 5D-3 will receive attention again in future years. One might recommend clearing of the quadrangle and consolidation of at least one corner. The ballcourt would also be relatively easy to restore to its approximate original condition. Some unresolved scientific questions could also be resolved without enormous expense, and the following stand out among lingering conundrums: What is the connection between East Plaza floors and Str. 5D-38? How did viewers climb up to the buildings on the two ballcourt ranges? Were sacrificed individuals buried within Str. 5D-43, as they were in a comparable structure at Seibal? Are burials to be found, as speculated, beneath Str. 5D-40, 5E-38, and 5D-Sub.26? What text was written in the first half of the facade inscription that still lies in pieces on the bench top of Str. 5D-42? Were sockets for three known alley markers (Column Altars 1, 2, and 3; TR. 33A) missed in the excavations of the ballcourt? What evidence for either storage or manufacturing may be found within unexplored marketplace rooms? Did a low platform or altar stand at the center of the market quadrangle as at Tenochtitlan? Are there remains of finished walls on the currently controversial entities arrayed on Plat. 5E-1?

Appendix: Platform Units

Units of Platform 5D-2

Unit	Page	Figure
1	9	9,12a,b,13b
2	8	9,12c
3	8,11	9
4	6	9
5	9	9,38c,44
6		38c
7	10	16d
8	5	19d
10	6	19d
11	11	13b
12		38c
13	8	9
15	7	19d
16	11	unillustrated
17	5	19d, 22c
18	7	19d
19	10	19d, 22c
20	10	46
21	7	38c
24	11	38c, 39b, 43b, 46, 48a,b
25	10	38c, 42a,c, 46, 48a
26	10	48a
27	10	2a
28	10	2a
29	11	53b, 54a, 59a,c, 60b
32	8	59a,c, 60b
33	10	38c
34	10	44
35	11	8f, 9, 11, 12a–c, 13a, 16d, 35, 37a–c, 38c, 39b, 42a,c, 43b, 45,
36	10	34, 35, 37c, 42a,c
37	11	46, 55
39	11	25b
40	11	24b, 27c,d, 32c, 34
41	10	23b, 32c
42	11	23b, 32d
43	11	32c, 34
44	10	34
45	11	57
46		32c
47	7	53a
49	7	48c, 53a
50	10	46, 55
51	11	3

52	10	42a
53	10	42a,c
54	10	37c
55	11	42c
56		42a,c
57	11	51c
58	10	51c
59	7	51c
60	7	51c
62	11	50a
63	10	50a
65	9	TR.14:FIG.254A
67	7	38c
68	10	38c
71	5	2b, 48c, 53a
72	6	2b, 48c, 53a
73	10	2b, 48c, 53a
74	10	2b, 48c, 53a
75	11	48c, 53a
76	10	54a
78	5	9
79	5	8f, 9
80	7	9, 13a
81	10	25b
82	11	25b
83	7	8f, 9, 12c, 13a, 16d, 38c
88	5	2b
91	7	23b
92	7	23b
93	11	TR.14:FIG.254A
94	7	19d
95		9
97	11	63b, 62

References

Acosta, Jorge, and Hugo Moedano Koer
    1946   Los Juegos de Pelota. In *Mexico prehispanico, culturas, deidades, monumentos,* 365–384. Mexico.

Becker, Marshall
    1971   *The Identification of a Second Plaza Plan at Tikal, Guatemala and Its Implications for Ancient Maya Social Complexity.* Ph.D. dissertation, University of Pennsylvania. Ann Arbor:University Microfilms.

Blom, Frans
    1932   Commerce, Trade and Monetary Units of the Maya. *Middle American Research Series, Publication* 4:533–550. New Orleans:Tulane University.

Broman, Vivian L.
    1960   Ceramic Testing Program. Photocopy.

Brundage, Burr Cartwright
    1972   *A Rain of Darts, the Mexica Aztecs.* Austin:University of Texas Press.

Carlson, John B.
    1991   Venus-regulated Warfare and Ritual Sacrifice in Mesoamerica: Teotihuacan and the Cacaxtla "Star Wars" Connection. *Center for Archaeoastronomy Technical Publication, No. 7.* College Park, Maryland.

Coe, William R.
    1962   A Summary of Excavation and Research at Tikal, Guatemala: 1956–1961. *American Antiquity* 27:479–507.
    1963a   Current Research (Tikal). *American Antiquity* 28:417–419.
    1963b   A Summary of Excavation and Research at Tikal, Guatemala: 1962. *Estudios de Cultura Maya* 3:41–64.
    1964   Current Research (Tikal). *American Antiquity* 29:411–413.
    1965a   Current Research (Tikal). *American Antiquity* 30:379–383.
    1965b   Tikal: Ten Years of Study of a Maya Ruin in the Lowlands of Guatemala. *Expedition* 8(1):5–56.
    1967   *Tikal: A Handbook of the Ancient Maya Ruins.* Philadelphia:The University Museum.
    1990   See TR. 14 below.

Coggins, Clemency
    1983   *The Stucco Decoration and Architectural Assemblage of Structure 1–sub, Dzibilchaltun, Yucatan, Mexico.* Middle American Research Institute, Publication 49. New Orleans:Tulane University.

Cortés, Hernando
    1962   *Hernando Cortés Five Letters 1519–1526.* Transl. J. Bayard Morris. New York: W.W. Norton and Co.

Culbert, Patrick T.
    1973   The Maya Downfall at Tikal. In *The Classic Maya Collapse,* ed. T. Patrick Culbert, 63–92. Albuquerque:University of New Mexico Press.

Demarest, Arthur
    1993   The Violent Saga of a Maya Kingdom. *National Geographic Magazine* 183(2):94–111.

Díaz, Bernal
    1956   *The Bernal Díaz Chronicles.* Transl. and ed. Albert Idell. New York:Doubleday.

Durán, Diego
    1971   *Book of the Gods and Rites and the Ancient Calendar,* transls. and eds. Fernando Horcasitas and Doris Heyden. Norman:University of Oklahoma Press.

Feldman, Lawrence H.
    1978   Inside a Mexican Market. In *Mesoamerican Communication Routes and Cultural Contacts,* eds. Thomas A. Lee and Carlos Navarrete, 219–222.

Papers of the New World Archaeological Foundation 40. Provo:Brigham Young University.

Ferree, L.
   1972   *The Pottery Censers of Tikal, Guatemala.* Ph.D. dissertation, Southern Illinois University. Ann Arbor:University Microfilms.

Gendorp, Paul
   1985   Los remates o coronamientos de techo en la arquitectura mesoamericana. *Cuadernos de Arquitectura Mesoamericana* 4:47–50. Universidad Nacional de México.

Greene, Virginia, and Hattula Moholy-Nagy
   1966   A Teotihuacan-Style Vessel from Tikal: A Correction. *American Antiquity* 31:432–434.

Hall, Alice, and Peter Spier
   1975   A Traveler's Tale of Ancient Tikal: A Portfolio of Paintings by Peter Spier. Text by Alice J. Hall. *National Geographic Magazine* 148(6):799–811.

Harrison, Peter
   1970   The Central Acropolis, Tikal, Guatemala: A Preliminary Study of the Functions of Its Structural Components during the Late Classic Period. Ph.D. dissertation, University of Pennsylvania. Ann Arbor:University Microfilms.

Haviland, William A.
   1963   Excavation of Small Structure in the Northeast Quadrant of Tikal, Guatemala. Ph.D. dissertation, University of Pennsylvania. Ann Arbor:University Microfilms.

Hellmuth, Nicholas M.
   1971a   Possible Streets at a Maya Site in Guatemala New Haven, Conn. Photocopy.
   1971b   Preliminary Report on Second Season Excavations at Yaxha, Guatemala. New Haven, Conn. Photocopy.

Jones, Christopher
   1969   The Twin Pyramid Group Pattern: A Classic Maya Architectural Assemblage at Tikal, Guatemala. Ph.D. dissertation, University of Pennsylvania. Ann Arbor:University Microfilms.
   1982   See TR. 33A below.

   1991   Cycles of Growth at Tikal. In *Classic Maya Political History: Hieroglyphic and Archaeological Evidence*, ed. T. Patrick Culbert, 102–127. Cambridge: Cambridge University Press.

Larios, Rudy, and Miguel Orrego
   1983   *Reporte de las investigaciones arqueológicas en el grupo 5E-11, Tikal.* Parque Nacional Tikal:Instituto de Antropología e Historia de Guatemala.

Lowe, Gareth W.
   1966   Current Research (Tikal). *American Antiquity* 31:460–463.

Maler, Teobert
   1911   Explorations in the Department of Petén, Guatemala, Tikal: Report of Explorations for the Museum. *Memoirs of the Peabody Museum of Archaeology and Ethnology, Harvard University* 5(1):3–91.
   1971   Bauten der Maya aufgenommen in den Jahren 1886 bis 1905 und beschrieben von Teobert Maler. In *Monumenta Americana 4*, ed. Gerdt Kutscher. Ibero-amerikanischen Institut. Berlin:Gebr. Mann Verlag.

Marquina, Ignacio
   1964   *Arquitectura prehispanica.* 2nd ed. Instituto de Antropología y Historia, Mexico.

Maudslay, Alfred P.
   1889–1902   *Biologia Centrali-Americana,* eds. F. Ducane Godman and Osbert Salvin. London:R. H. Porter and Dulau.

Millon, René
   1973   *Urbanization at Teotihuacán, Mexico.* Vol. 1. Austin:University of Texas Press.

Morley, Sylvanus Griswold
   1938   *The Inscriptions of Petén.* Vol. 3. Carnegie Institution of Washington, Publication 437.

Pollock, H. E. D.
   1980   The Puuc: An Architectural Survey of the Hill County of Yucatan and Northern Campeche, Mexico. *Memoirs of the Peabody Museum of Archaeology and Ethnology, Harvard University* 19.

Ruppert, Karl
 1924 Report of Karl Ruppert on the Secondary Constructions in the Court of the Columns. In *Yearbook of the Carnegie Institution of Washington*. Washington, D.C:Carnegie Institution of Washington.
 1952 *Chichen Itza, Architectural Notes and Plans*. Carnegie Institution of Washington, Publication 595.

Satterthwaite, Jr., Linton
 1939 Evolution of the Maya Temple—Part I. *The University Museum Bulletin* 7(4):2–14.
 1952 Sweathouses. *Piedras Negras Archaeology: Architecture* V(1–4). The University Museum, University of Pennsylvania.
 1961 See TR. 8, below.

Scarborough, Vernon L.
 1991 Courting in the Southern Maya Lowlands: A Study in Pre-Hispanic Ballgame Architecture. In *The Mesoamerican Ballgame*, eds. Vernon L. Scarborough and David R. Wilcox, 129–144. Tucson:University of Arizona Press.

Smith, A. Ledyard
 1982 Major Architecture and Caches. In *Excavations at Seibal, Department of Peten, Guatemala*, ed. Gordon R. Willey. Memoirs of the Peabody Museum of Archaeology and Ethnology, Harvard University 15:1.

Spores, Ronald
 1965 The Zapotec and Mixtec at Spanish Contact. In *Archaeology of Southern Mesoamerica, Handbook of Middle American Indians*. 3:2, ed. Gordon R. Willey, 962–987. Austin:University of Texas Press.

Stern, Theodore
 1950 The *Rubber-Ball Games of the Americas*, ed. Marian W. Smith. Monographs of the American Ethnological Society 17. New York: J. Augustin.

Stresser-Péan, Guy
 1971 Ancient Sources on the Huasteca. In *Archaeology of Northern Mesoamerica, Handbook of Middle American Indians* 11(2), eds. Gordon F. Ekholm and Ignacio Bernal, 582–602. Austin:University of Texas Press.

Strömsvik, Gustav
 1952 The Ball Courts of Copan. In *Contributions to American Anthropology and History* 11(55):183–214. Carnegie Institution of Washington, Publication 596.

Taladoire, Eric
 1981 Les terrains de jeu de balle (Mésoamérique et sud-ouest des Etats-Unis). *Etudes Mésoaméricaines*, Series II:4. Mission Archéologique et Ethnologique Française au Mexique.

Tedlock, Dennis, transl.
 1985 *Popol Vuh, The Mayan Book of the Dawn of Life*. New York:Simon and Schuster.

Tourtellot III, Gair
 1990 Burials: A Cultural Analysis. In *Excavations at Seibal, Department of Peten, Guatemala*, ed. Gordon R. Willey. *Memoirs of the Peabody Museum of Archaeology and Ethnology*, Harvard University 17:2.

Tozzer, Alfred M.
 1911 A Preliminary Study of the Prehistoric Ruins of Tikal, Guatemala. *Memoirs of the Peabody Museum of Archaeology and Ethnology, Harvard University* 5(2):93–135.
 1957 Chichen Itza and Its Cenote of Sacrifice. Memoirs of the Peabody Museum of Archaeology and Ethnology, Harvard University 11–12.

Tozzer, Alfred, ed.
 1941 *Landa's relacíon de las cosas de Yucatan* (translation). Papers of the Peabody Museum of American Archaeology and Ethnology, Harvard University 18.

Willey, Gordon R.
 1990 General Summary and Conclusions. In *Excavations at Seibal, Department of Peten, Guatemala*, ed. Gordon R. Willey. *Memoirs of the Peabody Museum of Archaeology and Ethnology, Harvard University* 17(4).

Tikal Reports (see TR. 12: Appendix B and pp. 57–61)

TR. 5: Shook, Edwin M., and William R. Coe
 1961 *Tikal: Numeration, Terminology, and*

Objectives. University Museum Monograph 20, University of Pennsylvania, Philadelphia.

TR. 8: Satterthwaite, Linton
    1961   *Excavation near Fragment 1 of Stela 17, with Observations on Stela P34 and Miscellaneous Stone 25*. University Museum Monograph 20, University of Pennsylvania, Philadelphia.

TR. 11: Carr, Robert F., and James E. Hazard
    1961   *Map of the Ruins of Tikal, El Peten Guatemala*. University Museum Monograph 21, University of Pennsylvania, Philadelphia.

TR. 12: Coe, William R., and William A. Haviland
    1982   *Introduction to the Archaeology of Tikal, Guatemala*. University Museum Monograph 46, University of Pennsylvania, Philadelphia.

TR. 13: Puleston, Dennis E.
    19XX   *The Settlement Survey of Tikal*. University Museum Monograph XX, University of Pennsylvania, Philadelphia.

TR. 14: Coe, William R.
    1990   *Excavations in the Great Plaza, North Terrace and North Acropolis of Tikal, Vols. I–V*. University Museum Monograph 61, University of Pennsylvania, Philadelphia.

TR. 15: Harrison, Peter D.
    forthcoming   Excavations in the Central Acropolis of Tikal.

TR. 19: Haviland, William A.
    1985   *Excavations in Small Residential Groups of Tikal: Groups 4F-1 and 4F-2*. University Museum Monograph 58, University of Pennsylvania, Philadelphia.

TR. 23H: Coe, William R., and Luis Luján
    forthcoming   Investigations of Causeways. In H. Stanley Loten et al., *Miscellaneous Investigations in Central Tikal*.

TR. 25A: Culbert, Patrick T.
    1993   *The Ceramics of Tikal: Vessels from the Burials, Caches and Problematical Deposits*. University Museum Monograph 81, University of Pennsylvania, Philadelphia.

TR. 27A: Coe, William R.
    forthcoming   The Artifacts of Tikal: Ornamental and Other Special Material.

TR. 31: Trik, Helen, and Michael E. Kampen
    1983   *The Graffiti of Tikal*. University Museum Monograph 31, University of Pennsylvania, Philadelphia.

TR. 33A: Jones, Christopher, and Linton Satterthwaite
    1982   *The Monuments and Inscriptions of Tikal: The Carved Monuments*. University Museum Monograph 44, University of Pennsylvania, Philadelphia.

TR. 35: Coe, William R., and William A. Haviland
    forthcoming   The Burials, Caches and Problematical Deposits of Tikal.

Other Publications on Tikal from University Museum Publications

TIKAL REPORTS 1–11: Facsimile Edition of the Original Tikal Reports 1–11
1986. University Museum Monograph 64. 432 pp. Hard. ISBN 0–934718–74–1

TIKAL REPORT 13: The Settlement Survey of Tikal
Dennis E. Puleston
(William A. Haviland, editor)
1983. University Museum Monograph 48. x + 50 pp., 76 figs., appendices, biblio. Hard. ISBN 0–934718–47–4

TIKAL REPORT 14:
Excavations in the Great Plaza, North Terrace and North Acropolis of Tikal
William R. Coe
1990. University Museum Monograph 61. 6 separate vols.: 3 casebound vols. of text, 1100 pp., 157 tables, 3 charts; 2 casebound over wire-bound vols. of figs., 333 figs. including maps, sections, photos, and numerous foldouts; map box with 31 oversize plans and sections. Hard. ISBN 0–934718–66–0

TIKAL REPORT 19:
Excavations in Small Residential Groups of Tikal, Groups 4F–1 and 4F–2
William A. Haviland
1985. University Museum Monograph 58. xvi + 200 pp., 60 figs., 4 foldouts. Hard. ISBN 0–934718–58–X

TIKAL REPORT 25A
The Ceramics of Tikal: Vessels from the Burials, Caches and Problematical Deposits
T. Patrick Culbert
1993. University Museum Monograph 81. xi + 345 pp., 155 figs. (inked illustrations) accompanied by long descriptive captions, 5 tables, index. Hard. ISBN 0-924171-20-0

TIKAL REPORT 31: The Graffiti of Tikal
Helen W. Trik and Michael E. Kampen
1983. University Museum Monograph 57. vi + 11 pp., 133 figs. Hard. ISBN 0–934718–56–3

The Rulers of Tikal: A Historical Reconstruction and Field Guide to the Stelae
Genevieve Michel
1989. PUBLICACIONES VISTA. xii + 148 pp., 43 pls., site plan, biblio. Paper. ISBN 0–9626221–1–7
(DISTRIBUTED FOR PUBLICACIONS VISTA, GUATEMALA)

UNIVERSITY OF PENNSYLVANIA MUSEUM
of Archaeology and Anthropology